Catering and Hospitality
NVQ/SVQ 2

Serving Food and Drink: Table and Function

Student Guide

SECOND EDITION

Ann Bulleid, Pam Rabone, David Rimmer, Caroline Ritchie, Tim Roberts, Nick Wilson

Text © Ann Bulleid (NG1), Pam Rabone (2NG4), Caroline Ritchie (NG2, 2NG3), David Rimmer (2NC1, 2NC5), Tim Roberts (2NC3), Nick Wilson (2NC2, 2NC4), 1994, 1996
Original line illustrations © Stanley Thornes (Publishers) Ltd 1994, 1996

First published in 1994 by:
Stanley Thornes (Publishers) Ltd
Second edition 1996

Reprinted in 2002 by:
Nelson Thornes Ltd
Delta Place
27 Bath Road
CHELTENHAM
GL53 7TH
United Kingdom

02 03 04 05 06 / 13 12 11 10 9 8 7 6 5 4

A catalogue record for this book is available from the British Library

ISBN 0 7487 2591 1

Page make-up by Columns Design Ltd

Printed in Great Britain by Scotprint

Contents

Acknowledgements

The authors and publishers gratefully acknowledge the help and advice of all those without whom the preparation of this book would not have been possible: Barry Eustice and Trish Smith for their very considerable contribution to Unit 2NC1, and Sarah Brazil for her contribution to Unit 2NC3; also Jeffrey T Clarke, Ron Evans, Bill Moorcroft and Gerry Shurman. They would also like to thank Gee's Restaurant, Oxford, for their help in providing photographs and artwork; Bass Taverns for their permission to use the cover photograph; Nick Wilson for the photograph on p.210; and Gilbeys (N. Ireland) and the German Wine Information Service for providing the wine labels illustrated in Unit 2NC3.

Maintain a safe and secure working environment

This chapter covers:

ELEMENT 1:   **Maintain personal health and hygiene**
ELEMENT 2:   **Carry out procedures in the event of a fire**
ELEMENT 3:   **Maintain a safe environment for customers, staff and visitors**
ELEMENT 4:   **Maintain a secure environment for customers, staff and visitors**

What you need to do

- Carry out your work in line with hygiene practices.
- Identify all company procedures for dealing with emergency situations.
- Comply with all relevant health and safety legislation.
- Take account of customers', staff and visitors' reactions when involved with emergencies and deal with them accordingly.
- Take cautionary measures to warn customers, staff and visitors of hazards or potential hazards.
- Identify hazards or potential hazards and take appropriate action to deal with the situation.
- Ensure that safety and security procedures and practices are followed at all times in a calm, orderly manner.
- Work in an organised and efficient manner in line with appropriate organisational procedures and legal requirements.

What you need to know

- Why it is important to comply with health and safety legislation.
- Where and from whom information on health and safety legislation can be obtained
- Why and what preventative actions are needed to maintain a safe environment.
- What action to take when dealing with an emergency situation such as fire, accident or the discovery of a suspicious item or package.
- Why preventative action must always be taken quickly when a potential hazard is spotted.
- How to identify and deal with safety hazards or potential safety hazards for customers, staff and visitors.
- Why suspicious items or packages should never be approached or tampered with.
- Why suspicious items or packages must always be reported immediately.
- Why it is important to use correct lifting techniques.
- The procedures for ensuring the security of the establishment and property within it.
- Why keys, property and storage areas should be secured from unauthorised access at all times.
- What action to take when challenging suspicious individuals.
- What action to take when establishment, customers' or staff property is reported missing.
- Whom to contact in the event of an emergency and the information they will need.

INTRODUCTION

When dealing with customers the image you project can say a lot about the way the company operates. People are more likely to use a restaurant or food outlet if they have confidence in the way the staff take care of their appearance and follow good hygiene practice when dealing with food and drink.

Besides looking good, everyone involved in the service of food and drink has a duty under the Food Hygiene Regulations to protect the food from risk of infection through careful storage and handling. You will find this covered in more detail in *Unit 2NC1*.

As someone involved in the service of food and drink there are a number of points you need to be aware of about the way you dress, your habits and your cleanliness that can greatly reduce any risk of food poisoning to yourself, your colleagues and your customers. Attention to these will also increase customers' confidence in their visit to your restaurant.

In food areas in particular there are legal requirements laid down which influence all aspects of the way you work.

ELEMENT 1: Maintain personal health and hygiene

Take care of your appearance

FOOD HYGIENE REGULATIONS

The Food Hygiene (General) Regulations 1970, particularly those related to people involved in the preparation and service of food, identify and lay down the legal requirements for the main risk areas.

This legislation has been amended and updated by *The Food Safety Act* 1990 which is now the main 'enabling Act' under which any future regulations will be passed. The features contained within the 1970 regulations are retained within this new Act and have been amended, where necessary, to reflect the tighter regulations contained within the new Act.

The new Food Safety Act came about as a response to genuine public concern about the risks associated with food preparation and production and the increases in the numbers of incidents of food related illnesses.

The Food Safety Act has been developed to take account and to impact on every stage of the food chain from its source to its presentation and consumption by the customer. This means there needs to be even more care and attention when dealing with the service of food and drink. The Act has increased the scope and impact of penalties and includes:

- the provision that it is an offence to supply food that fails to comply with food safety requirements
- strengthened powers of enforcement, including detention and seizure of food
- required training in basic food hygiene for all food handlers
- required registration of all food premises
- enablement of Environmental Health Officers to issue emergency Prohibition Notices to force caterers to stop using the food premises or equipment immediately.

Complying with legislation

The impact on an establishment if it contravenes hygiene regulations can be significant and could lead to lost business or even closure of the business. As an employee working within an establishment, you have a responsibility to comply with the regulations, to carry out your work to the standards expected and to ensure you attend any training in basic food handling you are required to.

The Environmental Health Officers (EHOs) are responsible for enforcing the regulations and have a number of powers which include:

1 entering food premises to investigate possible offences
2 inspecting food and, where necessary, detaining suspect food or seizing it to be condemned
3 asking for information and gaining assistance.

An EHO also has the power to issue Improvement Notices if they feel there is a potential risk to the public. They may also, where it is felt there has been a breach of the legislation, impose a Prohibition Order which closes all or part of the premises.

The Food Safety Act has increased the maximum penalties available to the courts and these include:

- up to two years imprisonment for offenders or the imposition of unlimited fines (in Crown Courts)
- up to £2,000 per offence and a prison sentence of up to six months (through Magistrates' Courts) – up to a maximum of £20,000.

There are also penalties for obstructing an Enforcement Officer.

Complying with the legislation is important as the fines may not just relate to an employer, but can also affect an employee who contravenes and fails to demonstrate hygienic working practices.

Finding out about current legislation

When you are working in an establishment which serves and prepares food you should be able to find out about the Food Hygiene legislation through your manager or supervisor.

There should be information and copies of the legislation available on the premises in which you work, so it is important you find out where this is kept and make use of it.

You will also find out further information through the training sessions your manager or supervisor will organise for you.

The library is a good source of information on this subject, and you should keep up to date through trade magazines and newspapers.

You will also find the local Environmental Health Office will be able to supply information should you need it.

Do this

- Find out where the establishment displays Food Hygiene information.
- Look out for new hygiene information related to your work in magazines and newspapers.

Your responsibilities under the hygiene regulations

In these regulations the food handler's responsibilities are clearly detailed and have formed the basis for the guidelines you will follow if you are involved in the preparation or the service of food and drink.

In the regulations it is stated that food handlers must:
- protect food from risk of infection
- wear suitable protective clothing
- wash hands after visiting the toilet
- not smoke, spit or take snuff in food rooms
- cover cuts or wounds with clean washable dressing
- report illness or contact with illness.

Much of the guidance for those involved in the service of food and drink in the restaurant is aimed at reducing the risk of bacterial food poisoning. By protecting the food from people through the wearing of a uniform or protective clothing and by ensuring that staff follow some basic guidelines for good personal hygiene the risks are greatly reduced.

Bacteria such as Staphylococcus is found naturally on the human body, particularly in the ears, nose, throat and on the hands.

Other bacteria can be carried in the intestines and can contaminate food through poor personal hygiene, for example, using the toilet and not washing your hands afterwards.

Some bacteria, such as Salmonella, can be transferred from one source to another through clothes, dirty hands and equipment.

The number of reported cases of food poisoning has been increasing in recent years and many of the outbreaks can be traced to people as the main cause of the spread of infection.

SOURCES OF FOOD POISONING

If you are involved in the service of food and drink in your establishment it is important to be aware of the most common sources of infection so that you can take practical measures to prevent poisoning outbreaks.

There are three main sources of food poisoning:
1 through *naturally occurring poisons* in, for example, poisonous plants such as toadstools, deadly nightshade
2 through *chemical or metal contamination*, such as pesticides, cleaning fluids, mercury, lead or copper. Food poisoning from this source can be caused through the chemical being inadvertently spilt into the food or drink
3 through *bacteria and germs*, such as Salmonella, Staphylococcus, Clostridium perfringens. These are naturally present all around us and can easily contaminate food unless we follow good personal hygiene practices. Bacteria are microscopic

Chemical contamination can occur accidentally

and invisible to the naked eye, so it is difficult to know when you may be carrying bacteria which may cause food poisoning. Bacterial food poisoning is by far the most common source of illness in humans.

PERSONAL HYGIENE

By following the basic principles of good personal hygiene when serving food in an establishment you can reduce contamination risks. This will benefit you, your customers, colleagues and employer.

Most of these principles are common sense and have a place in our daily life, but they need to be emphasised to ensure that you comply with your responsibilities under the Food Hygiene Regulations.

The points are in no particular order of importance as each one is essential to you in demonstrating good hygiene practice at work.

Clean hands

Washing your hands regularly prevents germs from contaminating food

Bacteria (germs) on your hands can be one of the main methods of spreading infection. Germs are easily transmitted by touching, for example, some dirty cutlery, then picking up food by hand to put on a plate for a customer. This moves the bacteria from one place to the other and could result in cross-contamination.

Or it may be that you have visited the toilet, returned to work without washing and now have bacteria on your hands. If you then return to the still room to, for example, make sandwiches, bacteria present on your hands can be easily transmitted to the food while you are preparing it. By washing your hands in hot soapy water after visiting the toilet you will be greatly reducing the risk of infection.

When involved in serving food and drink in the restaurant, it is important you bear the following points in mind.

Keep your hands clean
Wash your hands as often as necessary, but particularly:
● before starting work
● before handling food
● when moving between jobs
● after visiting the toilet
● after touching your nose, hair or ears
● after coughing and sneezing
● after smoking.

You will probably be aware that you are not allowed to smoke in the food preparation areas, in storage areas or when serving food. Some companies have gone as far as to ban smoking in their establishments altogether. This rule about smoking is to improve the atmosphere of the eating area for the customers, and to reduce the risk of contamination. When smoking you can easily transmit germs from your mouth to your hands and then to any items of food or equipment you handle. Smoking can also lead to ash being dropped into food and drink, contaminating it and making it unpleasant for the customer.

Use disposable tissues in food areas
Germs are present in our ears, noses and throats. It is very easy to transfer bacteria to your hands by sneezing without using a tissue, coughing, spitting or picking your ears or nose, and you should never do this. If you need to use a tissue, use a disposable one and wash your hands immediately afterwards. Always use a tissue away from service areas to avoid your customers' attention.

Keep fingernails short, free from polish and use a nail brush to clean them
Bacteria can gather under nails and spread when your hands touch food. This is why

it is a legal requirement that all hand wash-basins in food and bar areas are equipped with nail brushes as well as soap and disposable paper towels or hot air dryers.

Avoid wearing nail polish, even clear polish, as it can hide the presence of bacteria under nails. Nail polish can also chip, fall into or onto food thereby contaminating it.

Wear only plain rings or jewellery
This will, of course, depend upon the particular operational standards where you work. Some establishments limit their staff to wearing plain rings and very little jewellery, whereas others are more flexible and allow a more ornate style.

The amount of jewellery allowed can be influenced by the style of the operation and the type of customers who frequent the establishment.

If you are involved in preparing or serving food it is important to remember that ornate jewellery can harbour bacteria and cause infection. Food particles can damage the stones, or cause them to become loose and fall out. Rings can also be a safety hazard as they can become hot and burn you or you may trap them in equipment.

Do this

- Find out the standards for wearing jewellery within your own establishment.
- Find out which areas are designated 'no smoking' areas in your workplace.

Keep hair away from food

Food can become very unappetising and off-putting to the customer if a stray hair has been allowed to fall into it. Apart from being unsightly, hairs also carry germs and can infect food.

If you are involved in serving food, or you often need to be in areas where the food is prepared, you may be required to wear a head covering to reduce the risk of loose hair falling into food.

Always:
- wear a head covering if required
- keep hair clean by washing it regularly.

This will reduce the risk of bacteria accumulating on hair and will improve your general appearance.

Do not comb or brush hair anywhere near food
Make sure that you always look smart and professional while on duty. Do not brush or comb hair behind a food service area, or in front of customers, as this can appear unprofessional and be off-putting to them. It can also result in stray hairs finding their way into food or drink. Always groom yourself in an appropriate area and away from customers.

Keep hair, moustaches and beards neat and tidy
This will reduce risks from bacteria carried on hair.

Different establishments vary the standards they set for the personal appearance of the staff employed. These standards will depend on the theme of the establishment, the house style, the uniform worn (if any) and the type of customers attracted.

Trim and tidy hair gives your customers the right impression, and reflects your own professionalism and pride in your work.

If you are involved in serving food you will be required to comply with the Food Hygiene Regulations. Long hair must be tied back or up, and kept away from your eyes. This will help discourage you from touching or playing with your hair when serving customers.

GENERAL HEALTH

People involved in the service of food and drink should be in general good health. Healthy looking staff can do a great deal to increase customers' confidence in the food and drink they consume. Healthy staff will also minimise the risk of infection, which, if serious, can lead to ill customers, lost trade and damaged reputation.

When employed in a job that involves handling food and drink you have a responsibility to be aware of some of the potential dangers.
● Do not work if you have any symptoms linked to food poisoning, or have been in contact with someone suffering from, for example: vomiting, diarrhoea, stomach pains or infections. Report your symptoms to your supervisor.
● Wash and shower daily to reduce body odour and risks from bacteria. Working in a busy establishment can often be a very hot activity. Customers will soon notice if you sweat too much and develop a strong body odour. This can make both them and you very uncomfortable, especially if you are in close proximity, for example, when clearing tables, and may mean they choose not to return to the restaurant.

> **MEMORY JOGGER**
>
> What should food handlers do when working with food to ensure they comply with the Food Hygiene Regulations?

Staff Sickness Notice

If you develop any illness involving vomiting or diarrhoea, or have come into contact with anyone with these symptoms, you must report it to your Department Manager before commencing work.

Other illnesses you must report to your Manager include: abdominal pain, skin rashes, fever, septic skin, lesions or discharges from your ear, nose or throat.

The Food Hygiene legislation requires you to report any sickness

● Cover cuts or bruises with clean waterproof dressings. Open sores or cuts can harbour germs and can look, to a customer or colleague, very unpleasant. If you are required to help with food preparation in the lead up to the establishment opening you will find that waterproof plasters in the first aid kit for a food preparation area are blue, so that they can be seen if they fall into the food.
● Avoid working with food if you have any wounds that are infected, unsightly and likely to cause danger to customers.
● Avoid bad habits such as:
  – licking fingers when preparing food
  – picking, scratching or touching your nose

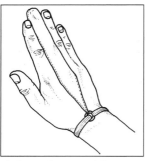

A dressed, covered finger

- – scratching your head or any spots
- – tasting food, or picking at food returned to the preparation area
- – coughing or sneezing over food
- – smoking
- – using hand wash-basins for washing food or utensils
- – tasting food with an unwashed spoon.

All of these habits can cause bacteria to spread and must be avoided at all times. They are also unpleasant for your customers and colleagues to see.

PROTECTIVE CLOTHING

Many establishments today require their staff to wear a uniform, or some form of protective clothing, such as an apron or a tabard. This is often a good idea as it can help project a particular image or style which complements the operation. Uniforms also help project a much more professional image and increase customers' confidence in the operation.

Uniforms, or any other form of protective clothing, can also be of benefit to you, reducing the wear and tear on your own clothes and perhaps minimising costs of buying new clothes for your job.

If you are provided with a uniform to wear you may find it will be your responsibility to ensure you wear it, keep it clean and in good repair.

There are a few guidelines to follow.

- *Wear protective clothing when in a food preparation area.* This can prevent the risk of transmitting bacteria from everyday or outdoor clothing. Everyday clothing can easily be contaminated by contact with pets, dirt and other people.
- *Keep your uniform in good condition,* with no tears nor missing buttons. Damaged protective clothing can look unsightly and be a danger to you if you catch it on equipment or edges of tables.
- Keep your uniform clean and change it daily. Uniform is often light-coloured and washable to show up food stains and dirt which can harbour bacteria. Avoid using aprons and glass cloths for drying your hands as this can lead to cross-contamination.
- *Do not wear protective clothing outside food areas,* for example, to travel to and from work as this can eliminate its effectiveness in protecting food from contamination.
- It is a good idea to *wear different shoes for indoors and outdoors* to reduce risks of infection. Alternating the shoes you wear ensures foot odour is kept to a minimum, helps reduce the strain on your feet and protects them.
- *Do not wear worn or open shoes* in case of spillages or falling items (such as trays or crockery) being dropped onto your feet. Open shoes offer little support if you slip on a wet floor, or trip. Low heeled, closed shoes give you the most protection and help you move quickly and efficiently about your place of work. Ensure your shoes are always clean and comfortable.
- Depending upon the style of the uniform, always ensure the socks, stockings or tights you wear are clean and complement the uniform to project a professional and hygienic appearance.

GENERAL APPEARANCE

When serving food and drink in the restaurant you will be the focus of attention for your customers. They will be looking to you to provide the level of service and professionalism projected by the company image. It will be this that will have attracted them into the restaurant in the first place. You represent your company to your customers, so it is essential that you reflect this in the way you deal with your customers and in the image you present. Your appearance will say a lot about you and the service the customer should expect.

Whether or not you have a uniform to wear ensure your overall appearance is professional and hygienic, by:
● making sure any make-up is not overdone and distracting to the customers
● not wearing heavy perfumes or aftershave as it may be unpleasant to the customers. Strong perfume or aftershave can be transferred to glasses and crockery, tainting the food or drink
● wearing deodorant to protect against perspiration and odours
● not carrying excess items in your pockets, such as pens, tissues, or money as this can look untidy and unprofessional.

Remember to:
1   check your appearance in a mirror before starting duty and take pride in your appearance and that of your uniform
2   follow good personal hygiene practice at all times whether in front of customers or not by:
   ● keeping yourself clean, washing your hair and body regularly
   ● wearing a clean uniform, protective clothing at all times and keeping it in good repair
   ● washing your hands regularly especially after visiting the toilet, touching your hair or face, smoking or preparing food
   ● using only disposable tissues when sneezing or blowing your nose – and disposing of them
   ● keeping all cuts and wounds covered with clean waterproof dressing.

Follow these basic practices, and you will enhance the service you provide as well as minimise any risks from food poisoning there may be to your customers, yourself and your colleagues.

Do this

● Find out what the correct uniform standard is for your job.
● Examine the uniform or protective clothing you have and check it is clean and in good repair.
● Check yourself against the points we have listed to see if you comply with personal hygiene requirements.

Case study

One day, when you are working a lunch shift in your establishment you notice a colleague has been quieter than usual and seems a little under the weather. She has been preparing the tables for lunch as usual but mentions to you she has been feeling sick and has had a bout of diarrhoea.
1   What is the potential risk to your customers in this situation?
2   What would you advise your colleague to do?
3   What action would you take in this situation?

What have you learned

1 Why is it important to comply with Health and Safety legislation?
2 Why is it important to wear correct clothing, footwear and headgear at all times?
3 Why should you report illness and infections?
4 Why is it necessary to wear protective clothing if you are involved in preparing and serving food?
5 Give five examples of good personal hygiene practice you must follow at work.
6 Where can you obtain information on current Health and Safety legislation?

ELEMENT 2:   Carry out procedures in the event of a fire

INTRODUCTION

Fires occur regularly on premises where staff are working and customers or visitors are present. Many, fortunately, are quite small and can be dealt with quickly. Others lead to tragic loss of life, personal injury and destruction of property.

Some of these fires could have been prevented with a little forethought, care and organisation. The commonest causes are misuse of electrical or heating equipment, and carelessly discarded cigarette-ends. People are often the link needed to start a fire: by acting negligently, perhaps by leaving rubbish in a dark corner; or by being lazy and taking shortcuts in work methods.

Fire legislation

The Fire Precautions Act 1971 requires companies to comply with certain legal conditions, such as those listed:
- providing a suitable means of escape, which is unlocked, unobstructed, working and available whenever people are in the building
- ensuring suitable fire fighting equipment is properly maintained and readily available
- meeting the necessary requirements for a fire certificate. On larger premises, the owners are required to have a fire certificate which regulates the means of escape and marking of fire exits. These premises must also have properly maintained fire alarms and employees and visitors must be made aware of the means of escape and the routine to follow in the event of a fire
- posting relevant emergency signs around the area giving people guidance on what to do and where to go in the event of a fire .

CAUSES OF FIRE

Fire hazards can exist wherever there is a combination of flammable materials, heat and oxygen. As part of your responsibility in ensuring the safety of yourself, colleagues and customers you need to be aware of some of the most common causes of fire.
- *Rubbish.* Fires love rubbish. Accumulations of cartons, packing materials and other combustible waste products are all potential flashpoints.
- *Electricity.* Although you cannot see it, the current running through your electric wiring is a source of heat and, if a fault develops in the wiring, that heat can easily become excessive and start a fire. Neglect and misuse of wiring and electrical appliances are the leading causes of fires in business premises.
- *Smoking.* The discarded cigarette end is still one of the most frequent fire starters.

MEMORY JOGGER

What are the main causes of fire in the working environment?

Damaged wiring

Disposing of waste correctly will help reduce fires from this source, but even so, remember that wherever cigarettes and matches are used there is a chance of a fire starting.

- *Flammable goods.* If items such as paint, adhesives, oil or chemicals are stored or used on your premises they should be kept in a separate store room and well away from any source of heat. Aerosols, gas cartridges and cylinders, if exposed to heat, can explode and start fires.
- *Heaters.* Portable heaters, such as the sort used in restaurants and offices to supplement the general heating, can be the cause of a fire if goods come into close contact with them or if they are accidentally knocked over. Never place books, papers or clothes over convector or storage heaters, as this can cause them to overheat and can result in a fire.

Preventing fires

Being alert to the potential hazard of fire can help prevent emergencies. Potential fire hazards exist in every area of the workplace, so regular preventative checks are essential as part of your everyday working practice.

- As far as possible, switch off and unplug all electrical equipment when it is not being used. Some equipment may be designed to be permanently connected to the mains (e.g. video recorders with digital clocks); always check the manufacturer's instructions.
- If new equipment has been installed, ensure that you are trained in its use and follow the manufacturer's instructions. If you are involved in carrying out maintenance on the equipment follow the schedule properly.
- Electrical equipment is covered by British Safety Standards, so look for plugs that conform to BS 1363 and fuses that conform to BS 1362.
- Ensure there are sufficient ashtrays available for smokers to use.
- Inspect all public rooms, kitchens, staff rooms and store rooms to ensure all discarded smoking equipment is collected in lidded metal bins and not mixed with other waste.
- As often as possible, look behind cushions and down the sides of seats to check a cigarette-end has not been dropped by mistake. You could check for this whenever customers have left an area.
- Ensure rooms and corridors are free of waste and rubbish, especially in areas where litter tends to collect, such as in corners and underneath stairwells.
- Place all accumulated waste in appropriate receptacles, away from the main building.
- Check that all external stairways and means of escape are kept clear.

MEMORY JOGGER

What can employees do in their daily work to help prevent a fire breaking out?

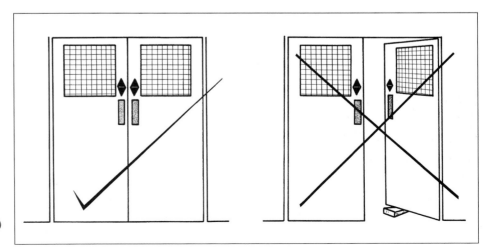

Fire doors used correcly (left) and incorrectly (right)

● Make sure that fire doors and smoke stop doors on escape routes are regularly maintained. These doors are designed to withstand heat and to reduce the risks from smoke. They must not be wedged open or prevented from working properly in the event of a fire.

IN THE RESTAURANT OR SERVICE AREA

Fire hazards

In a restaurant or service area there are additional hazards that you should be aware of. Note the following points.
● Any cooking operations should be kept under constant supervision.
● Electrical equipment (e.g. toasters) with faulty controls or thermostats can cause food (e.g. toast) to overheat, ignite and cause a fire. All equipment must be maintained and kept free from build-up of grease or dirt.
● Cloths, aprons and loose clothing should be kept away from any open flames (such as lamps, candles, etc.). It is very easy for fabric to catch alight and cause a fire to spread.
● Gas cylinders and methylated spirit or jelly containers used in the establishment should be in good condition and undamaged. Staff using the cylinders must be thoroughly trained in their use and aware of dangers from inadequate storage and damage to the cylinders.
● Flare lamps used for cooking, reheating or flaming dishes in the restaurant or service area must be regularly cleaned and maintained by trained personnel.
● Candle holders used on guests' tables must be checked before service, recharged where appropriate and maintained by trained personnel. Care must be taken to ensure candles are positioned on tables away from flammable material.
● In food service areas with open grills and barbeques, care must be taken to protect customers and staff from flames, smoke and heat generated by the equipment. Ensure you are trained how to light and replenish barbeques and open grills where appropriate.

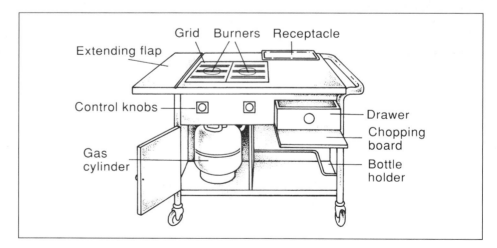

Guéridon trolley showing gas cylinder in place

● Any CO_2 cylinders in cellars must be properly secured and free from damage.
● If there is an open fire in the establishment, customers, visitors and staff must be protected from the flames by a fire guard.

Fire safety conditions

The following conditions must always be met within a working area.
● Fire doors should not be hooked or wedged open (see illustration on page 11).

Check that they close automatically when released. Fire stop doors held by magnets need to be closed from 11 p.m – 7 a.m.

● Fire extinguishers should be available, full and not damaged.
● Fire exit doors should be easy to use and secure.
● Emergency lighting should be maintained and visible at all times. Make sure that the lights are not obscured by screens, drapes, clothing, etc.
● Signs and fire notices giving details of exit routes must be available in all areas and kept in good condition.
● Alarm points should be readily accessible and free from obstruction.
● Fire sprinklers and smoke detectors must be kept clear of obstruction for at least 24 inches in all directions.
● Fire exit doors and routes must be kept clear at all times and in a good state of repair.

Do this

● Carry out a full survey of your own work area and identify any potential fire hazards. List the hazards under the following categories: combustible material, flammable liquids, flammable gases, electrical hazards.
● Discuss the potential dangers with your colleagues and agree ways of minimising the risk.
● Revise your own working methods to minimise fire risks.

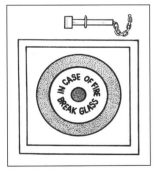

A break glass alarm

Discovering a fire

If you discover a fire, follow the sequence of events given below:
1 sound the alarm immediately
2 call the fire brigade
3 evacuate the area
4 assemble in the designated safe area for roll call.

Sounding the alarm

The function of the alarm is to warn every person in the building that an emergency has arisen and that fire evacuation procedures may need to be put into action. Most alarms are known as *break glass* alarms, and, as the name suggests, you have to break the glass to make the alarm sound.

Calling the fire brigade

The responsibility for calling the fire brigade falls to different people in different establishments. Often it is a receptionist or telephonist who will be expected to deal with the call. Make sure that you know who is responsible for this in your establishment.

When calling the fire brigade, be ready with the following information:
● your establishment's address
● your establishment's telephone number
● the precise location of the fire.

You may like to write down the necessary information about the establishment and keep it near the telephone in case of an emergency. If you do have to make an emergency phone call, make sure that you listen for the address to be repeated back to you before replacing the telephone receiver.

Evacuating the area and assembling outside

It is essential for everyone to be able to escape from danger. If you do not have specific duties to carry out in the evacuation procedures you should leave the premises immediately on hearing the alarm.

When evacuating the premises:
- ensure guests are informed immediately of the escape procedure and assisted in their escape in a calm but firm manner
- switch off equipment and machinery
- close windows and doors behind you
- follow marked escape routes
- remain calm, do not run
- assist others in their escape
- go immediately to an allocated assembly point
- do not return for belongings, no matter how valuable.

You and all of your colleagues should be instructed on what to do if fire breaks out. Customers and visitors should also be made aware of what to do in the event of a fire and should be made familiar with the means of escape provided. Although this is usually done by means of notices in all public areas (often in several languages), it is not always possible in an establishment. Be prepared to inform guests of escape procedures as soon as you hear the alarm sound.

Fighting fires

Fighting fires can be a dangerous activity, and is generally to be discouraged. Personal safety and safe evacuation must always be your primary concern. If a fire does break out, it should only be tackled in its very early stages and before it has started to spread.

Before you tackle a fire:
- evacuate everyone and follow the emergency procedure to alert the fire brigade. Tell someone that you are attempting to tackle the fire
- always put your own and other people's safety first; never risk injury to fight fires. Always make sure you can escape if you need to and remember that smoke can kill. Remember the rule: *if in doubt, get out*
- never let a fire get between you and the way out. If you have any doubt about whether the extinguisher is suitable for the fire do not use it; leave immediately
- remember that fire extinguishers are only for 'first aid' fire fighting. Never attempt to tackle the fire if it is beginning to spread or if the room is filling with smoke
- if you cannot put out the fire, or your extinguisher runs out, leave immediately, closing doors and windows as you go.

Fire fighting equipment

Types
On-premise fire fighting equipment is designed to be used for small fires only and is very specific to the type of fire. Hand extinguishers are designed to be easy to use, but can require practice and training in how to use them.

All fire fighting equipment is designed to remove one of the three factors needed for a fire: heat, oxygen or flammable material. Fire extinguishers are filled with one of the following:
- *water*. This type of extinguisher provides a powerful and efficient means of putting out fires involving wood, paper and fabric
- *dry powder*. These extinguishers can be used to put out wood, paper, fabric and flammable liquid fires, but are more generally used for fires involving electrical equipment
- *foam*. The pre-mix foam extinguishers use a combination of water and aqueous film, and are effective for extinguishing paper, wood, fabric and flammable liquid fires
- *carbon dioxide*. These extinguishers are not commonly in use, but can be used in situations where there is electronic equipment.

> **MEMORY JOGGER**
>
> What are the different types of on-site fire fighting equipment and the type of fires they can help control?

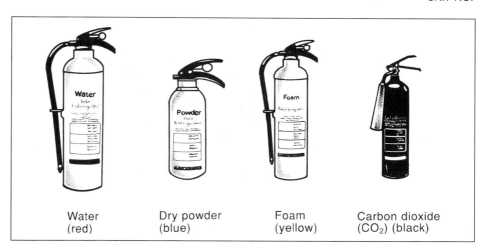

| Water (red) | Dry powder (blue) | Foam (yellow) | Carbon dioxide (CO_2) (black) |

Fire extinguishers

1 Fire extinguishers must be wall-mounted on wall brackets (unless designed specifically to be floor standing) and should not be used as door stops
2 When a fire extinguisher is discharged it must be replenished as soon as possible, and at least within 24 hours
3 Every establishment should have a scale drawing indicating the location of fire fighting equipment.

Fire blankets are also used to extinguish fires. These are made from a variety of materials: some are made of woven fibreglass while others have a fibreglass base and are coated with silicone rubber on both sides. Fire blankets are generally housed in a wall-mounted plastic pack with a quick-pull front opening. A fire blanket can be used to put a barrier between the user and the fire and removes the oxygen a fire needs to burn.

How to use a fire blanket

An establishment may also have fire hoses which are linked to the water supply. These can be used in the same situations as the red water-based extinguishers and are usually activated by the action of removing the hose from its mounting.

Maintaining equipment
Fire fighting equipment is needed in areas where there is a potential risk from fires. It is essential that equipment is:
● *maintained regularly and kept in good condition*. The fire brigade or your supplier will carry out annual checks and note on the extinguisher when the check was carried out

- *kept clear from obstruction at all times*. The equipment must be visible and readily available. Obstructions can prevent easy access and may result in unnecessary damage to the equipment
- *available in all areas of work*. Different types of extinguishers are needed for different fires, so the most suitable extinguisher should be available in the area. Guidance can be sought from the fire brigade or equipment suppliers
- *used by trained operators*. Fire extinguishers can be quite noisy and powerful and can startle you if you have not used one before. It is important that you know the best way of utilising the extinguisher to tackle a fire in the most effective way.

Complying with fire legislation

The fire legislation has been developed to ensure premises and working practices are safe for employees, customers and visitors. Failure to observe the regulations can lead to damage to property and, in more serious situations, loss of life. The legislation has been developed for everyone's safety and everyone has a role in ensuring they do not ignore fire notices and information provided about fire exits, and that they take part in fire evacuations and fire drills when necessary.

Finding out about the fire legislation

In your work area there will be notices and information posted around the building.

Details about the fire regulations will also be kept on site for you, your manager or your supervisor to refer to.

The local fire station will have a nominated Fire Officer who gives advice and guidance to establishments on how well they are complying with the regulations and identify any improvements in the evacuation drill that may be needed. The local Fire Officer will also be keen to give advice and support and, where appropriate, assist in the training of staff within the establishment.

Do this

- Find out where your nearest fire exits are located and the route you need to follow to reach your nominated assembly point.
- Identify the fire extinguishers available in your area and learn how to use them.
- Look out for potential fire hazards in your area and remove or report them immediately.
- Take part in practice fire drills in your establishment and learn to recognise the type of sound made by the alarm in your building.

Case study

You are carrying out a security check of your establishment and you notice that two of the fire extinguishers have been removed from their wall brackets and the fire exit near the delivery area is blocked with old cardboard boxes.

1 What would be you main concern if you found these problems?

2 What immediate action would you take?

3 What longer-term action could be taken to prevent this happening again?

What have you learned?

1 What are the possible causes of fire in the working environment?
2 What should you do first on discovering a fire?
3 What type of extinguisher would you use for putting out:
  ● an electrical fire?
  ● a fire on a guéridon trolley?
  ● a fire in a store room where chemicals are stored?
4 List four points you need to remember when evacuating your work area if the fire alarm sounds.
5 Why is it important to comply with your responsibilities under the fire regulations?
6 How does a fire blanket work in preventing a fire from spreading?
7 Why should fire escapes and exits be kept free from rubbish and doors unlocked when people are on the premises?

ELEMENT 3: Maintain a safe environment for customers, staff and visitors

INTRODUCTION

The safety of all who work in or visit an establishment should be foremost in the minds of everyone. A main part of an employee's work is to carry out procedures and comply with regulations which have been designed to encourage good working practices and to reduce the risks of injury to themselves and others. These regulations are also designed to make the working environment more comfortable and safe to work in.

The Health and Safety at Work Act 1974 set out to detail the responsibilities of employees and employers to take a 'general duty of care' and to place an emphasis on the need for preventative measures to be enacted and managed. The act encouraged the constant re-evaluation of systems and processes which prevent accidents and reduce risks to everyone in the establishment.

The Health and Safety at Work Act 1974 is an 'enabling Act' in that it imposes a general duty of care but has the flexibility to be adapted to suit future needs. Relevant regulations passed under the 1974 Act include:
● Health and Safety (First Aid) Regulations (1981)
● Reporting of injuries, diseases and dangerous occurrences (RIDDOR) (1985)
● Control of substances hazardous to health regulations (COSHH) (1988)

Under the *Health and Safety at Work Act (HASAWA)* 1974 there are certain responsibilities both employers and employees must comply with. Those given here are ones you should be particularly aware of.

EMPLOYERS' RESPONSIBILITIES

Employers must, as far as reasonably practicable:
● provide and maintain plants and systems of work that are safe and without risks to health
● make arrangements to ensure safety and the absence of risks to health in connection with the use, handling, storage and transport of articles and substances
● provide such information, instruction, training and supervision as will ensure the health and safety of employees

● maintain any place of work under their control in a safe condition without risks to health and provide at least statutory welfare facilities and arrangements.

These duties also extend to include customers and others visiting the premises.

MEMORY JOGGER

What are the employees' respon-sibilities under the *Health and Safety Act 1974?*

EMPLOYEES' RESPONSIBILITIES

As an employee you also have responsibilities and must:
● take reasonable care of your own health and safety
● take reasonable care for the health and safety of other people who may be affected by what you do or neglect to do at work
● cooperate with the establishment in the steps it takes to meet its legal duties
● report any physical conditions or systems which you consider unsafe or poten-tially unsafe to a supervisor.

These responsibilities have been drawn up for the benefit of everyone in the work-place, to ensure that the risk of accident or injury to anyone is minimised through promotion of a thoughtful and considerate approach to work practices. Customers place themselves under your protection as far as safety is concerned when visiting your work area.

Many working days can be lost through accidents, which more often than not are caused through carelessness and thoughtlessness. As a result the business suffers reduced productivity and, in serious cases, considerable trading time if forced to close while the premises are made safe.

Under the HASAWA, Health and Safety Inspectors (often under the umbrella of the Environmental Health Office) have the authority to place prohibition notices on premises if they persistently fail to meet the standards set by law. This might occur it there were a physical problem in the building or in equipment, or an outbreak of food poisoning caused by poor hygiene practice.

Whatever the cause, it is important that you and your colleagues have a positive and active approach to maintaining the safety of the environment in which you operate.

The Health and Safety Executive has the responsibility of advising on safety matters and of enforcing the HASAWA if the obligations of this Act are not met. This is one reason why serious accidents must always be reported to the Executive.

In the case of hotel and catering establishments, local authorities appoint their own inspectors: Environmental Health Officers who work with companies and colleges on matters associated with health and safety.

HEALTH AND SAFETY INSPECTORS

These appointed representatives have a number of powers under the Act which include:
● being able to enter premises at reasonable times
● to test, measure, photograph and examine as they see fit
● to take samples or dismantle equipment
● to view health and safety records, accident books, etc.
● to serve Improvement Notices requiring action within a period of not less than 21 days
● to prosecute *any* person contravening a statutory provision (penalty is a maxi-mum fine of £5,000 and/or term of imprisonment up to 2 years).

HAZARD SPOTTING

Much of the health and safety legislation is aimed at preventing accidents from happening and ensuring the environment is safe for everyone within it.

A hazard is defined as something with the potential to cause harm.

A risk can be expressed as the likelihood of that harm actually arising.

Some of the most common causes of accidents in the workplace are caused through basic mistakes, such as someone not cleaning up a spillage, or a cable left trailing across a walkway.

By being aware of the potential danger of hazards you will be able to contribute effectively to the safety of the area in which you work. The guidelines given here show areas in which you can start contributing towards maintaining a safe environment.

Cautionary measures

1   When you spot a hazard, or potential hazard, remove it immediately (if you can) and report the situation to your supervisor. Most organisations have a standard Health and Safety Report Form stating action to be taken and follow-up procedures.
    ● If you are unable to remove the hazard, as in the case of a doorway blocked by a delivery of goods, monitor the situation and if it appears the goods will not be moved quickly, report the problem to your supervisor.
    ● By taking immediate action over a potential hazard you will be contributing to your own well-being and that of your colleagues.
    ● Some hazards, however, may be due to poor working practices or faulty building design and they will need a different approach and more time to solve.
2   You may also need to place signs, such as 'Caution, Wet Floor' to warn others of the potential hazard they are approaching. In some cases you may even need to cordon off an area while you deal with, or make arrangements to deal with, the hazard.
3   Other cautionary measures will include ensuring you keep potentially dangerous items such as chemicals under lock and key, or out of reach of others.
4   Take note of all signs warning of dangers or potential hazards, especially those associated with:
    ● use of machinery
    ● hazardous chemicals
    ● cleaning fluids.

Safety points to remember

● Be constantly aware of obstacles on the floor or in corridors and remove them, returning them to their rightful place.
● Watch out for damaged floor coverings or torn carpets: it is very easy to catch your heel and trip over a carpet edge.
● Make sure electrical cables or wires never run across walkways. Always keep them behind you when you are working to reduce the risk of damage to them.
● Clean up spillages as soon as they occur. If grease is spilt use salt or sand to absorb the spillage before cleaning the area.
● If cleaning up spillages on non-porous floors use wet floor signs to warn people of the danger.
● Never handle electrical plugs with wet hands. Water conducts electricity: this can cause death.
● Never use equipment that appears faulty or damaged. You are increasing the risk to yourself by doing so. Report the problem immediately and ensure the equipment is repaired.

● Use a step ladder to reach to the top of shelves. Never stand on piles of cases or boxes.
● If lifting a load, make sure it is not too heavy or awkward for you to move on your own. If you need help, ask. Back injuries are among the most common reasons for people having to take time off from work.

Essential knowledge

Preventative action should always be taken quickly when a hazard is spotted. This is essential in order to:
● prevent injury to staff and customers
● prevent damage to buildings and equipment
● comply with the law.

RESTAURANT AND SERVICE AREA HAZARDS

In the restaurant service area there are some special hazards to be aware of. The following points show how these can be kept to a minimum.

● When using knives, always use the correct knife for the job you are doing. Use of incorrect knives can lead to accidents. Always leave a knife with its blade flat: if you leave the blade uppermost it would be very easy for you or a colleague to put a hand down on top of the blade and cut the palm of the hand. Never leave a knife immersed in water.
● If walking while carrying knives, always point the blade towards the floor, away from your body; or place it on a service plate or salver. If you were to trip when carrying the knife incorrectly you might accidentally stab someone or injure yourself.
● Always use a dry cloth when handling hot containers: wet cloths can transmit heat and burn you, causing you to drop boiling liquid or hot items on yourself or a colleague.
● Think about your customers, and ensure that they are protected from potential hazards as you are preparing the food service area. Check that table legs are level, table corners do not jut out awkwardly, space between tables is adequate and that walkways to kitchen and sideboard areas are clear. Restaurants are sometimes dimly lit and some clients may be unsighted, partially sighted or disabled; remember that an obstacle you may walk around easily can constitute a hazard to these guests.
● Ensure that you are trained in how to use hot water boilers, still sets, coffee machines, etc. before use. Both boiling water and steam can cause severe burns.
● Stack unused chairs and tables in a safe area and in a manner that does not cause a potential safety hazard or block access to those needing the equipment at a later date.

Much of the health and safety legislation focuses on people having a thoughtful and commonsense approach to their work and the safety of others. Many of the accidents which happen on premises, whether they be to staff, customers or visitors, occur as a direct result of someone not doing the right thing at the right time.

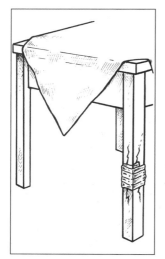

Faulty table legs can cause accidents

HAZARDOUS SUBSTANCES

The Control of Substances Hazardous to Health Regulations (1988) form part of the Health and Safety Regulations and lay down the essential requirements and a step by step approach to protecting people exposed to them. In the service area the most likely exposure to chemicals is through the use of cleaning and associated chemicals.

The COSHH regulations set out the measures employers and employees have to take. Failure to comply with COSHH constitutes an offence and is subject to penalties under *The Health and Safety at Work Act* 1974.

Substances hazardous to health include:
● those labelled as dangerous (e.g. toxic, corrosive)
● those where exposure over a long time is thought dangerous (e.g. pesticides)
● harmful micro-organisms
● substantial concentration of dust of any kind
● any material, mixture or compound used at work, or arising from work activities, which can harm people's health.

In a service area or bar hazardous cleaning substances may include bleach, ammonia, chlorine, detergents, methylated spirits, solvents, pipe cleaning fluid.

COSHH requires an employer to:
● assess the risk to health arising and state the precautions needed
● introduce appropriate measures to prevent or control the risk
● ensure the control measures are used
● where necessary, monitor the exposure of employees
● inform and instruct employees on a regular basis.

COSHH requires an employee to:
● know what risks there are in using certain substances
● understand how these risks are controlled
● take the necessary precautions.

When storing hazardous substances it is important:
● they are stored in a locked area
● they are clearly labelled in a securely capped container
● to have First Aid instructions and method of summoning assistance
● to have a system of work related to their use.

REPORTING HAZARDS

Under the HASAWA, every company must have a procedure in place for employees to report potential hazards they have identified. In some companies there may be *Safety Representatives* whose role is to bring the hazard to the supervisor's attention. The Safety Representative may be part of a *Health and Safety Committee* who will meet regularly to deal with matters of safety and to ensure appropriate action is taken.

Your department may have a standard Hazard Report Form which you would complete to help you and your supervisor deal with the hazard through a formalised procedure. You may also be involved in carrying out regular safety audits in your department aimed at ensuring that planned preventative work is implemented.

Under *The Health and Safety at Work Act* it is your responsibility to be aware of potential hazards and to take the necessary action to prevent them from becoming actual hazards.

Do this

● Carry out a hazard spotting tour of your area highlighting potential dangers and noting any actions needed.
● Find out how you are required to report health and safety hazards in your place of work.
● Examine the equipment you use in your department. Is the wiring in good condition? When was the equipment last serviced? Discuss any problems found with your supervisor.

DEALING WITH SUSPICIOUS ITEMS AND PACKAGES

In any area of work there may be times when an unattended item, package or bag raises suspicion. This could lead to an emergency, and, if not handled correctly, may result in danger or injury to people in the area.

Because of the 'chance' or transient nature of custom, food service establishments are a prime target for terrorists. It is important to treat any suspicious item seriously. Be aware of the danger it potentially contains and be prepared to inform people of your suspicions quickly and calmly.

A suspicious package which is not dealt with immediately may result in serious injury to people in the area or serious damage to the building. It is an essential part of your daily work to keep alert to dangers from suspect packages and follow laid down procedures when dealing with the problem.

Recognising a suspicious item or package

It is difficult to give precise guidance about where you may discover a suspicious package, or what size or shape it might be. Either of the types of package listed below might raise your suspicions.
- Something that has been left unattended for some time, such as a briefcase next to a chair, or a suitcase left in a reception area.
- Something that looks out of place, like a man's holdall in the ladies' cloakroom, or a full carrier bag near a rubbish bin.

A full carrier bag left next to an empty rubbish bin might be enough to arouse suspicion

In fact, anything that sticks out in your mind as somewhat unusual. Always check on and under tables and chairs when guests leave; if you find anything left behind, politely remind the relevant guests.

On discovering a suspicious item
- Do not attempt to move or touch the item. The action of moving or disturbing the item may be enough to start off a reaction leading to an explosion or fire.
- Remain calm and composed. Try not to cause panic by shouting an alarm or running from the item. People and property can be injured through a disorderly or panicked evacuation.
- Report the matter to your supervisor or the police immediately. Check your establishment's procedures to find out whom you should inform.
- If possible, cordon off the area and move people away. It may be difficult to do this without causing people in the area to panic, but it is essential that no one attempts to move or touch the item, so you will need to warn people to keep clear.
- At some point it may be necessary to evacuate the building, or the part of the building nearest to the suspect package. This may be a decision taken by your supervisor, or the police if they are involved. If it is thought necessary to clear the area, follow your company procedures for the evacuation of the building.

MEMORY JOGGER

What are the actions to take if you discover a suspicious item in or around your area of work?

22

REPORTING A SUSPICIOUS ITEM

If you are reporting a suspicious item make sure you are able to tell your contact:

1 what the suspicious package looks like:

2 the exact location of the suspect device:

3 the precautions you have taken so far:

4 the existence of any known hazards in the surrounding area, e.g. gas points:

5 the reason for your suspicion:

6 any witnesses to the placing of the package or item:

Essential knowledge

- Suspicious items or packages must never be approached or tampered with in case they contain explosive materials which may be set off.
- Suspicious items or packages must always be reported immediately, to prevent serious accidents occurring involving bombs and explosives.

Do this

- Carry out a survey of your work area to identify places where suspicious items or packages could be left.
- Find out what procedures your establishment follows for dealing with suspect packages.
- Carry out regular checks in your area.

DEALING WITH AN ACCIDENT

Within the normal course of your work you may be required to deal with an accident or an emergency resulting in someone sustaining an injury. Often these injuries are not life threatening, but occasionally they may be serious enough to warrant the person involved being taken to hospital, or being unable to carry on their work for that day.

Most organisations have several people trained in dealing with emergencies and administering first aid. These *first aiders* are often spread around the different departments to ensure that someone is available at all times. Organisations are legally required to have trained first aiders on the premises and to display a list detailing their place of work and contact telephone number on notice boards.

First aiders are usually the people who deal with an emergency before a doctor or an ambulance arrives (if necessary). They have a responsibility to respond to emergencies as they arise, and are trained to diagnose the course of action needed to deal with the injured person. You would immediately call a first aider when an accident occurs.

Recording an accident

All accidents need to be reported as soon after the event as practicable. Any accident is required by law to be reported and recorded in an accident book located on the premises. Any accident resulting in serious injury must be reported to the Health and Safety Executive within three working days. Your establishment should have procedures for dealing with this.

In the case of an accident to a member of staff, ideally the person who received the injury would complete the accident book. However, it may be necessary for an appointed person to report the accident on their behalf.

The following information is mandatory:
1 the date and time of the accident
2 the particulars of the person affected:
   - full name
   - occupation
   - nature of injury or condition
3 where the accident happened
4 a brief description of the circumstances.

If an accident happens to a customer or visitor there will probably be different records available. Check the type of records kept by your own establishment.

Accident record keeping is important, not only to comply with the legal requirements under Health and Safety legislation, but also to ensure details are available for possible insurance claims. Accident reporting can also be a great help when analysing trends and identifying where there may be a need for preventative training.

Complying with the regulations related to accidents

The current regulations governing the notification and recording of accidents are contained in the *Reporting of Injuries, Diseases and Dangerous Occurrences Regulations* (RIDDOR) 1985. These regulations are about ensuring that a company has procedures in place to manage the reporting of accidents. They are separated into five main areas.

1 Fatal or specified major accidents or conditions.
2 Notifiable 'over three days' injuries.
3 Reportable diseases.
4 Dangerous occurrences (whether there is an injury or not).
5 Other accidents.

Each establishment is responsible for ensuring there are procedures in place which enable employees to comply with the regulations. Failure to follow the RIDDOR requirements can lead to prosecution under the Act.

Do this

- ● Establish where the Accident Recording Book is located.
- ● Find out whether there are different procedures and records for accidents involving customers and visitors to those involving staff for your establishment.
- ● Find out the procedure for reporting accidents to the emergency services.

Who is a *first aider*?

The term *first aider* describes any person who has received a certificate from an authorised training body indicating that they are qualified to render first Aid.

The term was first used in 1894 by the voluntary First Aid organisations and certificates are now offered by St John Ambulance, St Andrew's Ambulance Association and the British Red Cross. The certificate is only valid for three years, to ensure that first aiders are highly trained, regularly examined and kept up to date in their knowledge and skills.

First Aid organisations (left to right): St John Ambulance, St Andrew's Ambulance Association, British Red Cross

When a first aider is dealing with the casualty their main aims are to:
● preserve life
● prevent the condition worsening
● promote recovery.

Their responsibility is to:
● assess the situation
● carry out diagnosis of the casualty
● give immediate, appropriate and adequate treatment
● arrange, without delay, for the casualty to be taken to a hospital or to see a doctor if appropriate.

Giving information to the first aider
Once the first aider arrives at the accident they will need certain information from
you before they begin their treatment.

Be prepared to tell them as much as you know about:
● *the history of the accident.* How the accident happened, whether the person has
  been moved, what caused the injury
● *the symptoms.* Where the casualty is feeling pain, what other signs you have
  observed, whether the symptoms have changed
● *the treatment given.* What has already been done to the casualty and whether the
  casualty has, to the best of your knowledge, any other illness or is receiving treatment or medication.

Initial response to an accident
Whether you are a first aider or not, in the event of an accident it is the initial
response to the situation and the way laid-down procedures are followed that can
make the difference to the treatment received by the injured person.

You need to know what immediate response you should give if a person near you
sustains an injury. Many of the points are common sense, and will depend upon the
extent of the accident and the speed with which you can contact the relevant people.

When dealing with accidents the following points are important.
● *Remain calm when approaching the injured person.* The injured person will probably
  be frightened by the situation they are in, or may be in pain, and they will benefit
  from someone taking control of the situation. This may help reduce the feeling of

MEMORY JOGGER

What would you do if you were not a *first aider* and you were in the vicinity when someone had an accident?

Initial response to an accident

26

panic, helplessness or embarrassment they may be experiencing.
- *Offer reassurance and comfort.* Keep the casualty (if conscious) informed of the actions you are taking by talking in a quiet, confident manner. Do not move the person but keep them warm, covering them with a blanket or a coat if necessary. By keeping them warm you are minimising the risk of shock which can often cause the condition of the injured person to deteriorate. By preventing them from moving you are allowing time for them to recover and reducing the possibility of further injury.
- *Do not give them anything to drink.* If the casualty is given something to drink they may not be able to have an anaesthetic if necessary. A drink may also make them feel worse and may cause nausea.
- *Contact or instruct someone else to contact a first aider.*
- *Stay by the casualty* if you can, to reassure them and ensure they do not cause further injury to themselves.
- *Minimise the risk of danger* to yourself, the injured person and any other people in the area.

In the case of:
1 *gas or poisonous fumes*: if possible, cut off the source
2 *injury from electrocution*: switch off at the source – do not attempt to touch the injured person until they are clear of the current
3 *fire, or collapsing buildings*: move the casualty to a safe area after temporarily immobilising the injured part of the person.

Do this

- Find out the name and work location of your nearest first aider (a list should be displayed in your work area).
- Find out how you can become a first aider.

CONTACTING THE EMERGENCY SERVICES

If either you or your supervisor decide that assistance is required from the emergency services, or you have been asked to call them by the first aider you will need to pass on certain information:
1 *your telephone number,* so that if for any reason you are cut off, the officer will then be able to contact you
2 *the exact location of the incident.* This will help the ambulance or doctor to get to the scene of the accident more quickly
3 *an indication of the type and seriousness of the accident.* This will allow the team to bring the most appropriate equipment and call for back-up if necessary
4 *the number, sex and approximate age of the casualties involved.* If possible, you should also explain the nature of their injuries
5 *any special help you feel is needed.* For example, in cases where you suspect a heart attack.

It might be a good idea to write down the information you need to pass on before calling the emergency services.

If you do call 999, you will be asked to state the service required: in the case of accidents you would normally state 'ambulance'. The officer responding to your call will be able to pass on messages to any other emergency services necessary, such as gas or fire.

Establishment procedures
Procedures vary from company to company as to who has authority to call the emergency services so it is important that you find out how you are expected to deal with the situation in your own place of work.

CORRECT LIFTING TECHNIQUES

One of the most common sickness problems related to work is back injury. It affects not only those in manual jobs but also it can affect sedentary workers. Under the Health and Safety Regulations, the Manual Handling Operations Regulations are intended to reduce the risk of injury and sets out simple steps to take to reduce such injury. Back injury can put people out of work for a while as well as have a long term debilitating effect on a person's health. Prevention of back injury is a must.

When lifting at work where there is a risk of injury, there are a number of questions to consider. For example, in the longer term:
● can the lifting operation be eliminated?
● is the lifting operation unnecessary?
● can the lifting operation be automated?
● could the lifting operation be mechanised?

As well as these longer term issues it is also important that an employee gives thought to how they are going to move an object – before they do it. They could:
● 'walk the route' to check how to lift and move the object without causing injury
● get someone else to help if the load is heavy
● get someone else to help if the load is bulky or an awkward shape
● use lifting techniques which do not put strain on the back, such as that shown in the picture below, illustrating the correct way of lifting a heavy object.

If an employee is required to lift as part of their job, under Health and Safety legislation it is important they are trained in manual handling techniques. And, having been trained, it is then the responsibility of the employee to work to the laid-down procedures

The correct way to lift a heavy object

DISCLOSABLE INFORMATION

During the time you are at work there may be people who ask you questions. These may be general questions about the operation, or may be specific about one aspect of the business. It is important when this happens you are discreet and careful about what you say. It may be by answering these questions there could be a breach of security, or have a more indirect effect on the business (e.g. an idea being used by a competitor).

If you are unsure what you can or cannot say to someone about the business or how it operates, it is best to say nothing and to check with your manager or supervisor.

It is also a useful idea to mention to your manager or supervisor about the questions you have been asked. It may alert him and avoid a problem in the future.

Reporting unusual/non-routine incidents

Throughout the working day it is likely you and your colleagues have been busy. Much of the work involves patterns of work and routines. If something disturbs that routine or seems out of the ordinary it is important these incidents are reported to the appropriate person (usually your manager or supervisor)

It may be the incident does need further action to be taken, but it also may result in a bigger problem being avoided. In cases where you see something which is a little bit out of the ordinary it is important it is reported.

FINDING OUT ABOUT AND COMPLYING WITH THE REGULATIONS

Health and safety is a responsibility of us all. Failure to comply with the requirements laid down in the Acts may lead to an occurrence which could lead to prosecution. An injured person may be able to sue their employer, or a fellow employee for breach of their statutory duty. This could lead to damages being awarded through the Civil Courts, or being prosecuted in the Criminal Court.

Information about the health and safety aspects of your work should be made available by your manager or supervisor.

There may be a *Health and Safety at Work* handbook available when you join an establishment detailing your responsibilities and those of your colleagues.

There will also be information available in the form of posters, statutory notices posted around the building and on staff notice boards.

During training sessions you will be given information about the regulations and how they affect your work. You should also be given guidance on working practices (such as lifting techniques) which will ensure you do not put yourself or others at risk from injury.

Case study

The area in which you are working is very busy and there are often piles of crockery, cutlery and trays of glasses as well as tables and chairs used for functions stored in the back of the restaurant. The area is used as interim storage prior to functions and you have to work around these items. Recently you have been asked, as part of your job, to help with function room set-ups and to move the tables and chairs to the correct rooms. You are happy to help as it means you are learning more about the set-up and running of functions.

1   Before you get involved in this job what are the main health and safety points to remember?

2   What should you find out from your supervisor?

3   What steps should you take to ensure you are complying with the HASAWA?

What have you learned

1 Why is it important you are aware of your responsibilities under *The Health and Safety at Work Act* 1974?
2 What are the main responsibilities for employees under the HASAWA?
3 Why is it important to be involved in and carry out hazard-spotting exercises?
4 Why is it important to report any suspicious packages or items you may spot?
5 What might make you become suspicious about a package or item?
6 Why must accidents be reported?
7 Where can you find the Accident Register/Book in your establishment?
8 Why is it important to use correct lifting techniques?
9 Who can provide you with up to date information about health and safety matters?
10 List five potential health and safety hazards in your area of work.

ELEMENT 4: Maintain a secure environment for customers, staff and visitors

---

INTRODUCTION

Maintaining effective security should be the concern of everyone working within an establishment and is an essential part of good business practice. There may be staff within your own organisation employed as Security Officers whose role will include all aspects of protecting people on the premises, looking after the security of the building and the property contained within it.

Effective security practices can help protect the profit of the business by reducing the likelihood of losses through, for example:
- *theft*, whether through break-ins causing damage to the building or through walk-outs where customers leave without paying for their service
- *fraud*, by customers or staff
- *missing stock*.

Profitability can be affected both by the immediate loss of property or damage to the building and by bad publicity, which can damage the business through loss of custom.

YOUR ROLE

Whether or not there are security staff employed within your organisation, you will find there are many situations within your working day where you need to be security conscious. It is easy to become complacent or lazy in your working habits, which can lead to an opportunity being seen and seized by a thief. A common example of this is a member of staff leaving a cash drawer open after transactions for speed or ease of use, allowing a customer to remove cash from the till when the cashier turns away.

Daily work patterns may also present an opportunity to be exploited by a thief. When we work in an area we become familiar with our surroundings, used to seeing things in a certain place and following procedures in a certain way. It is often these patterns that are observed by potential thieves and which can lead to break-ins or thefts.

Being aware of potential breaches of security and knowing how to report them or the action to take is an essential starting point. Think about the way you work and how security conscious you are. Make sure that you always follow the basic security practices listed overleaf.

MEMORY JOGGER

What are the guidelines to follow to help ensure there are no breaches of security in your working area?

- Handle all cash transactions away from the customer and preferably out of their sight.
- Keep display materials beyond the reach of any customers and as far away from main entrances as possible, making it difficult for people to remove the items without being spotted.
- Keep security issues and procedures confidential: you can never be sure who might overhear you discussing a sensitive issue.
- Keep your own belongings, such as handbags or wallets, secure and out of sight in a locked compartment or drawer.
- Keep alert to anyone or anything that looks suspicious, for example: an occupied car parked outside the building for a long period of time, boxes or ladders placed near to windows, fire exits left open.
- Keep keys, especially master keys, under close supervision. You will probably find that your establishment has a log book for recording the issue of keys.

It is important for you to follow any particular security procedures that are in place in your establishment. These procedures are there both for your benefit and to minimise any loss to the business.

Do this

- Think about your working day. List the things you do where attention to security is essential.
- Now write down your ideas for improving security within your job. Discuss your ideas with your supervisor.
- Find out what security procedures you are required to follow within your work area.

DEALING WITH LOST OR MISSING PROPERTY

From time to time company, customer or staff property may go missing. This can be due to a variety of reasons, such as:
- customer property may have been left behind
- company property may have been moved without people knowing and may, in fact, be misplaced rather than lost
- a member of staff may have been careless about returning property, such as dirty linen to the linen room, or crockery to the crockery store
- items may have been stolen from the premises. You may hear this type of loss called *shrinkage* or *pilfering*, especially when referring to food or liquor missing from refrigerators or cellars.

In most establishments there will be procedures for dealing with any missing property. If you discover that property has gone missing it is important you follow the correct procedure. The type of information you should report will probably include:
- a description of the missing item/s
- the date and time you discovered the item/s were missing
- the location where item/s are normally stored
- details of any searches or actions taken to locate the item/s.

In some cases your organisation may decide to report the loss to the police. This is common where the item missing is of value or where a substantial amount of goods has gone missing. In some organisations all losses are reported to the police whether theft is thought probable or not. If the police are involved, you may be required to give them information, so it is essential for you to be clear on the circumstances of the losses.

Essential knowledge	Keys, property and areas should be secured from unauthorised access at all times in order to:
	● prevent theft
	● prevent damage to property
	● prevent damage to the business from loss of customer confidence.

RECORDING LOST PROPERTY

In most establishments there are procedures for recording lost property. This usually covers personal property lost by customers, visitors or staff rather than property which may have been deliberately removed from the premises.

If someone reports they have lost an item it is usual for this to be recorded in a Lost Property Book. An example page from a book is shown below.

● The information required should be recorded clearly and accurately. This information can then be used as a reference point for any property found on the premises.

● When recording lost property it is particularly important to take an address or telephone number so that the person can be contacted should the item/s be found.

● If you find property it is your responsibility to report the find so that it can be returned to the appropriate person.

LOST PROPERTY RECORD					
Date/time loss reported	Description of item lost	Where item lost	Lost by (name, address, tel. no.)	Item found (where, when, by whom)	Action taken

A page from a Lost Property Book

● In some organisations, found property is retained for a period of, for example, three months and then either returned to the person who reported it or sent to a charity shop.

SECURING STORAGE AREAS

Throughout the building there will be areas designated as storage, whether for customers or staff. These areas can often be used by a variety of people in the course of a day, so security of the area and the contents is essential.

Storage areas, particularly those allocated for use by customers such as coat racks or cloakrooms, are especially sensitive and can lead to a great deal of damage to the business if items from such areas are lost or go missing. Store rooms, refrigerators, freezers and cellars often contain a great deal of stock which constitutes some of the assets of the business and must be protected from potential loss.

Some items can be easily removed from the premises and are therefore of particular concern.
● *Small items* such as glasses, ashtrays, cutlery, etc. can be easily concealed in a handbag or carrier bag and removed without too much difficulty
● *Larger items* such as candlesticks or table lamps can also be removed, but will generally need more thought and planning beforehand.
● *Valuables* such as money and credit cards can be easily removed from coat pockets if left unattended in a cloakroom, or at a table when a customer goes to the cloakroom during their meal.

It is sometimes extremely difficult to make an area completely secure, especially as the premises are often host to a large variety of people. It is therefore important to minimise the risk as much as possible by following some fundamental guidelines.

Before we explore those guidelines, complete the exercise below. This will help you to identify areas which are not as secure as they could be. This may be due to a lost key, poor working practice or laziness on the part of the staff concerned.

Do this

● Draw up a list of all of the designated storage areas within your work area and indicate whether they are secured storage areas (i.e. lockable) or unsecured storage areas. Make sure you include every area in your list, including those made available for customers, staff and the storage of company property.
● Once you have drawn up the list, tick those areas which are kept secure at all times. Identify the gaps, then discuss with your colleagues ways of improving the security of these areas.

SECURING ACCESS

By carrying out regular checks you could highlight the need for improvement and increase the security of your area.

The following points show how you might prevent unauthorised access to certain areas.
● Where access to storage areas is restricted to certain people ensure you comply with the rule. If you see anyone you think could be unauthorised report it to your supervisor, or ask the person to leave the area.
● If you have been issued with a duplicate or master key keep it safe at all times. Ensure you follow any recording procedures there might be when you take and return the key.

MEMORY JOGGER

How could you ensure you secure the areas within your establishment where access is restricted?

- Never leave keys lying around or in locks: this is an open invitation to an opportunist thief.
- Never lend keys to other staff, contractors or visitors; especially master keys. If you have been issued with a master key, you have responsibility for the access to that particular storage area.
- Follow any organisational procedures regarding the reporting of lost keys. It may be necessary to trace the lost key or have a new lock fitted to ensure the security of the area.
- If you are working in a secure area, e.g. a liquor store room, always lock the room when you are leaving, even if only for a few moments.
- When closing the restaurant, check all windows, shutters and doors are secure and the area including toilets has been cleared of customers.

These guidelines are by no means exhaustive, but should help you maintain security within your area of work and raise your awareness about the potential risks.

Do this

- Add your own ideas to the guidelines listed above, taking into account the list of storage areas you drew up earlier.
- Keep the list in a prominent position, such as your notice board or locker to remind you about the 'do's and don'ts' of effective security practice.

DEALING WITH SUSPICIOUS INDIVIDUALS

Since you are working in the business of hospitality, there will inevitably and frequently be strangers within the building.

As part of your job you should keep yourself alert to the presence of strangers in areas reserved for staff, i.e. in the staff restaurant, offices and corridors.

Non-staff may have a legitimate reason for being there: they may be visiting or delivering some material. On the other hand, they may have found their way in and be looking for opportunities to steal.

An individual may seem suspicious to you for a number of reasons. The following list will give you some pointers to potential problems, but remember that behaviour and situations may or may not indicate that an offence is taking place. An individual fitting any of these descriptions might be said to be acting suspiciously:
- someone wearing an incorrect uniform, or a uniform that is ill-fitting or worn incorrectly
- someone asking for directions to certain areas where you would not expect them to work; for example, someone wearing kitchen whites and asking directions to a bedroom
- someone carrying company property in an area not open to them
- someone who appears lost or disorientated (remember however that the person *may* be an innocent new employee)
- someone who just *looks* suspicious: perhaps they are wearing heavy clothing in summer, or carrying a large bag into the restaurant. Large bags or coats can be used to remove items from your premises
- someone who seems nervous, startled or worried, or is perspiring heavily
- someone booking into accommodation without luggage
- a customer asking for details of someone else staying in the establishment. (In this case, it is better to pass on the enquiry rather than give out information to a stranger.)

MEMORY JOGGER

What would you need to do if you notice someone acting suspiciously?

Responding to a suspicious individual

If you see someone on the premises you do not recognise, or who looks out of place it is important that you:

1   challenge them politely: ask if you can help them, or direct them to the way out
2   report the presence of a stranger to your supervisor immediately.

Procedures for dealing with strangers will vary depending upon the establishment in which you work.

In all cases, *do not put yourself at risk*. Do not approach the person if you feel uncomfortable or potentially threatened by them. Merely reporting any suspicions you have, whether about customers, staff or visitors, can often be of great help to the security of the business.

Do this

- Find out what procedures are laid down by your organisation for dealing with people acting in a suspicious manner.
- Discuss with your supervisor how you think you might challenge someone should you need to.

Case study

The hotel is fully booked with a conference and the restaurant has been busy as usual. A non-resident has been to you to report that she thinks someone has stolen her handbag from the table at which she has been sitting with her friends during the evening.

1   What would you do if faced with this situation?
2   How would you record the incident?
3   What would you report to the manager?

What have you learned

1   Why is it essential to maintain secure storage areas within your establishment?
2   List any potential security risks within your own area.
3   Why is it important you are aware of these risks?
4   Which keys, property and areas should be secured from unauthorised access at all times?
5   What should you ensure you do when leaving a secure area?
6   What should you do if you see someone acting in a suspicious manner?
7   How can you reduce the risk of items being taken from your own work area?
8   Why is it important you give only disclosable information to others?
9   Why is it important to report all unusual non-routine incidents to the appropriate person?

Get ahead

1   Find out about the *recovery position* in first aid. When would you need to use this? Why is it effective?
2   Find out what immediate response you could give in the case of burns and scalds, fainting, strokes and heart attacks.
3   Talk to your security officers. Find out what kind of events they commonly deal with in your establishment.
4   Invite a fire prevention officer to your establishment to talk about fire prevention and fire fighting in more detail.

Maintain and deal with payments

This chapter covers:
ELEMENT 1:   **Maintain the payment point**
ELEMENT 2:   **Deal with payments**

What you need to do

- Follow all your establishments procedures with regard to the handling of cash and all other accepted methods of payment.
- Work efficiently and calmly under pressure, and within the required time.
- Follow your establishment's procedures regarding the security requirements and guarantees for all methods of payment.
- Replenish audit rolls, receipt rolls and customer bills as appropriate.
- Complete all opening, closing and handover procedures correctly.
- Ensure sufficient change is always available for use.
- Enter the correct price or code and inform the customer of the amount due.
- Receive cash, token and voucher payments, and give change when required.
- Issue receipts.
- Acknowledge the receipt of non-cash payments
- Produce the accompanying documentation efficiently, accurately and neatly.
- Store the payment and accompanying documentation securely.
- Be aware of all the security aspects involved in the handling of cash.
- Ensure that the payment point is secured from unauthorised access.
- Report or deal with any unusual or unexplained behaviour or situations in accordance with company procedures.
- Deal with customers in a polite and helpful manner at all times.
- Comply with all health and safety regulations at all times.

What you need to know

- Why you must be correctly prepared at the beginning of your shift with all the opening and handover procedures completed, and why you must complete all handover or closing down procedures at the end of the shift.
- Why you must follow company procedures at all times especially when actually handling cash, handing over change or handing over cash to authorised persons.
- Why you should never hand over cash to unauthorised persons and always maintain customer bills accurately and securely.
- How to look after and change as appropriate receipt and audit rolls.
- Why you should always have a sufficient amount of change and how to anticipate and deal with any shortages of change before they arise.
- Why security both of the cash and of access to the payment point are so important.
- The establishment's procedures for processing non-cash payments.
- How to authenticate all forms of non-cash payments.
- How to prepare the appropriate documentation to accompany non-cash payments.
- How to deal with any problems or

discrepancies that occur.
- All the prices in the restaurant, and the codes for them on the cashiering machines, if applicable.
- How to issue a bill, calculate change, issue change (if applicable) and how to issue a receipt.
- How to deal with vouchers and tokens.
- How to deal with customers in a polite and helpful manner at all

times, and work swiftly and efficiently.
- How to work swiftly and efficiently, so that all work is done correctly by the required time.
- How to deal with unexpected situations.
- The procedures of your establishment for dealing with cash, token and voucher payments.

INTRODUCTION

MEMORY
JOGGER

Whom do company
procedures protect?

Cash handling is often an important part of the job of food service personnel. It is also one of the most vulnerable areas and one that is open to fraudulent behaviour. For these reasons security is of vital importance when handling cash: not only of the cash but also of customer accounts and the back-up paperwork. Anyone who handles large amounts of cash is a target for thieves and conmen. Non-cash payments are not as vulnerable to simple theft as cash payments, however, they are more vulnerable to fraud. Another potential problem is that the credit card company or bank may refuse to honour the payment. They have the right to do this if the credit payment is not accepted correctly. You must never lose sight of the fact that any form of payment is always potentially fraudulent, as are any refund claims. The cash handling procedures within your establishment will have been designed to reduce the risk of theft and fraud, and your own vulnerability. You must therefore familiarise yourself thoroughly with these procedures and follow them carefully. If you do not understand why something is done in a specific way, ask your supervisor, but never deviate from the procedure without authorisation because the system may have been designed specifically to protect you and other members of staff.

ELEMENT 1:	Maintain the payment point

OPENING, CLOSING AND HANDOVER PROCEDURES AT A PAYMENT POINT

In most food service operations customers are able to pay a bill at any time during opening hours, but in residential catering establishments, such as hotels and hostels the facility to pay bills may be available to customers 24 hours a day, seven days a week. However, there are always fairly regular high and low activity periods in establishments, although the actual routine will vary from establishment to establishment. Thus there are fairly standard shifts for most staff. Examples are as follows.
- An early shift will start sometime between 10 a.m. and 11 a.m. and go on until mid-afternoon, around 3 p.m.
- A late shift will start around 3 p.m. and continue until around 11 p.m.
- Some restaurants are open until 1–2 a.m. In this case they are often closed during the afternoon. If not, in an area with a lot of tourism, the changeover between the early and late shift usually takes place around 5–6 p.m.
- In other places, such as industrial canteens, those handling cash may work straight shifts with no handover being necessary.

This means that the payment point is open for all of the time that the restaurant is open, and the food service personnel, if they handle cash, upon starting or finishing a shift will have to go through various different procedures depending upon what time of day or night they are starting or finishing.

In some establishments you may be responsible for handling your own bills, and operating your own payment point. In other restaurants there will be one member of staff whose sole job is to operate the payment point. Whatever your main duties are, the procedures which you will have to follow when operating a payment point are still the same.

Opening a payment point

When a start is made early in the morning, or as an establishment opens, you would be considered to be *opening a shift*. You would perform the following tasks.

- Fetch, or receive the float and any other monies from where they have been stored overnight. This would normally be some sort of safe and would be authorised by the duty manager.
- When you have received the float you should count it, in the presence of the manager or supervisor who is issuing it to you. Both of you would then agree on the amount that has been handed over. In most establishments there will be a book which you will sign to this effect.
- Set up the payment point ready for the customers who will eat that day.

Date	Time	Amount	Till number/ Department	Issued by/ Handed over by	Received by

The top section of a page from a Float Received Book

MEMORY JOGGER

So that you can operate the payment point efficiently what materials should you always have available?

- Ensure that the till or other billing machine is ready for use, and put the float securely in the cash drawer. How you ensure that the till or other billing machine is ready for use will vary from establishment to establishment. In essence it means that you will ensure that the till rolls are in and working. In some restaurants you will have to ensure that the paperwork necessary to create bills is available.
- Check to see if any transactions took place after the payment point had closed down at the end of the previous shift. This will mean that you will have to check with any staff who were on at night to see what transactions took place and make sure that they are recorded correctly. In an hotel restaurant this might entail you making sure that these late meal charges have been transferred to the reception payment point to be entered onto the customers' bills.
- You should also check to see if there are any special charges, discounts or promotions to be applied to the bills.
- There may well be a handover book in which any such details have been noted which you should consult.

The exact procedure will depend upon the policy of each establishment, which you will have to learn. Always follow your establishment's procedure and if in doubt ask your supervisor.

Handing over a payment point

In a restaurant which is open for more than eight hours it is normal for there to be a handover of the cashier's duties. Normally it takes place during the afternoon; this is because it is usually the quietest time of the day. The handover takes place when the late shift takes over from the early shift. The following points and tasks should

Restaurant staff counting the float

be noted, but the exact order in which they are carried out will depend upon the individual establishment.
- The payment point does not close during this procedure, which is why it is referred to as a *handover period*.
- During this time the till rolls will be read, or some other computerised reading will be taken to show how much business has been done to this point. The cash, and other forms of payment, will be totalled up against the readings, and the float removed. The float should be the same amount as it was when the payment point was opened in the morning, and the cash, or other forms of payment should total the reading from the cash machines.
- The float will be formally handed over, and recorded as it was in the morning, and the till roll and takings removed by an authorised person to a secure place for banking.
- It is important to discuss any relevant points which have arisen during the shift to ensure that the handover is efficient. For example, perhaps not all the bills from lunch time are in because some people came in for a late lunch, or the float is running short of change and action should be taken now, etc.

Closing a payment point

At the end of the working day, the payment point will be closed down. The payment point closure procedures are along the lines listed here.
- A reading of all the business done to date will be taken, and the till roll removed.
- The takings will be counted against the cash point reading, and the float will be counted out again, but this time it will be handed back to management for safe storage over night.
- All the customers' bills will need to be completely up to date, and, if applicable, made available to the authorised night staff.
- The handover/shift comment book will also need to be completed.

Exactly how these activities will be completed will vary from establishment to establishment and be based upon its size and the number of payment points that it has. Remember that you must never deviate from your establishment's procedure because it is designed to safeguard you as much as anyone else.

Remember the following points
- If you do not open, close and hand over at a payment point correctly, the cash takings for the restaurant may be recorded incorrectly and mistakes will be very hard to trace.
- In some restaurants whoever handles cash is required to make up any cash discrepancies at the end of their shift from their own pocket.
- If you do not open, close and hand over at a payment point correctly all mistakes may be attributed to your shift and you may have to make up any cash discrepancies, whether or not the error occurred during your shift.
- Even when you are very rushed never accept or hand over cash unless it has been signed for, or authorised in some way.

Do this

- Find out what type of till or billing machines your establishment has and where they are. Ask your supervisor how they work, and if there is more than one type of machine, why they are not all the same.
- Write down for yourself what you are supposed to do when opening, closing or handing over at any of these payment points.
- Find out who is authorised to hand over the float to you and to whom you should give it back.
- Ask your supervisor what is the establishment's policy about cash shortages, or excesses.
- Find out how people who want to pay their bills during the night would do so (if this is applicable to your establishment).
- Discuss with your supervisor, and then make a list of all the types of things which should be written in the handover book, or discussed during a shift handover.
- Find out where the customers' bills are kept whilst the payment points are closed.
- Find out how you would get access to the bills if you were opening up a payment point by yourself.

HOW TO MANAGE A FLOAT

The float which you receive at the beginning of your shift is to enable you to give change to your customers. It is not possible for you or the management to know exactly how all of the customers will pay, whether they will use cash, vouchers or some form of credit, or whether, if they give you cash, they will give you the exact amount or require change. This means that from time to time the change in your cash drawer could run out. You should never let this happen. If a customer is in a hurry to pay and leave they do not want to wait whilst you try to find change for their bill, they will simply become annoyed at your inefficiency. To prevent this happening you should always follow the procedure described here.

1. When the change starts to run low you must notify an authorised person about the situation. They will probably ask you what kind of change you are running low on and how much more you think you need. This is something that you will learn to judge accurately as you become more experienced.
2. The change will then be brought to you by an authorised person, and they will usually ask you to give them the same amount of money back in large denomination notes. You may or may not be asked to sign for this transaction, it will depend upon company procedure. The total amount of money in your till should not be affected by this activity.
3. In some establishments when you receive the float, the exact breakdown of the float will be recorded, in others just the total amount.
4. Periodically during the day authorised persons will remove the cash from all of the cash drawers. This is to prevent the build up of cash, which would make the payment point a tempting target for thieves. When this happens, and when you are extracting the float from the takings at the end of the day, you should try to

make sure that the money remaining in the cash drawer, or making up the float, is in small change so that change is always available for the customers' benefit.

5   On some shifts everyone may pay by non-cash methods, so that you never run out of change. On other days everyone may pay by large denomination notes and you run low frequently. This is a fact of business life, and you should not worry if you have to request more change frequently. You will not be able to provide an efficient service to the customers if you do not have the right equipment, in this case enough change.

6   Never allow yourself to run out of change, so that in a panic you take change from other members of staff and then have to try to extract it from the cash point at a later date.

Essential knowledge	Make sure you have sufficient change available at all times. This will enable you to: ● give the customer correct change in the appropriate denominations ● carry out cash transactions efficiently ● keep the customer satisfied.

Do this 	● Find out the float size for each payment point in your restaurant, and if possible why it is set at that level. ● Write down the procedure within your establishment for requesting extra change. Make a special note of who is authorised to do this. ● Find out whether or not you have to list the exact breakdown of the float when you receive it and when you hand it back. ● Ask your supervisor to explain to you how they become aware of the fact that they are running short of change. ● Ask your supervisor if, because of the types of customer who eat at your restaurant, you require more change at certain times than others.

DEALING WITH AUDIT ROLLS, RECEIPT ROLLS AND CUSTOMER BILLS

Whenever you handle cash, tokens or vouchers there should be some paperwork to back up your action. This is for your own protection as well as to enable the establishment to judge how efficiently its business is running. It also enables any queries in the future to be traced back to the source and understood. Perhaps a customer may have paid twice, both the husband and wife accidentally paying. The restaurant will want to confirm that this is what happened before they give a refund, and also why it happened so that they can prevent such an error occurring again.

There are two main ways of compiling and recording this information, and complying with legal requirements, either by using a conventional electronic till or via a computerised payment point.

On a conventional mechanised, electronic till there will be two rolls of paper. One is a till roll, or receipt roll, and one is the audit roll. When a payment takes place the details of the payment will automatically be printed onto both rolls. The receipt roll will be pushed out of the machine so that it can be given to the customer as proof of purchase, and the audit roll will remain within the machine, and have printed on it an exact replica of the information on the receipt roll.

At the end of the day, when the payment point is closed down, and perhaps during the day, during handover periods, an authorised person will cause a total of the

Conventional till with receipt roll and audit roll

business to date to be recorded on the audit roll (and it may also appear automatically upon the receipt roll as well). They will then take away the relevant part of the audit roll and compare it with the actual takings to date, to make sure that there are no discrepancies. You, the billing machine operator, will not be able to access the audit roll, but will be able to see it. You will have access to the receipt roll. At the beginning of each shift you should check to ensure that there is enough of each roll to last throughout the shift. If customers are held up whilst the till rolls are being replenished it will make them impatient, and make the restaurant look inefficient.

In a computerised payment point it is more likely that there will not be an audit roll. Instead there will be a program to which only authorised persons have access, and this program will automatically record each use of the payment point.

In both types of machine the receipt roll may be replaced by the customers' bills. This would be quite legal as long as the items on the bills are printed out by the machine and not recorded by hand. The customers' bills then act as their receipt.

Obviously therefore you must make sure that there is a plentiful supply of bills available for use during the shift, whether they be individual bills or an automatic feed supply to the payment point.

The exact procedure will vary from establishment to establishment, and from machine type to machine type.

Do this

- Find out what kind of audit rolls, receipt rolls, and customer bills are used in your restaurant. Are they the same for each payment point?
- Find out where the replacements are kept and if access to them is restricted.
- Make a list of who is authorised to read the audit rolls or programs. Make a note of their job titles as well.
- During a quiet period ask your supervisor to show you how to change the receipt roll of any machine that you are likely to have to use.

If all the customer bills are numbered ask your supervisor what to do if you have made a mess of a bill and it cannot be used. (Do not worry if you damage one or two bills at the beginning, your restaurant will have a procedure for dealing with this event.)

SECURITY AT THE PAYMENT POINT

Given that cash is such a temptation for thieves, it is obvious that when you handle cash you have to be very careful about security. You also have a duty to ensure that the customer is only asked to pay for those meals and beverages which they have consumed, and that they are charged for every item of food and drink consumed.

You should remember the following points.
- Any amount of cash is always a temptation to a thief.
- Members of staff are just as likely to steal from an establishment as a stranger.
- It is almost impossible to prove who is the real owner of a specific piece of currency. If £50 goes missing from the cash drawer and some people in the vicinity of the till have over £50 in their pockets how do you prove who is the thief, or that none of them are?
- While you are the operator of a payment point you are responsible for all the cash moving through that area. You are therefore responsible for any discrepancies between what should be there and what actually is there.
- If unauthorised persons gain access to customers' bills, they may alter the totals for their own illegal reasons. The customer will therefore not be charged correctly, with serious consequences for the business.

In some establishments payment points may be physically separate from other parts of the restaurant, and even be within a secure cubicle.

The payment point may be near the entrance to the restaurant, allowing customers to be greeted while service is not interrrupted

In other establishments the payment point is incorporated within the food service personnel's service point or sideboard.

If you are authorised to deal with payments during a shift then you are responsible for the security and safety of all the money in your cash drawer and for the safety and confidentiality of the customers' bills.

There are several golden rules which you should observe at all times:
- never leave an unsecured payment point unattended for any period of time
- whenever you have to leave a payment point unattended, for example, when serving a customer, make sure that the payment point is securely locked
- never hand over cash, tokens or vouchers to, or receive cash from, anyone, even an authorised person, without the correct explanatory paperwork
- never allow anyone except the customer or a properly authorised person to look at the customer's bill
- never allow anyone without proper authorisation into the area of the payment point
- if you have to make an adjustment to a customer's bill, get the proper authorisation and signature before you do so
- whenever you have the smallest doubt about the honesty of anyone's actions immediately contact your supervisor.

Beyond this, each establishment will have a security procedure which has been set up to deal with each payment point's security needs. You must always follow this procedure.

Essential knowledge

It is essential that payment points are secured from unauthorised access:
- to prevent strangers or members of staff stealing from the payment point
- to make sure unauthorised persons do not see customers' accounts
- to prevent anyone tampering with the payment point, for example by making false charges or adjustments to customers' accounts
- to prevent damage to the payment point.

Do this

- From time to time when you are in charge of a payment point you may need to leave it; you may need to go to the toilet for instance. Find out what is the procedure within your establishment if this type of situation should arise.
- Make a list of all those people who are authorised to have access to the customers' bills, and why they have that authorisation.
- Discuss with your supervisor and then make a list, of when you should hand over monies, to whom, why, and what is the required authorisation.
- Do the same activity but with monies received.

DEALING WITH CUSTOMERS AND UNEXPECTED SITUATIONS

The society in which we live teaches us to have certain expectations of what we should expect to happen in various situations. For instance customers eating in a restaurant have the belief that their bill will be ready for them immediately they call for it. This should be true. Sometimes it may not be, if for example you have a problem with the till. Another problem which may occur is when a customer finds out at the end of a meal that they have not bought any means of payment with them, perhaps they changed before they came out and left their money in the pockets of their other clothes. If you are unable to assist a customer straight away, or the problem is beyond the scope of your authority, remember to remain polite and calm at all times, and contact someone who can help you deal with the situation.

Anticipating customer needs will enable you to prevent most problems. If most people finish their meal between 2 and 2.30 p.m. make sure all the bills are up to date by 2 p.m. This is an example of being aware of a potential problem and defusing it before it occurs. The ability to do this comes through observation and experience.

You cannot, however, anticipate all potential problems. If a customer walks towards a payment point wearing a heavy coat on a summer's day, it may be that they have a gun or other weapon under the coat, as they intend to try to rob the establishment. It may also be a customer who has just come to this country from a much hotter one, and is finding the British summer a little cold. If someone comes into the restaurant and has a cup of coffee which they drink very, very slowly and watches what is going on, it may be a person with dishonest intentions; it may also be a person who is early for an appointment and is merely killing time.

When you are responsible for a vulnerable area, like a payment point, you must learn to become aware of all unexpected behaviour because of the potential trouble it could indicate. However, you must not overreact, and possibly embarrass a genuine customer who happens to be behaving oddly.

Bearing in mind that you must never leave an open payment point unattended, the following points are useful guidelines as to what you can do and what you should not do.

- If you have any reason to believe that there is something unusual going on you must immediately do something and not let it pass hoping that nothing will happen.
- You should always follow the restaurant's policy in dealing with the situation. This would normally be to contact your supervisor, or the security department, if your establishment has one, and report your suspicions.
- Approaching a potentially suspect person by yourself may not be a wise thing to do, nor possible if you are alone at the payment point. It could be dangerous.
- Being aware of suspect behaviour also means keeping an eye out for packages, etc. left lying unattended. These may have simply been forgotten, or they may be much more dangerous even, possibly, a bomb.

Do this

- Find out your establishment's policy for reporting unusual or suspicious behaviour.
- Ask your supervisor, and other members of staff about problem areas which frequently arise. Find out how they deal with them.
- Make a note of when you have a problem at a payment point. After a week or so look at your notes and see if some problems are occurring regularly. If they are, discuss with your supervisor how you could anticipate them, and so prevent them from happening.

Case study

There was an accident on the way to work which blocked the traffic, and so you were late arriving for your shift. You had a very busy session and now you are cashing up at the end of your shift. The payments in your till do not match with the till readings.
1   How do you know that there is a discrepancy?
2   What action must you take?
3   What action can you take in the future to prevent this from happening again?

What have you learned ?

1 Why must you strictly follow your establishment's procedures with regard to the operating of a payment point?
2 What problems may you cause yourself if you do not open, close and hand over a payment point correctly?
3 What is a 'float'?
4 Why should you always have a sufficient amount of change available in the cash drawer?
5 What is the difference between an audit roll and a receipt role?
6 Why shouldn't the cash handler on duty have access to the audit roll or program?
7 Why must the customer have a receipt of some description?
8 Why must it be printed out by the cash machine?
9 What should you do if an unauthorised person wants access to a payment point?
10 Why should you never hand over any monies without the proper authorisation documents?
11 What should you do if you think that someone is behaving in an unusual fashion?
12 Why shouldn't you approach them directly?

ELEMENT 2:   Deal with payments

COMPILING A CUSTOMER'S BILL

In places like supermarkets the customer's bill is often created by swiping the bar code on an item over a computer reader. This reader then tells the cash register how much to charge for the item, and then when all the items have been 'read' it totals up the amount automatically. The cashier does not need to know the price of any item individually, and so they have quite an easy task when compiling a bill. This procedure cannot easily be followed in the service industries: you cannot put a bar code on a portion of freshly cooked spaghetti, for instance, or a glass of wine.

Even in a restaurant where the menu is short and rarely changes and the billing machine can be pre-programmed with the price of each item, you still need to know the code or symbol for each item in order to press the correct key.

This means that you must be very skilful and accurate when compiling a bill, and know exactly what price to charge, or code to use, for each item of food and drink that the customer has purchased. Obviously you will not be able to remember the prices and codes of everything which the customer can buy, especially in a very large restaurant, or if there is a very long menu or wine list, therefore the restaurant will have a set of procedures for keeping you up to date.

The basic components of a bill in a restaurant are food and drink. The menu may either be an à la carte one where each item is charged separately, or a table d'hôte menu, where there is a set price for a certain number of dishes. There may also be special dishes of the day, at special prices, or promotions where a small amount of wine is included with the meal. There are also the beverage charges to be added to the bill.

The basic principles behind compiling a bill do not vary however, whatever is on the bill. They are as follows.
● You must know what types of charges should be on the bill, whether a customer ate from the à la carte menu or the table d'hôte one, etc.
● If when you come to compile the bills you notice that one type of charge appears to be missing you should check. This can be done by contacting the appropriate department, e.g. the dispense bar and asking if the customer had anything to

Mr Eaton			
V.A.T. reg no. 423 1654 39		**Date** 14-9-96	
Couverts 5 Dinners @ £8.50		42	50
Cafe 4 Coffees @ £1.25		5	00
Wine 2 × 23 @ £11.50		23	00
Spirits —			
Liqueurs 1 Drambuie / 1 Tia Maria		2 / 2	50 / 50
Beers —			
Minerals 1 Mineral Water		1	50
Cigars and tobacco			
Table no. 4		**Total £** 77	00
No. covers 5			
04214			

An example bill

drink with their meal. They may have only had tap water so no beverage charge would occur, but this is unusual.

● Once you are sure that you have collected all the charges you must ensure that you enter the correct figure on the bill. If the customer is one person you must charge for only one portion of everything, and if they are entitled to any discounts etc. they must receive them, and so on.

● When all the charges are entered onto the appropriate cash register, they can be totalled, ready for presentation to the customer, or sub-totalled, if the customer is not yet leaving and may use some other services, for example they may decide to have liqueurs after their meal. Common sense should tell you what is the most suitable action to take.

When compiling a bill the most difficult part may be ensuring that the customer is charged the correct amount for any food or drink which they have consumed. This can be a problem:

(a) because you are not expected to remember all the possible prices within the restaurant, and

(b) because the restaurant may offer special discounts, or packages to certain people at certain times, so that the normal prices do not apply.

In order to prevent this problem occurring there should be appropriate price lists at the payment point and if any of the customers are receiving special rates you should be given details of this before the customer arrives at the restaurant, or begins the meal.

Entering checks into a cash register

In some establishments which are highly computerised, it may not be part of the duties of the person operating the payment point to compile the bill because the charges are entered at source. In this case you may merely be required to total and print bills as and when required.

For instance food service personnel may take a food order on a computerised hand-held pad. This will automatically inform the kitchen of the dish ordered as well as informing the payment point to start compiling this new bill.

Whatever system is used in any part of your establishment, there will be a set of guidelines for you to follow so that you will know, once you have collected all the necessary charges, how to record them and create a bill. Whatever system is used you must take great care to make sure that the correct figure or code is entered correctly onto the right bill and that it is ready for presentation at the appropriate time. The bill should then be totalled and made ready for presentation to the customer when the customer requires it.

For certain bills it may be possible to anticipate when the customer is most likely to call for their bill. In these cases you can have the bill already prepared in advance, so as to prevent possible delays if many bills are likely to be required at once. Likely busy periods are immediately after lunch and dinner.

You should also remember the following points.
● It is illegal to charge a price other than the one advertised for any food or beverage.
● All basic prices must be displayed for the customer to see easily, whether for food, drink, accommodation or other services.
● It is very bad for the reputation of any establishment to accidentally over- or under-charge the customers.
● A messy bill, with lots of corrections, would indicate that the establishment, and its staff, are very inefficient.

MEMORY JOGGER

What four points are important to remember when presenting customers' bills?

Untidy, disorganised payment points will alienate customers

A well organised till drawer

Do this

- Find out if your restaurant uses a manual, computerised or semi-computerised system for compiling bills.
- Learn how to compile the bills according to your establishment's procedures for any payment point which you are likely to have to operate. For example you may have to work in two different food service points at some time during your training.
- Make a list of those bills which are compiled for immediate presentation and those for which you will receive payment at a later date.
- If your restaurant uses codes to compile bills make a list of all the codes and what charges they represent.
- Make a list of all the different price lists within your establishment. Check to see that they are available at the appropriate payment point.

PRESENTING AND ACKNOWLEDGING A CUSTOMER'S BILL

There is always an appropriate time to present a bill to a customer, normally upon request. The bill may be presented either by the person working at the payment point, if the customer collects it themselves, or by a member of staff who takes the bill to the customer. This depends both upon within which department the bill is required, and upon establishment procedure.

When a customer asks for their bill it should be presented in a written format; normally it is printed by a cashiering machine, but in some establishments it is handwritten. In this case great care should be taken to ensure that the writing is clear and legible. The customer should be given the bill in a written format so that they can see what charges are on the bill and therefore how the total amount was arrived at. The customer should be allowed time to study the bill, if they choose to do so, before the actual payment is collected.

When the bill is presented it should be done so discreetly. That is to say so that only the customer receiving the bill can see what charges are on it. There are several reasons for this.

- The customer may be entertaining someone else, perhaps for business or as a treat, and they would prefer the other person not to know how much was spent.

Bills should be presented discreetly

- The customer may simply not want the rest of the world to know how much they did or did not spend, or what discounts they received, etc.

When creating or totalling a bill it is essential that the correct prices or codes are used, otherwise the bill will not be correct and unnecessary delays and embarrassment will be caused whilst the errors are corrected. It is also essential to use the correct price and code when accepting payment in any form. The correct price must be entered so that:

- you can give the correct change, if applicable
- he reading on the receipt roll, and audit roll match the amount of payment received
- you charge the customer the correct amount of money.

A bill with a receipt attached

The correct code or ledger information (a bill that is not being paid immediately may be sent to a company for payment, and is called a ledger payment) must be entered when receiving payment so that the accounts department will know how much money to expect in cash and how much in other forms of payment. This information will either be indicated on the keys of the billing machine or, if your establishment uses a computer, there will be a list of codes available at the payment point. You must make yourself familiar with the establishment procedure and codes.

Once payment has been made, even if it is for a non-cash payment, the customer must receive a machine printed receipt showing the amount that they have paid. If the bill was created by machine rather than by hand then it can be used for this purpose. However, if the bill was handwritten the customer must be given a receipt from the billing machine's receipt roll as proof of the transaction.

The exact procedure will vary from establishment to establishment and from machine to machine.

Do this

- Find out if your restaurant creates its customers' bills manually or by machine. If more than one system is used, find out why.
- Find out how your establishment presents bills to different types of customers and in different departments, if applicable.
- Make a list of why some bills are presented in one fashion and some in another.
- Make a list of all the codes which are used when operating a payment point within your restaurant, and what they mean.
- Find out what types of receipts are issued at each payment point that you are likely to work at, and learn to create them yourself.
- Ask your supervisor if there are specific times of the day when certain customer bills are most likely to be required. If there are, ask why these busy times occur and what action you can take to anticipate them so that you will be able to react swiftly and efficiently to them (what work should you have done in advance, what should you have checked?).
- Ask your supervisor what you should do if someone other than the customer, another guest perhaps, says that they have come to collect the bill on the customer's behalf.

THE ACCEPTANCE OF CASH PAYMENTS, RECEIPTS AND CHANGE

You may not always be able to give change to a customer, it depends upon what method they choose to pay by, but you are always able to, and by law must, give a printed receipt for each transaction which takes place.

Once a customer is satisfied that their bill is accurate they will pay.

Cash payment means payment using the coinage and or, printed money of the country which you are in. If a customer pays by this method they are entitled to the appropriate amount of change, again in the coinage or printed money of that country.

When voucher or token payments are made no cash changes hands. This is a method of payment where the actual exchange of cash took place before the customer visited your establishment. For instance, an employer may purchase Luncheon Vouchers for their employees and include them as part of their pay package. Each voucher represents a certain cash value, as written on it, and can be exchanged for food in those establishments which accept this type of voucher or token. When the customer has consumed their meal they will pay for it using these vouchers instead of money. If the meal comes to £5.60 and the customer gives £6.00 worth of vouchers or tokens they would not normally be entitled to any change.

Bill showing an allowance against a person for a meal

Some tokens or vouchers may be a form of part payment. Sometimes organisations promote themselves by having special offers. They may say, for instance, that at the weekend a child can eat for free, if the child's parents, or two adults have a full meal. When this type of token or voucher is presented at the payment point, a certain portion of the bill is not charged to the customers, i.e. the child's food, but the rest is, i.e. the adults bar and restaurant bills.

A printed, itemised bill showing an allowance against a person for a meal

Although a customer is not entitled to change if they do not use up all the facilities available on a voucher or token, for instance if they did not have their free bottle of wine because someone in the party was taking antibiotics at the time, the management might say that they could use up the unused facilities on their voucher at another time. However, this would be a decision which the manager would make and not you.

Whatever method of token or voucher payment is used you must make sure that it is one which is accepted by your restaurant. There should be a list of those which are acceptable at the payment point. Normally, if a customer is going to settle their account using a voucher or token they will tell you when they arrive, or check in advance (perhaps by telephone) before they use the voucher or token. However, there may be customers who present the voucher when they ask for their bill. If the voucher or token is one which is accepted by the restaurant it would simply be accepted and the appropriate information recorded on the bill. If, however, it is not a token or voucher which is acceptable to the restaurant, then you would have to say that you cannot accept it and ask for some other form of payment. If there are any problems here, perhaps with the customer insisting that the voucher should be accepted, then you should be courteous and polite, explaining that you are not able to help them, and ask your supervisor to deal with the problem. Problems often arise if people do not read the expiry dates, or exact terms on free/special offers.

When a voucher or token is accepted in lieu of a cash payment it must be cancelled immediately so that it cannot be used again. There are various methods for doing this. There may be a section on the token or voucher which should be filled in by you, it may be company policy to write cancelled across the voucher or token, or the restaurant may have special date stamps which can be used to show when the voucher was accepted and by what department.

A cancelled voucher

Assuming that everything is fine, the payment in cash, token or voucher form should be accepted, cancelled where appropriate, and stored in the correct compartment of the cash drawer.

As soon as the payment has been placed in the cash drawer it must be closed, for security reasons, to make it less vulnerable to theft, etc. See *Essential knowledge* on page 66. On some machines it is not possible to start a second transaction unless the cash drawer has been fully closed from the first one.

If cash, tokens or vouchers are not placed neatly in the cash drawer then it will be much harder, and much slower, finding change when it is necessary, and if the notes are muddled up into different denominations it is quite easy to give out the wrong change.

Once payment in any form has been accepted the customer is entitled to a printed receipt. The receipt does not necessarily have to show the exact breakdown of the bill, but should show where and when the transaction took place, how much it was for and what type of service it covered, e.g. accommodation, food, the use of leisure facilities, etc. If the customer's bill was printed by the billing machine then it can act as the customer's receipt. This saves the customer from having to have an extra piece of paper to carry around with them, and saves you time in having to produce the receipt. If the customer's bill is also their receipt, it is customary for the bill to be in duplicate or triplicate. This means that it will have one or two, self-duplicating, copies.

A disorganised till drawer

A triplicate bill

The top copy of the bill is given to the customer, with their change if any, and acts as their receipt. The bottom copy/ies are kept by the restaurant and used by the accounts department to make sure that all transactions have been correctly charged for, and all monies taken correctly recorded.

If the customer's bill was handwritten they would have to be given a printed receipt from the till roll (see page 51).

Exactly what you will have to do will depend upon the type of billing machines that your establishment uses, the vouchers and tokens they accept and the establishment's procedures for accepting payment. You must find out all this information as quickly as possible.

Do this

- Make a list of all of the vouchers and tokens which your restaurant accepts.
- Make a list of how to cancel them once they have been accepted.
- Find out what is the restaurant's policy if a customer wants to pay with a voucher or token which the restaurant does not normally accept.
- Find out if the billing machines tell you how much change you should give a customer when they pay by cash, or if you have to work it out.
- Find out what type of receipts your establishment issues, are they the same for all payment points?

ACCEPTANCE AND VALIDATION OF NON-CASH PAYMENTS

There are various types of non-cash payments. Each must be treated slightly differently, but no matter which establishment you work in the basic acceptance and validation procedures for each type of payment remain the same. The main types of payments are as follows:

- cheques e.g. bank, giro or building society cheques; sterling traveller's cheques; Eurocheques
- credit cards e.g. Access/Mastercard; Visa/Barclaycard
- charge cards e.g. American Express; Diners Club
- direct debit cards e.g. Switch; Visa.

CHEQUES

Cheques are issued by banks and building societies. If you are presented with a normal cheque then it means that the customer has an account with the issuing establishment into which they pay money with which their cheques will be paid. A normal cheque can only be used in the country and currency in which it was issued. This means that a cheque from a Barclays Bank anywhere in the UK can be accepted anywhere within the UK and the amount written on it will be in pounds sterling.

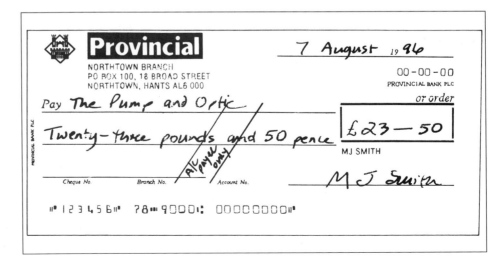

A cheque that has been filled in

TO 30833

A Eurocheque is similar to a normal cheque but it can be accepted anywhere within the European Union and written in any currency. This means that a customer from France can bring a Eurocheque, issued by a bank in France, to the UK and pay for goods and services in sterling.

A Eurocheque that has been filled in

A sterling traveller's cheque is slightly different. In this case the customer will usually have bought, by paying cash, the traveller's cheques from a financial institution, for instance Thomas Cook or American Express, because carrying traveller's cheques is safer than carrying large amounts of cash around. When your establishment accepts the traveller's cheque they will eventually get their money from the issuing financial institution, which already has the customer's money.

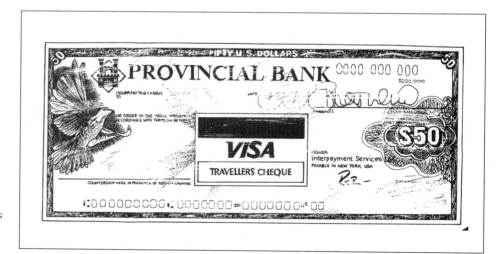

A traveller's cheque that has not yet been countersigned that has been filled in

People tend to carry cheques with them rather than cash if they are not sure how much their bill will come to and because it is a safer method of carrying money than carrying cash. If cheques are stolen then the customer can report this to the issuing company and they can cancel them, and no money is lost. This is not possible with cash. This means however, that when accepting a cheque payment you must always consult the establishment's cancelled/invalid lists. These lists will also record the number of any bank cards which are no longer valid and which should also not be accepted in payment.

ACCESS INVALID CREDIT CARD LIST 25.2.96

Card Number	Expiry Date
5534 9948 7535 9630	10/97
7984 5555 2341 9804	9/97

An invalid/cancelled cheques, credit card list

A bank guarantee card

A bank card is a small plastic card issued by a bank or building society which contains information to enable an establishment to verify the ownership of a cheque.

Bank, building society and Eurocheques should all be supported by the relevant bank card. The bank card has a cash figure on it, usually a multiple of £50, and the signature of the customer. This is to enable you to check that the bill total is not for more than the issuing establishment will accept (the cash amount on the bank card) and by checking the signature on the card against the signature on the cheque you can make sure that the cheque has been written by the correct person. Traveller's cheques are usually supported by a passport or official ID card. Here you will be able to look at the photograph and signature and establish the identity of the customer. If there is no supporting card or passport you must not accept the cheque.

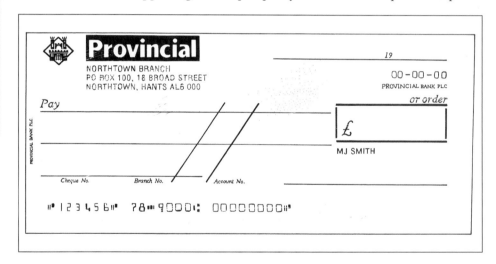

A blank cheque. Compare this with the completed cheque on page 55

BASIC PROCEDURE FOR ACCEPTING BANK, BUILDING SOCIETY AND EUROCHEQUES

1 Show the customer the bill, so that they can write out the amount owing on the cheque.
2 Take the filled out cheque from the customer and check the following points:
   ● the date is written in correctly
   ● the amount, both in writing and figures, is written correctly
   ● the signature on the cheque is the same as that on the bank card
   ● that the signature is written on the original paper strip (if a new one has been pasted to the bank card then when you run your thumb over the back of the card it would catch on the different surface)
   ● if your establishment has a validation machine hold the card under the ultra violet light to check that the hologram is a true one and not a two dimensional fraud
   ● the bank card is valid, not out of date, etc.
   ● that it is the correct bank card; you can check this by making sure that the sort code on the cheque is the same as the sort code on the bank card (except with a Barclays Bank card because the bank card is also able to be used as a credit card under certain circumstances)

● the total of the bill does not exceed the guarantee figure on the bank card (if it does you must follow your establishment's procedure for dealing with the cheque).

3 Compare the bank card and cheque with the cancelled/invalid list, make sure that it does not appear on it.

4 Write the card number on the back of the cheque (you may also be asked to write down other information but that will depend upon your establishment's procedures).

5 Place the cheque in the cash drawer.

6 Give the customer back their bank card, plus a copy of the bill, and a printed receipt if applicable.

If the bill total is for more than the amount guaranteed on the bank card your establishment will have a set of procedures for you to follow. This usually means that other information is entered on the back of the cheque, so that if the cheque is not honoured (paid) by the issuing company the customer can be traced and asked to pay by another method.

Your establishment will also have a set of procedures to follow if the cheque or bank card number show up on the withdrawn list. Make sure that you are familiar with them and follow them, always remembering to be as discreet and tactful as possible. If you accept payment from a cheque or bank card which has been withdrawn, the issuing company will not honour the cheque and your establishment, and perhaps you, will lose money. If, on the other hand, you retain an invalid card correctly you may be financially rewarded.

In some establishments cheques are not handwritten, they are printed out by the billing machine. In this case the above procedures remain the same except for point 1. The procedure would now be to:

1 Show the customer the totalled bill, and take a cheque from them. Print the cheque on the billing machine and return it to the customer for checking and signature.

Then continue as before.

BASIC PROCEDURE FOR ACCEPTING STERLING TRAVELLER'S CHEQUES

Before accepting a sterling traveller's cheque you should note the following:

● An unauthorised traveller's cheque is one on which the second signature is not yet filled in. The first one was filled in when the customer bought the traveller's cheques.

● Traveller's cheques are issued for standard amounts, e.g. £5, £20, £50, etc. This means that when a customer uses this method to pay, the amount on the traveller's cheque is unlikely to be the same as the amount on the bill.

● If the value of the traveller's cheque is greater than the value of the bill then you should give the customer change for the difference. For example if the bill is for £79.50 and the customer gives traveller's cheques worth £80, then they would be entitled to 50p change. If on the other hand a customer's bill came to £55 and they gave the cashier £50 worth of traveller's cheques then the difference would have to be made up, usually by the customer paying £5 in cash.

● Often a customer may use more than one traveller's cheque to pay for one bill. For example they may use two £50 cheques to pay for a £100 bill. This is an acceptable, standard practice.

● Customers who are entitled to change may only be given change in sterling. Only banks and other licensed premises are legally allowed to issue foreign cash.

Accepting a sterling traveller's cheque

1 Show the customer the totalled bill.

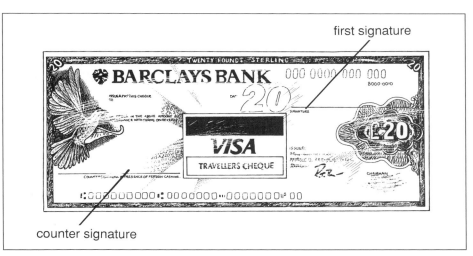

first signature

counter signature

A sterling traveller's cheque, not yet authorised

2 Accept from the customer unauthorised traveller's cheque(s), usually for more than the total of the bill.

3 Accept from the customer an authorised form of identification, usually a passport or an official ID card.

4 Ask the customer to date the traveller's cheque, and countersign it (that is to enter the second signature). This second signature should only be entered in front of the person receiving the payment so that they can authenticate the signature.

5 Check the signature, and the photograph, in the passport or on the ID card against the signature and person in front of you.

6 If it is your establishment's procedure write down the passport or ID card number on the back of the traveller's cheque.

7 Receive the difference between the total of the traveller's cheques being offered and the total of the bill, if applicable.

8 Give the correct change, the identification documents and a printed receipt to the customer.

9 Place the traveller's cheque(s) safely and correctly in the cash drawer.

CREDIT CARDS AND CHARGE CARDS

Some cards are issued by banks, like Barclays, and others are issued by large financial institutions, like American Express. Some are only acceptable within the UK and some are acceptable internationally. Not all restaurants accept all credit and charge cards. This is because they have to pay commission to the issuing company. Your restaurant will have a list of those charge and credit cards which it accepts, and you should familiarise yourself with it so that you only accept the listed cards.

Credit cards

As far as accepting payment by credit or charge card is concerned, you will follow the same basic procedures. This is because the main difference in the type of card is how the establishment receives its final cash payment from the issuing company. Another difference which you will notice is that the internationally accepted cards, which tend to be charge cards, normally have a higher guarantee limit, and the restaurant will have a higher floor limit for this type of card.

A cheque is guaranteed by a bank card, and checking against the cancelled/invalid list. A charge card or credit card payment is guaranteed by the card's printed limit, by the floor limit of the restaurant, by an authorisation code and by checking the cancelled/invalid list.

Floor limits

- The 'floor limit' is the restaurant's credit limit, that is the maximum amount that can be accepted without authorisation for a credit or charge card payment. Its purpose is to reduce the potential for fraud.
- Normally there is a different floor limit for each type of card which the establishment accepts.
- If the total of a bill exceeds the floor limit an authorisation code must be obtained from the issuing company otherwise they may refuse to honour the payment.

Authorisation codes

An authorisation code is needed whenever the bill total is for more than either the card's stated limit, the restaurant's floor limit or both. In this case you must contact the issuing company by following the restaurant's procedure. This will normally be to telephone a special number. You will give the issuing company the following information:
- the name of the restaurant
- the reference number of the restaurant
- the name, number and expiry date on the card
- the total of the bill.

The issuing company, if everything is fine, will then give you a number. This is the authorisation code. It guarantees that the issuing company will reimburse the restaurant for the total of that bill even if the customer should run out of money. Once an authorisation code has been obtained no adjustments may be made to the customer's bill. If one has to be made a new authorisation code for the new amount must be sought.

If there is a problem then you will be asked to retain the card and inform the customer why you are doing so. If this happens your restaurant will have a standard procedure to follow to help you do this; probably it will recommend that you contact your supervisor.

Always remember that when a card is cancelled, whilst it may be that the customer is trying to defraud your restaurant, it could also be that they are a genuine customer whose last payment simply got held up by something like a postal strike. If they are a genuine customer they will be deeply embarrassed, and would not want anyone else to know what has happened. Therefore you must be discreet. In all circumstances you must follow your restaurant's procedures, as well as asking for another form of payment.

Basic procedure for accepting credit and charge cards

In some restaurants the method of accepting credit and charge cards is manual and in others it is incorporated into a computerised system. The procedures vary slightly from one another so both are described below. It may also be useful for your future career to learn both systems.

MEMORY JOGGER

What are floor limits and authorisation codes?

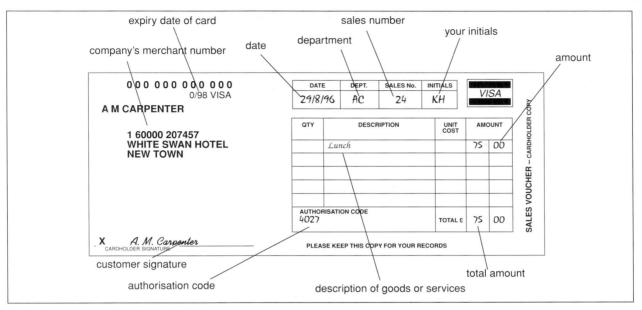

Labels around the credit card form:

- expiry date of card
- sales number
- your initials
- company's merchant number
- date
- department
- amount

Form contents:

0 00 000 000 000
0/98 VISA
A M CARPENTER

1 60000 207457
WHITE SWAN HOTEL
NEW TOWN

DATE	DEPT.	SALES No.	INITIALS	VISA
29/8/96	AC	24	KH	

QTY	DESCRIPTION	UNIT COST	AMOUNT	
	Lunch		75	00

AUTHORISATION CODE
4027

| | TOTAL £ | 75 | 00 |

SALES VOUCHER – CARDHOLDER COPY

X   A. M. Carpenter
CARDHOLDER SIGNATURE

PLEASE KEEP THIS COPY FOR YOUR RECORDS

- customer signature
- authorisation code
- description of goods or services
- total amount

Blank credit card form

A manual acceptance system

1 Give the customer the totalled bill.
2 Accept from the customer the credit or charge card.
3 Check that this is a card which is accepted by your restaurant, and the floor limits for this type of card.
4 Check the following details on the card:
   ● that it is still valid, i.e. the expiry date has not yet been reached
   ● the cash guarantee limit of the card
   ● check that the signature is the original one by running your thumb over it: if a new paper strip has been added with a new signature written on it your thumb will catch on the edge of the new strip
   ● if your restaurant has a validation machine place the credit or debit card under the ultra violet light to check that the hologram is real, not a two-dimensional fraud
5 Take a blank voucher and the credit card, and run them through the imprinting machine.

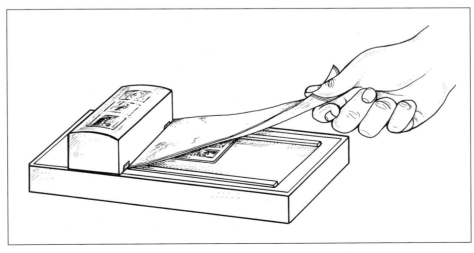

A credit card and voucher
in an imprinter

6 Write the following information onto the voucher:
- date
- department, if applicable
- sales number, if applicable
- your initials
- a brief description of what is being paid for, like 'lunch'
- the amount of the bill in the amount section and the total section
- the authorisation code, if applicable

7 Give the voucher back to the customer to sign.
8 Check the signature of the customer on the voucher against the signature on the card. (The card may be valid, but it may not be the owner of the card who has presented it to you.)
9 Give the customer the customer's copy of the voucher, their card and a printed receipt.
10 Place the restaurant's copies of the vouchers in the correct place in the cash drawer.

A mechanised acceptance method
1 Give the customer the totalled bill.
2 Accept from the customer a charge or credit card.
3 Check that it is a card which is accepted by the restaurant.
4 Swipe the card through the appropriate machine (there will be a machine through which to swipe the card, or it will be incorporated as part of the billing machine). The machine will automatically check the card and provide an authorisation number. When the checks have been successfully completed the machine will print out a duplicate voucher.
5 Ask the customer to sign the voucher.
6 Check the signature on the voucher against that on the card. (Again, the card may be valid, but it may not be the owner of the card who has presented it to you.)
7 Give the customer the customer's copy of the voucher, their card and their copy of the bill.
8 Place the restaurant's copies of the voucher in the correct place within the cash drawer.

In some restaurants there may be a combined manual and mechanised system. Here the normal procedure would be for you to validate the card by swiping it through an authorising machine and entering the total of the bill. The machine would automatically show the authorisation code on a digital display, and you would complete processing the card via the manual system. This system is more popular now than an entirely manual system, because it saves time and all cards can be validated quickly and efficiently at any time of day or night.

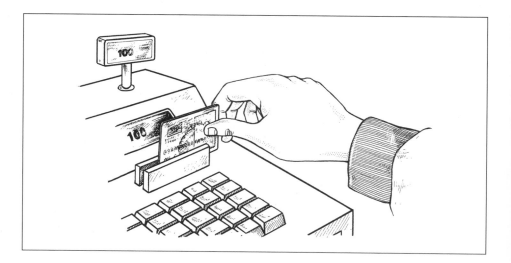

An authorisation machine

If at any stage you are not happy with the transaction, you cannot get an authorisation code, the signatures do not look the same (even after you have asked the customer to sign for the second time on the back), etc. then you should not accept the payment, but, following the restaurant's procedures should get assistance from another member of staff.

This is especially true if the payment point is very busy because if you take a long time to deal with one customer others will be starting to ask where their bills are and become very frustrated. It is also very difficult to be discreet when there is a problem with lots of other people around, like customers and waiters, all trying to collect or pay bills, and therefore able to overhear any conversation which might be going on.

DIRECT DEBIT CARDS

These are cards which directly debit the customer's bank account with the total of the bill, and place that amount into the restaurant's bank account. It is therefore similar to accepting cash, in that there is no waiting period for the payment. However, the procedure for accepting payment by this method is very similar to the mechanised credit or charge card system. The most common card of this type is a Switch card.

Many people choose to carry them in preference to cash, as a security measure. Restaurants are happy to accept them because as long as they are correctly accepted the restaurant is guaranteed its money straight away.

Basic procedures for accepting a direct debit card

1   Give the customer the totalled bill.
2   Accept from the customer the direct debit card.
3   Check that it is a card which is accepted by the restaurant.
4   Swipe the card through the appropriate machine (there will be a machine through which to swipe the card, or it will be incorporated as part of the billing machine). The machine will automatically check the card. When the checks have been successfully completed the machine will print out a duplicate voucher.
5   Ask the customer to sign the voucher.
6   Check the signature on the voucher against that on the card. (The card may be valid, but it may not be the owner of the card who has presented it to you.)
7   Give the customer the customer's copy of the voucher, their card and their copy of the bill.

As with any other form of non-cash payment, if you are not happy with any part of the acceptance or validation procedure you should follow your restaurant's procedure for dealing with problems in a non-cash payment situation. This will normally involve explaining the problem to a more senior member of staff, in the first instance.

DEALING WITH ERRORS OR SPOILT CHEQUES OR VOUCHERS

From time to time, especially when you first start training, you will make errors. Your supervisors expect a few problems to occur, and there will be an establishment policy for dealing with them. However, when a cheque or voucher is spoilt or written incorrectly there are several basic steps to follow which will be part of your establishment procedure. These steps are the following.

Cheques

1   If any part of the cheque is written out incorrectly (often it is the date), the customer can cross the error through, write down the correct information and initial the error.

2 As long as the cheque is still clearly legible it will not matter if there is more than one correction on it, but all the corrections must be initialled by the customer.

3 If there are a lot of corrections it is better to cancel the cheque by tearing it up in front of the customer so that they can see you doing it, and giving them the torn cheque if they require it. In this case a new cheque would be written out.

Credit or charge cards

1 If there are any errors the voucher must be voided.

2 The voucher should be torn up, in front of or by the customer, and they should be given the torn voucher if they require it.

3 A new voucher should be written out.

If your establishment has a mechanised method of accepting credit or charge cards and you make an error, perhaps in the amount of the bill, when you are creating the voucher there will be a method of cancelling the voucher immediately. Your company will have a procedure for this, there is probably a void key on the machine, and you must always follow this procedure keeping all paperwork that is generated by the error, i.e. the incorrect voucher and the cancellation slip. These should be placed in your cash drawer and handed over at the end of your shift.

Do this

- Write down the procedure for accepting a cheque if it is for more than the guaranteed cash limit on the card.
- Make a list of forms of ID other than a passport acceptable to your establishment when accepting sterling traveller's cheques.
- Make a list of all the credit cards and charge cards which your restaurant accepts.
- Make a list of your establishment's floor limits for each card which is accepted.
- Find out where the cancelled/invalid lists are kept. Make sure that there is one beside the cash point.
- Write down exactly what you should do if you are at all worried about accepting a non-cash payment.
- Find out whether your restaurant uses a manual or mechanised credit and charge card authorisation system, and learn how to use it.
- Write down the procedure which your restaurant uses to cancel unusable cheques and vouchers.

SECURITY OF THE PAYMENT POINT

Given that any form of payment is a temptation to dishonest people, it is obvious that security of the payment point is very important. If unauthorised persons gain access to a payment point they will be able to gain access to the customers' bills, as well as cash and other forms of payment.

If a person gains access to the payment point they may be able to find out unauthorised information about various customers of the establishment. For example, if a celebrity is dining they may not want fans, press or other interested people to know that they are dining in the restaurant, as they would like to enjoy their meal uninterrupted. The information gained can also be used more seriously, perhaps in a legal situation such as a divorce court.

Unauthorised people may also behave in other dishonest ways, for example they may alter the totals of the customers' bills, e.g. lower their own. They may also simply steal, i.e. remove cash and other valuable items.

For these reasons payment points must be kept secure, and are sometimes physically separate from the other parts of the restaurant, and can even be within a secure cubicle.

MEMORY JOGGER

Why must you never leave the payment point unattended?

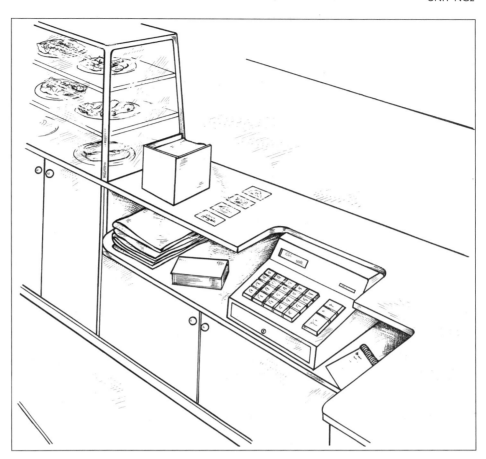

The cash machine should be positioned away from the access end of the service station

In other establishments the payment point is incorporated within the main service station (see above).

If you are the person authorised to deal with payments during a shift then you are responsible for the security and safety of the contents of your cash drawer and for the safety and confidentiality of the customers' bills.

There are several golden rules which you should observe at all times.
● Never leave the payment point unattended for any significant period of time.
● If you have to leave the payment point unattended, perhaps to serve a customer, make sure that the payment point is securely locked.
● Never allow anyone except the customer, or a properly authorised person to look at the customers' bills.
● Never allow anyone without proper authorisation into the area of the payment point.
● If you have to make an adjustment to a customer's bill, get the proper authorisation and signature before you do so.
● If you have to void a voucher or cheque actually tear it up in front of the customer so that they can be certain that it has been destroyed.
● Whenever you have the smallest doubt about the honesty of anyone's actions immediately contact your supervisor.

Beyond this, each establishment will have a security procedure which has been set up to deal with each payment point's security needs. You must always follow this procedure.

Essential knowledge	It is essential that payment points are secured from unauthorised access:
	● to prevent members of the public or members of staff stealing from the payment point
	● to make sure unauthorised persons do not see customers' accounts
	● to prevent anyone tampering with the payment point, for example, by making false charges or adjustments to customers' accounts
	● to prevent damage being done to the payment point.

Do this

● From time to time when you are in charge of a payment point you may need to leave it, you may need to go to the toilet for instance. Find out what is the procedure within your restaurant if this type of situation should arise.

● Make a list of all those people who are authorised to have access to the customers' bills, and why they have that authorisation.

● Discuss with your supervisor and then make a list, of when you should hand over any form of payment, to whom, why, and what is the required authorisation.

DEALING WITH REFUNDS

You may be the first person to hear about a problem for which a customer feels that they are entitled to a refund. This is because the payment point is where they settle their account. When dealing with such customers you should remember the following points.

● From time to time refunds either in cash or credit will need to be made by all establishments.

● Not all refunds are the results of errors, or bad service, etc., however, most are.

● A customer requiring a refund will usually be unhappy about something and therefore will require especially sympathetic handling.

● Applications for refunds are as open to abuses such as fraud, just as payments are.

● Because all applications for refunds are potentially fraudulent, all refunds must be appropriately authorised.

● The issuing of a refund must be authorised and recorded. If cash is handed over without being recorded, the person who handed it over is open to accusations of cash discrepancies, i.e. theft.

● All applications for refunds must be recorded so that management can take action to prevent the problem re-occurring.

There are three basic reasons why a customer may ask for a refund, but in each case they may be, or appear to be very angry, and so need to be treated very politely and diplomatically. The reasons are as follows.

1 If something has gone wrong, for example the customer asked for chicken breast from a roast chicken and was served a drumstick, then they are entitled to be angry. If they requested a birthday cake in advance, and it did not arrive at the end of the meal, they are caused great inconvenience. This means that when you are dealing with them you will have to be especially tactful.

2 A customer may be 'trying it on'. That is to say seeing if they can get a price reduction even if they are not really entitled to it. A senior member of staff after investigating the incident will have to give authorisation, after they have become satisfied that the incident has occurred. This type of customer usually appears very angry in order to intimidate the establishment's staff. This is why a senior member of staff should investigate it and deal with the problem.

3 A customer may have a problem, but they may have caused it themselves, for example when they ordered their meal they did not mention that they were allergic to bacon, but a hock was used in the preparation of the lentil soup, and so the

soup made them ill. Again a senior member of staff will have to investigate the incident, and make a decision about whether or not the guest is entitled to some form of compensation.

In all these cases it is you who often gets the first blast of anger. Your restaurant will have a procedure to deal with this. If you follow it and remain calm the incident can be defused and remedies offered, but if you take the customer's anger personally and become angry in return the problem will get worse. For more information about how to deal with customer complaints see *Unit 2NG3*.

Your restaurant will have a procedure for validating and issuing refunds. You must never deviate from this procedure because it is designed to protect staff as well as the restaurant.
- Issuing a refund means giving money away from the business. It can only be done if a senior member of staff has authorised it.
- Giving money away means that the money in your cash drawer will be short. You must have documentation to justify the shortage.
- As a refund claim is as potentially open to fraud as any other payment transaction, the claim must be validated before the refund is issued.

Most establishments will follow the same basic rules and only the fine detail will vary from establishment to establishment. The basic procedure is as follows.
1 The restaurant becomes aware of a problem. This may happen in two ways.
   - In the first incident the restaurant's staff become aware of the problem, and

Mr Eaton			
V.A.T. reg no. 423 1654 39	**Date** 14 -9- 96		
Couverts 5 Dimers @ £8.50		42	50
Cafe 4 coffees @ £1.25		5	00
Wine 2 x 23 @ £11.50		23	00
Spirits —			
Liqueurs 1 Drambuie 1 Tia Maria		2 2	50 50
Beers —			
Minerals 1 Mineral Water		1	50
Cigars and tobacco Sub Total:		77	00
Credit 1 x No. 23 wine		11	50
Table no. 4	**Total £**	65	50
No. covers 5			
04214			

A customer's restaurant bill with a reduction against the meal

alert the appropriate senior member of staff. For instance a customer who has arranged a surprise party at the restaurant asked for flowers for the ladies to be available upon arrival, and paid in advance for them as it was an unusual request. The flowers have not arrived (they were sent elsewhere in error) and the florist has closed for the day. Here the management know that there is a genuine problem before the customer is aware of it and complains, and can work out the remedial action to take, e.g. arrange for champagne to be available upon the party's arrival and debit the cost of the flowers from the total of the bill.

● In the second type of incident the customer becomes aware of the problem first. For instance they may have ordered one bottle of wine with their meal but the cost for two has been put on their bill. Your first action, after apologising, would be to contact the appropriate senior member of staff. The senior member of staff will quickly investigate the incident.

2   Once the senior member of staff is sure that the incident happened then they will authorise you to make a refund. They will do this by writing up the incident in a Refund Book, which will be similar to the example given here.

Date	Details	Cash Refund	Credit Refund	Authorised By	Cashier

A page from an example Refund Book

3   If the refund is a *cash refund* then cash is removed from the cash drawer and given to the customer. There will normally be a duplicate book for the customer to sign saying that they have received the cash, with the bottom copy going into the cash drawer to justify the reduction in cash. If the refund is a credit refund, that is to say that there is an adjustment made on the customer's bill, then no cash changes hands but when the customer comes to pay their bill there will be a reduction on it for the agreed amount.

4   If the refund is a *credit or charge card refund* then you will have to fill in a voucher which is very similar to a credit or charge card voucher. However, it will say refund. You will take an imprint of the customer's card, or run it through an authorisation machine, according to your restaurant's procedures. The customer will sign the voucher and retain their copy. However, when the customer eventually receives their statement from their credit or charge card company they will find that the refund amount has been deducted from their statement, not added on to it.

RIVERSIDE RESTAURANT

CREDIT NOTE

Name ....   Date ....

Address ....   Issued by ....

....   Authorised by ....

....

Credit to the value of: ....

A credit/refund voucher

As previously mentioned, if your establishment has a mechanised method of accepting credit and charge card payments, and you make an error which you notice before the voucher is signed there will be a method of voiding the voucher which you have just created. Always follow your establishment's procedure for doing this.

5   If the senior member of staff is not satisfied that the refund is justified then they will not authorise it, they will deal with the customer in private away from the public work areas. If there is no authorisation you must never give out a refund, even if it is only for a tiny sum like 50p, because you may not know the whole story.

In all restaurants the basic procedures will be as described above, however there will be variations in the documentation to be completed and in the members of staff who are authorised to issue refunds. You must learn the procedure for your restaurant.

Do this

● Find out what is your restaurant's procedure for dealing with applications for refunds.
● Find out who is authorised to give refunds in your restaurant.
● Find out where the refund authorisation book is kept
● Find out if there is a special key on your billing machine which is used to indicate that a credit refund has been given.
● Over a period of a month make a list of all the refunds which you are authorised to deal with. Analyse the list and see if any of the incidents occur regularly. Discuss them with your supervisor.
● Ask your supervisor how they deal with very angry customers, and learn some techniques from them for handling people who are upset or angry.

DEALING WITH CUSTOMERS AND UNEXPECTED SITUATIONS

Customers expect an efficient service at all times. This should be true. Sometimes it may not be. If you are unable to assist a customer straight away remember to remain polite and calm at all times, and if you are unable to deal with the customer at all, contact someone who can.

Anticipating customer needs will enable you to prevent most problems. If most people eat lunch between 12 noon and 2 p.m. make sure that all the documentation for creating bills is ready by 11.30 a.m. This is an example of being aware of a potential problem and defusing it before it occurs. The ability to do this comes through observation and experience.

You cannot, however, anticipate all potential problems. If a customer walks towards a payment point with a folded paper held in both hands, it may be that they have a gun or other weapon under the paper, as they intend to try to rob the establishment. It may also be a customer who has a strange way of holding their newspaper.

If someone comes into the restaurant and just orders a mineral water which they take a very long time to drink, whilst sitting and watching what is going on, it may be a person with dishonest intentions; it may also be a person who has arrived early for an appointment nearby and who is merely killing time.

The ability to deal well with unexpected situations comes mainly through personal experience, and observing how others deal successfully with incidents. The restaurant's procedure for dealing with unexpected incidents has been set up to provide a set of guidelines to work within, but common sense is also required.

When you are responsible for a vulnerable area, like a payment point, you must learn to become aware of all unexpected behaviour, because of the potential trouble it could indicate. However, you must not overreact, and possibly embarrass a genuine customer who happens to be behaving oddly. Bearing in mind that you must never leave an open payment point unattended, the following points are useful guidelines as to what you can do and what you should not do.

A customer who may have criminal intentions

- If you have any reason to believe that there is something unusual going on you must immediately do something, such as contacting your supervisor, and not let it pass hoping that nothing will happen.
- You should always follow the establishment's policy in dealing with the situation. This would normally be to contact your supervisor, or the security department, if your establishment has one, and report your suspicions.
- Approaching a potentially suspect person by yourself may not be a wise thing to do, nor possible if you are alone at the payment point. It could also be dangerous.
- Being aware of suspect behaviour also means keeping an eye out for packages, etc. left lying unattended. These may have simply been forgotten, or they may be much more dangerous.

Do this

- Find out what is your establishment's policy for reporting unusual or suspicious behaviour.
- Consciously try to become aware of anyone who is behaving in an unusual fashion when they enter a vulnerable area, like a payment point.
- Ask your supervisor, and other members of staff about problem areas which frequently arise. Find out how they deal with them.
- Make a note of when you have a problem at a payment point. After a week or so look at your notes and see if some problems are occurring regularly. If they are, discuss with your supervisor how you could anticipate them, and so prevent them from happening.

Case study

A group of customers in your restaurant have just finished their meal. They said that they had had a great time. However, when they come to pay they offer you a voucher for a promotion which finished last week and which your restaurant no longer accepts.

What should you do: (a) immediately and (b) to prevent future incidents like this occurring?

What have you learned

1 If a customer gives you a form of payment which is more than the total of the bill, under what circumstances should you not give them change?
2 Why must vouchers and tokens be cancelled immediately?
3 Why must cash drawers be kept closed when not in actual use?
4 Why must the customer be charged the correct price for a good or service?
5 Why should the customer be able to look at the bill before they pay it?
6 Why must price lists be displayed?
7 Why must printed receipts be given?
8 What do you need to guarantee a bank, building society or Eurocheque?
9 What do you need to guarantee a sterling traveller's cheque?
10 Which type of cheque can you give change to?
11 In what currency?
12 If an error is made on a credit or charge card voucher what is the most secure way of voiding it?
13 What credit cards and charge cards are accepted by your restaurant?
14 How should all cheques and vouchers be held securely at a payment point?
15 Who should cheques and vouchers be given to and why?
16 Why must all refunds be authorised?
17 Who is able to authorise refunds?
18 What should you do if a refund is not authorised?
19 Where should a refund be recorded if it is a) a cash refund, and b) a credit refund?
20 Why must you remain calm and helpful all the time?
21 Why shouldn't unauthorised people have access to a payment point?
22 Why must you never leave a payment point unattended?
23 Why must you report all unusual situations?
24 Why must you follow company procedure at all times?

Get ahead

1 Find out what 'fidelity bonding' means.
2 Learn how all the payment points in your establishment work, not just the ones in your area.
3 Find out how all the charges on a customer's bill are arrived at, and how they get to the various payment points in the establishment.
4 Find out what a 'ledger' payment is, and how the account is settled with your establishment.
5 Find out why your establishment only accepts certain vouchers and tokens.
6 Find out why some vouchers and tokens can only be used at certain times.
7 The government says that customers must have a printed receipt for each transaction, it will protect them. From whom or what will it protect them and how?
8 Your establishment should have a list of procedures which you must follow when operating a payment point. Some of those procedures are to protect the establishment, some are to protect the cash handlers, some cover both areas. Identify which procedures protect the establishment, which the cash handlers, which both. How do they do this?
9 Find out why it is useful for management to have the details of all refunds recorded. What use do they make of this information?
10 Find out what are the most common reasons for your senior staff to refuse to give a refund. What do they do when this type of situation occurs?
11 Find out how much commission your restaurant pays for each type of credit or charge card it accepts.
12 Find out why your restaurant accepts the cards they do.
13 Find out how long it takes for the restaurant to actually receive the money in the bank if they accept payment by any non-cash method.
14 Make a list of the most common ways that conmen are able to defraud restaurants using non-cash payment methods.
15 Find out the legal position if very confidential information about customers is given out to unauthorised persons by your restaurant.

UNIT 2NG3

Develop and maintain positive working relationships with customers

---

This chapter covers:

ELEMENT 1:   **Present positive personal image to customer**
ELEMENT 2:   **Balance needs of customer and organisation**
ELEMENT 3:   **Respond to feelings expressed by the customer**
ELEMENT 4:   **Adapt methods of communication to the customer**

What you need to do

● Learn to deal with all customers in a polite and professional manner at all times.
● Learn to work efficiently under stress.
● Learn to identify all individual customer needs accurately and anticipate them, where possible.
● Learn how to help customers without being pushy or rude.
● Identify how your establishment requires you to present yourself.

● Make sure that you maintain the required standards of behaviour and personal presentation at all times.
● Identify the equipment and supplies which you will need to work efficiently.
● Make sure the equipment is available, up to date and in good working order.
● Learn to work within current health and safety, and all other relevant, legislation.

What you need to know

● What standards of behaviour and personal appearance your establishment expects you to maintain.
● Why you must always be polite and courteous to customers.
● What equipment you will need for each job that you may be asked to do.

● How to maintain and replenish that equipment.
● How to constantly seek to improve your relationships with your customers, within the professional limits of your establishment.

INTRODUCTION

When serving food and drink in the restaurant, one of the most important tasks is dealing with customers. For most customers you will be the first and last person they deal with. This means that how you behave is crucial to how the customer perceives the rest of the establishment, and whether or not they enjoy their meal. You will have to develop great skills of tact and diplomacy in order to be able to cope with all the situations which will arise, and learn to remain calm under all circumstances. Without customers you will have no work.

73

ELEMENT 1:   Present positive personal image to customer

All customers are individuals and need to be treated as such. Most of the work involved in dealing with customers will be routine, and you will easily be able to help them if you have a good enough knowledge of your restaurant, what food is served, the way it is served, the facilities available within the rest of the establishment, if applicable, and the local environment.

However, you must also remember that you have obligations, or limitations upon your behaviour, with regard to the establishment that you work for, some of which are legal requirements. So you must try to achieve a balance between the needs of the customer and the limitations of the establishment.

When you are at work, especially in a food service area you are acting as the public representative of your establishment, and how you behave will affect how the customers think about your establishment. Sometimes, when you are very busy, you may feel very pressured, for instance if your customers cannot make up their minds what to order and there are several customers to serve. If you snap at the customer, ask them to hurry up perhaps, they will become offended, and very difficult. Remember your customers have come out to enjoy themselves, do a business deal, or drown their sorrows, not to deal with your problems.

You must learn to deal efficiently with these pressures in a way that pleases the customer and enables you to use your time most effectively. For instance, if the customer cannot decide which main course to have, you can recommend one or two, which will both speed up their decision making, and make them feel that you have contributed positively to their enjoyment. You could also suggest coming back to take their order later if they are enjoying their discussion about what to have. Then you can serve someone else who knows what they want, but neither group of customers will feel neglected, and the first group will feel that you understood just what they wanted – thinking time.

You must not forget your first group of customers, if they have chosen to think awhile, otherwise you risk losing the positive images which they have about the establishment.

If the customers require assistance which you are unable to give, perhaps about the different types of port served, ask your supervisor or another member of staff for assistance. However, you should never be unable to serve a customer because you have forgotten to prepare some equipment correctly for your shift.

When you first start work you will not know about every product which the establishment sells, nor how to present them but you must make it a priority to find out as soon as you can, so that you are able to:

- answer customer enquiries correctly, and make positive recommendations when required
- ensure that all the equipment which you need to serve your customers is available, e.g. service equipment, order pads
- work as efficiently as possible, because you know what you are serving and how it should be served
- give your customers the best, most efficient service possible
- reduce pressure on yourself at busy times, so that you can react more positively to your customers requirements.

Your establishment will set certain standards of behaviour and personal appearance for all staff. For instance you may be required to wear a uniform. This is partly to help create the correct establishment image, but also for hygiene and safety reasons. For more information on health and safety at work see *Unit NG1*.

However, your behaviour as much as your appearance will affect how the customer

---

MEMORY JOGGER

Why must you always be polite to customers, even when you are very busy?

MEMORY JOGGER

Why must you make sure that all the equipment and supplies you need for your shift are ready before you start?

perceives you, and the establishment will have standards of behaviour which they will expect you to maintain. For instance, in all establishments you will be required to present a cheerful face to all of your customers, no matter how much your feet hurt, etc., but in some establishments you will need to go out into the restaurant and serve the customers at their table while in others you will be required to wait behind the food counter and assist people as they come to you.

From time to time you may notice that a customer needs something, and be able to offer it to them before they request it, for instance a new napkin, or more water. When this happens you should provide what the customer needs before they have to ask for it because the customer will feel that they have been well looked after, and so will feel more positive about your establishment. They may even stay longer and place another order!

Essential knowledge

- A customer will always respond positively to a positive member of staff and negatively to a negative one.
- Organisational standards are designed to enable you to provide the customer with the level of service which they expect.
- If you do not prepare your equipment and supplies correctly at the start of your shift, you will not be able to work efficiently.

Do this

- Make a list of all the equipment and supplies you need to have ready at the start of each shift in order to do your job efficiently.
- Find out how to order new supplies when that is necessary.
- Find out how to have equipment repaired if it should become faulty.
- Ask your supervisor what standard of dress and behaviour is expected of you, and always stick to it.
- Ask your supervisor about legislation relating to safe working practices.
- Practise smiling even when you are under pressure.

Case study

A new member of staff has just been employed. They do not like the material that the uniform trousers, which you all have to wear, is made from. Neither do you. They suggest, as only you two will be in the food service area for the next shift that you wear your own trousers.
1   *What would you like to do?*
2   *What are you going to do?*
3   *Why?*

What have you learned

1 Why must you always be courteous, even when you are very busy?
2 Why must you always maintain the standard of behaviour required by your establishment?
3 How can you find out what these standards are?
4 How can you build a positive working relationship with your customers?
5 Why should you do so?
6 Why must you always be properly prepared at the start of your shift?
7 Where do you get more equipment and supplies from when you need them?
8 Why must you maintain health and safety regulations?

ELEMENT 2:   Balance needs of customer and organisation

In order for you to be able to balance the needs of your customers and the abilities of your establishment, you must have a detailed knowledge of your establishment's facilities. You must also be aware of what type of information is confidential, and the legal requirements in force. This will enable you to deal with most of the situations you are likely to find yourself in. It is important to remember the following points.

- Help the customer whenever you are able to do so.
- Identify all company procedures for dealing with customer needs.
- Only give that information to customers which is within your authority.
- Identify what senior management are available and at what times, should any difficulties arise outside your ability to act.

To help you deal with any situation that might arise you need to know:

- why you must always try to assist your customers
- why you should not give assistance to a customer which is beyond your authority
- what assistance you are unable to give
- why you are unable to give that assistance
- when to get assistance from your supervisor
- how to record any incidents.

Essential knowledge

- A comprehensive accurate knowledge of the menu, dish composition, drinks available, methods and times of service will enable you to answer 90 per cent of enquiries and describe the establishment's facilities and products professionally to a customer.
- Inaccurate information will result in angry and embarrassed customers.
- When you are unable to deal with an enquiry or request, someone else *will* be able to, and the enquiry, or request, must be passed to them as soon as possible so that the customer's needs can be attended to swiftly.
- Some information is confidential and it must never be given out. To do so may break the law and/or cause the customers (or staff) great embarrassment.
- Not all comments require action, but all should be acknowledged so that the customer does not feel ignored.
- Comments which need action, good or bad, should be passed to the appropriate person for action as soon as possible.
- You can have a direct bearing upon the success of the business if you encourage the customers to use facilities which they might not otherwise have done.
- If you over promote – 'hard sell' – you may put the customers off, and prevent them from using one of the establishment's other facilities.

DEALING WITH CUSTOMER ENQUIRIES

Enquiries fall into two categories, those that require confidential information and which you may not answer and those which require non-confidential information which you may answer.

Non-confidential enquiries

Many customers have a belief that any member of staff will be able to answer any query that is put to them, and nine times out of ten you should be able to do so. This is because although you will be asked many questions most of them will be about the same subjects. As long as you know about these areas you will be able to help. Most questions fall into the four categories listed below.

1 *One type of question will be about the establishment and its facilities.* This means that you are as likely to be asked if you can heat a baby's bottle, as the opening times of the restaurant and what type of food it serves. You must therefore make sure that you know what facilities your establishment has, when customers can use them, and if there are any extra charges, perhaps for specialised food requests, such as a kosher meal. You must also be able to direct the customers accurately to any part of the establishment that they wish to get to.

2 *Another common query will be about local facilities,* e.g. how to get to the local station, what time mainline trains run, numbers of local taxi companies and so on. If you have a good working knowledge of the facilities or have easy access to guides and other sources of information again you will be able to help. If your establishment is a hotel then it will have a reception desk, and may have a concierge's or porter's desk. It may be company policy that they deal with certain enquiries and bookings. In this case you should explain to the customer and direct them to the correct place.

3 *Some queries may require that the customer needs to speak to another member of staff,* perhaps they have special dietary needs, or want to make a special party booking. In this case you should locate the required member of staff and enable the customer and staff member to talk to each other. In order to deal with this type of enquiry you will have to know the names and responsibilities of all the supervisory staff in the establishment and how to contact them.

4 *Customers may ask you for a particular product that you sell.* For instance, when ordering a customer may ask, 'Can I have a Perrier water please?'. If you serve them another type of mineral water you will not have provided them with what they asked for, and in fact, will have broken the Trades Descriptions Act. You must always be accurate. What you could have done would have been to say, 'I'm sorry we don't have Perrier water, but we do have … (whatever type of mineral water your establishment serves)'. The customer then knows what type of drink they are getting and you remain within the law. You would also be breaking the law if you said that the gateaux on the dessert menu were freshly made on the premises when, in fact, they were bought in.

5 *Sometimes customers may ask you questions to which you do not know the answers.* In this case you should tell them that you do not know, but that you will find out or pass them on to someone who can help them. If you give out the wrong information, because you think that it may be right, you may actually cause the customer a lot of inconvenience and embarrassment. For instance if you say that there is a vegan dish on the menu and the customer orders it, when it arrives and turns out to be a vegetarian dish the customer will be unable to eat it, and be angry and upset. An even worse incident would occur if you were to say that the establishment has easy access for wheelchair users, perhaps to a telephone enquiry, but when the customer arrived they found out that it did not and they were unable to enter the establishment without help.

It is not possible for you to be able to anticipate every single thing that all the customers could possibly ask you, but if you say that you do not know it will give you a breathing space to find out the answer or to find out whom to pass the enquiry onto. When customers ask very unusual questions they do not normally expect you to be able to answer them immediately, but they do expect that whatever answer they get will be accurate.

Confidential enquiries

From time to time you may be asked for information which it would be indiscreet for you to give out, or for confirmations of details that you are not authorised to give. In this situation you must exercise great tact and diplomacy. For instance, in a hotel restaurant, if someone came to you and asked the room number of another guest in the restaurant you have no way of knowing whether or not the other guest wants anyone else to know a) if they are staying at the hotel and b) in which room

Do not give misleading information to customers

they are staying, if they are. Your establishment will probably have a code of practice for this type of situation. This does not mean that you should be unhelpful though. You can always say that you will take and pass on a message.

Customers may also ask odd questions about the products which you sell such as who supplies them, or even, how much money is made by the establishment. You will need to be very tactful as well as discreet in replying to these enquiries, without disclosing information which you have no authority to give.

Remember though, if you do take a message, you must see that it reaches its destination, whether it is for a customer or a member of staff. The message may be very important, or trivial, but you do not know which. To pass on information accurately you should always write it down at the time that you take it.

If it is a formal message, e.g. a complaint, there will be an establishment procedure to follow, and forms to fill in. For more details see page 81 on customer complaints. If it is an informal message, e.g. 'Mary Ward has been called away and so is unable to wait for Lesley Mason', a note on a memo pad will be sufficient, as long as the message is passed to Lesley Mason upon arrival at the restaurant

You should remain calm, professional and discreet in these circumstances as it is nothing to do with you why one person may or may not want to talk to another, nor why one person might enquire after something or someone else. However, if you give out information which you do not have the authority to give out, you may inadvertently break the law, and/or cause your company great embarrassment.

MEMORY JOGGER

What should you do if one customer asks about another one?

DEALING WITH CUSTOMER COMMENTS

It is always important to treat all comments seriously. If a customer has been sufficiently motivated to bring some point to the notice of a member of staff, then you should have the courtesy to listen politely, so that the customer feels that they are being taken seriously, and are important.

Customer comments differ from customer enquiries in that they are not asking you something, they are telling you something. This may be good or bad and may or may not require you to take some form of action.

A comment might range from someone saying that they like the floral arrangement on the table, to someone saying that the soup appears to be rather salty. In the first case no action other than an acknowledgement of the guest's comment is required. In the second case the message should be passed on to the supervisor and/or chef immediately so that they can take remedial action.

From the establishment's point of view, dealing with a comment quickly and efficiently may prevent a major problem occurring. If a guest says that the soup is rather salty, and it is, swift action will prevent other customers from eating something which is actually unpleasant and would prevent them from enjoying their meal.

If the comment is favourable, for instance the customers said that the food or service in the restaurant had been extremely good, this should also be passed on as it encourages the staff concerned to keep up their standards of service.

PROMOTING THE ESTABLISHMENT'S FACILITIES CORRECTLY

You will often be asked many questions about the establishment. To be efficient and professional, as we have established, you will need to know about all of the features of your restaurant and possibly the other facilities of your establishment. Having this knowledge means that there may be times when you can encourage a customer to use more of your establishment's facilities than they had originally intended.

Most of the facilities of any restaurant are promoted using the menu and wine lists. These are usually given to the customer upon their arrival in the restaurant and in an hotel are included as part of the guest packages in the bedrooms. However, simply because something is handed out to a customer does not mean that it will be read. This is especially true if the customers are foreigners, as they may not be able to read English, or if the customer has poor or bad eyesight.

Your customers may not order certain dishes because they do not know that they are available in your restaurant or because they are not aware that your restaurant can cater for their specialist needs. When a customer asks where they may be able to eat ethnic food for example, if your menu has a suitable dish you can draw their attention to it, or suggest that they might like to talk to the chef about their dietary requirements.

Not all of the establishment's services remain the same all of the time. It may be company policy to offer special packages or promotions at certain times of the year, such as at Christmas. You need to become aware of these activities so that you can promote them to your customers.

The more that the facilities of your establishment are used the more likely it is that it will remain in business.

> **MEMORY JOGGER**
>
> Why should you try, continuously, to help the customers?

Case study

You have taken a booking for a group of customers for next week. The customer making the booking mentions that one of the party has coeliac disease. This is an allergy to wheat.

1. *What would you do immediately?*
2. *What information would you pass on to which other people?*
3. *What is your establishment's procedure for communicating this type of information?*
4. *What must you **not** do?*

Do this

- Make a list of all of the special features of your menu and wine list which your customers may like, and, if applicable, when they are available.
- Make a list of all the reference books that it would be useful to have available in the restaurant (such as telephone directories). If they are not available ask your supervisor why.
- If your establishment has a concierge's or porter's desk find out what types of enquiries they deal with.
- Make a list of all of the supervisors in your establishment, what they are responsible for and how you would contact them, e.g. via a paging system, or a telephone extension or some other method.
- Write down your establishment's policy on the handling of written messages if there is no one available to deal with a specialist enquiry immediately.
- Ask your supervisor what your company's policy is on giving out any type of information about the guests in your establishment.
- Write down what you should do when someone asks you for information which it would be indiscreet and against company policy to give out.
- Write down how you feel when you are praised for doing something well.
- Discuss with your supervisor, and then make a list, of those types of comments which should be passed on and those which should just be acknowledged.
- Find out your establishment's method of passing on comments and make yourself familiar with it.
- From your tariff, menu or beverages lists highlight those special features that could be offered as an alternative when a customer asks about a local facility, e.g. if a foreign visitor asked about a traditional pub, would your establishment's bar be a suitable alternative?
- Make a list of all of the special activities coming up in your establishment so that you can recommend them at the appropriate time.

What have you learned

1 What knowledge should you seek in order to be able to answer 90 per cent of the questions you will be asked without difficulty?
2 Which is the most unprofessional: a) to be unable to answer a query immediately or b) to give inaccurate information?
3 Why is some information confidential?
4 What should you do if you are unable to answer a question?
5 What is the difference between a comment and an enquiry?
6 Why should good as well as bad comments be passed on?
7 In what ways can you directly influence the success of the establishment?
8 Even when promotional material is available why should you draw customers' attention to the special facilities of the menu or beverages list?
9 Why are you a sales person as well as a provider of food and drink?
10 What is a 'code of conduct'?
11 What problems can result if you say that your establishment has facilities or serves products which it does not?

ELEMENT 3: Respond to feelings expressed by the customer

Whenever strong feelings are aroused in a customer it is important that you find out why. The customer may be very happy with the service that they have received, but often these feelings are raised because they are not. Customers may also become very upset by something over which the establishment has no control, but which they must deal with as it has affected a customer, such as a customer having their pocket picked before they enter your establishment, and thus no money to pay for what they have just ordered. As mentioned before when customers are very happy, they usually just pass comment, so when they start to express a strong feeling about something it is serious and you *must* listen. These feelings will usually be expressed either as complaints or incidents. There are several important points to remember.

● Learn to observe whenever a customer is feeling very strongly about something.
● Learn how to identify an incident from a complaint and assess its seriousness.
● Learn how to prioritise your response to the event.
● Be able to identify, quickly, any incident or complaint you are unable to deal with and refer it to the appropriate person as soon as possible.
● Become familiar with your establishment's procedure for dealing with those events which have aroused strong feelings within your customers.
● Learn how to reassure a customer that they are being taken seriously.

Before dealing with feelings expressed by customers there are several things you should bear in mind.

● Why an angry or upset customer must be dealt with straight away.
● Why tact and diplomacy are very important.
● Why any complaint or incident must be accurately identified and its seriousness assessed.
● Why the situation should be resolved as soon as possible, either by you or the appropriate person.
● Why it is important to deal with all incidents quickly and seriously.
● When an incident is beyond your ability to respond to it, how and to whom to refer it.
● Why you must follow the company procedure when dealing with and recording complaints or incidents.

Essential knowledge

● A person who is angry or upset does not always act in a rational fashion.
● A customer who is angry or upset will be very impatient.
● If you do not start to deal with a customer who is upset immediately, they will simply become more angry and more irrational.
● As a representative of the establishment you are responsible for any problems which your customers come across.
● All complaints or incidents are serious, because they have caused upset to your customers who are no longer satisfied with your establishment.
● When some incidents occur, as in the case of lost property or an accident to a customer, the establishment may have a legal responsibility.
● You must never admit responsibility for an incident, because you may have committed the establishment to some legal liabilities in the future.

DEALING WITH CUSTOMER COMPLAINTS

When dealing with a customer who has a complaint you must *always remember that they will be angry*. Perhaps not yet angry enough to shout and threaten, but certainly unhappy enough to get extremely short with you if you do not act in a very efficient and diplomatic way. This would be true even when you, personally, are not responsible for the problem, because you as a representative of the establishment bear a collective responsibility for everything that happens within it. You must remember, therefore, to remain calm and polite no matter how upset the customer may get with you. Do not take the anger personally.

In order to defuse the situation as swiftly as possible you should follow the course of action recommended below, always remembering to act within your establishment's policy.

- *The first thing to do is to immediately acknowledge the guest and apologise to them*. If they are not attended to swiftly, all it will do is make them more angry.
- *Listen very carefully, without comment*, unless the customer asks you to say something. Remember that when someone is angry they often tell you about lots of minor things before they get to what is really wrong. If you jump in too soon you may prevent the customer from explaining the real reason for their annoyance. Sometimes just by describing what has made them so angry will enable the customer to become more rational and calm.
- *Start to deal with the complaint immediately*, with the customer able to see that you are taking them seriously and actually doing something. You can also tell the customer what you are doing, e.g. returning the well-done steak to the kitchen in order to exchange it for a rare one as was ordered.

The situation and the customer should now become calmer.

When listening to the customer's complaint you should have a calm, but interested expression on your face. This is one time when a smile could be taken as a sign of a lack of interest or seriousness, and could make the situation worse.

MEMORY JOGGER

What should you do if a customer has a complaint?

When listening to a customer's complaint have a calm, but interested expression on your face

Types of complaint

Some complaints are very easy to deal with. Examples of these are as follows.
- If the taxi a customer has ordered has not arrived, you can phone up and find out why there is a delay.
- If the customer wanted to order a drink in the lounge area and the bar person has gone missing, you can take the order and pass it directly on to the bar.

However, there are other complaints which you cannot do anything about at the time. Examples of this could be as follows.

- A customer may say when leaving that they had asked for no mushrooms with their meal as they are allergic to them, but they had found one in the sauce.
- A customer says, as they are leaving, that the mineral water which they had ordered did not arrive.

In this type of case you should write down all the details of the incident, the date, the name of the customer and what the problem is, and then you should pass on this information to your supervisor, or other appropriate person as soon as possible (according to your establishment's code of practice), and tell the customer that this is what you are going to do. For example, it would be appropriate to thank the customer for drawing your and the establishment's, attention to the problem of another customer who is making personal remarks about people in the restaurant in a rather loud voice so that they can be overheard and possibly cause annoyance, etc.

MEMORY JOGGER

Why must you respond fast and accurately to customers' feelings?

If you are unsure about what to do, or if the customer is being very difficult to deal with, rather than allow the situation to deteriorate, you should ask your supervisor to deal with the customer. If you allow the customer to get angry with you, then this will be another thing for them to complain about.

If the customer is allowed to leave the restaurant still feeling that the problem has not been dealt with then that dissatisfaction is what they will remember about your establishment and is what they will describe to their friends as typical of it. This will seriously damage the reputation of the establishment.

DEALING WITH CUSTOMER INCIDENTS

There are many things that can happen to customers while they are dining in your establishment. In most cases, no matter what the incident is, they will report it to you. This is especially true if the customers are strangers to the area or from overseas, and so unfamiliar with the locality or the regulations of the country. As a consequence, unlike when dealing with enquiries, you will often not be able to help immediately, and will have to report the incident or redirect the customer.

As with a customer with a complaint, a customer who has been involved in some incident – they may have lost their wallet perhaps – and is in an agitated frame of mind, or has been mugged and is feeling frightened and vulnerable, will need to be reassured that they are being taken seriously in a very tactful manner.

The first thing to do is to listen, very carefully, to what the customer says has happened. Then you will be able to decide what action to take. It may be helpful to jot down some notes.

When property is found in an establishment, it should be recorded in a lost property book, and stored for safekeeping (see *Unit NG1*). If the customer remembered paying for something in the bar, and was now unable to find their wallet, you could check with the bar, and with the lost property book to see if it could be located. If the action was not successful you would have to record and report the incident according to your establishment's procedures.

However, some incidents may be much more serious, such as if a customer is mugged or a child lost outside the establishment. In this type of incident, where outside bodies such as the police have to be involved, senior management may also be involved and you must become familiar with company procedures for reporting such incidents to the appropriate person as soon as possible.

No matter how serious the incident is, nor how agitated the customer is, you must remain calm. If you do not then you will not be able to find out what has happened and take the appropriate action.

Do this

- Find out your establishment's policy about how to deal with a complaint or incident.
- Find out if your establishment has a book in which complaints or other incidents are recorded, and if it has, how to fill it in.
- Find out where the lost property book is kept.
- Find out who has the authority to deal with very serious complaints.
- With a friend, pretend that one of you is a waiter and one of you is a customer with a complaint. See if the 'waiter' can deal with the incident to the 'customer's' satisfaction.
- Make a list of the things that make you angry at work, and another list of how you think that these problems could be sorted out. Discuss this with your supervisor.
- Ask your supervisor what was the most serious incident that they have been involved in and how they dealt with it.

Case study

A customer orders one gin and tonic, one vodka and tonic, one gin and bitter lemon and one pint of lager. By accident you serve two gin and tonics. The customers start to drink and then you realise what you have done.
1   *What action should you take?*
2   *What laws have you broken?*
3   *How are the customers likely to react?*

What have you learned

1   In what sort of mood will a customer with strong feelings be?
2   Where are incidents involving your customers likely to take place?
3   Why should all incidents be treated seriously, no matter how trivial?
4   What might be the consequences of unnecessarily delaying dealing with an incident?
5   What will be the consequences of dealing with an incident swiftly and efficiently?
6   Why must the problem be solved before the customer leaves the establishment?
7   Why might you find yourself doing things which are not, strictly speaking, within your job description?
8   Will your management always be unhappy to receive complaints?
9   What is the procedure within your establishment for dealing with complaints that you cannot solve immediately?

ELEMENT 4:   Adapt methods of communication to the customer

Accurate communication with your customers is essential if you are to be able to provide them with whatever service they require. Not all communication is verbal, body language is also important, as can be supplementary methods of conveying information to people with special needs, e.g. the hard of hearing.

There are several things you must learn in order to communicate effectively with customers.
- Learn how to communicate with people from different cultures, of different ages, and with differing needs.
- Learn how to ascertain if the communications have been understood correctly by both parties.
- Identify other personnel within the establishment who are able to communicate by different methods, e.g. a foreign language or sign language.
- Learn how to respond to people with different needs.

You also need to know other factors.
- The importance of communicating accurately with your customers.
- Why it is particularly important to establish a good rapport with customers from the moment they enter your establishment.
- What facilities there are within your establishment for people with special needs.
- All the facilities which your establishment is able to offer to its customers.
- When and how to seek assistance when there is a problem in communicating with a customer.

Essential knowledge

- You may be the first representative of the establishment that the customer meets. You may also be the only and last person, so the impression that you make on them will colour their views about the rest of the establishment and what they tell their friends or colleagues.
- If you do not understand a customer you will not be able to help them satisfactorily.
- If you smile most people will smile back and feel relaxed.
- Non-verbal communication is as important as verbal communication.
- A person with individual specific needs wants useful, accurate information not embarrassed sympathy.

VERBAL AND NON-VERBAL COMMUNICATION

Verbal communication is using speech. *Non-verbal communication* is the information which you convey by your body language. For instance if a customer comes up to you and you continue with what you are doing, without acknowledging them in any way, they will feel ignored and angry. You may be busy, perhaps answering a telephone enquiry from another customer. However, you can still smile at the new customer who is waiting, they will then know that you have seen them, and will be with them as soon as you can. They will feel noticed and welcome.

Make customers feel welcome

Verbal communication is also an important skill for you to develop, and you should try to become aware of the following points.

- Customers must be able to understand what is being said to them.
- You should, therefore, be very careful about the words you use and their pronunciation.
- If you use a slang word the customer may never have heard of that word, or never have heard it used in that context, and so not understand you.
- If you do not enunciate your words clearly, you slur them, or mumble instead, even the most intelligent and patient customer will not be able to understand you and will become dissatisfied.
- Just because a customer does not respond to you immediately, it does not mean that they are either rude or stupid. It may mean that they are hard of hearing, or that they are having difficulties trying to respond in a language not their own.

Welcoming and addressing your guests

Everyone likes to be made to feel welcome when they arrive somewhere, especially if they may have had a long and difficult journey. Saying 'Good morning' or 'Good afternoon' with a smile on your face as soon as the customer appears is a very good start. If you know the customer, they may be a regular visitor, or have been staying for a while, use their name to personalise the conversation, e.g. 'Good afternoon, Mr. Johnson, it's nice to see you again', or 'Good morning, Mrs Smith, how can I help you?'

Useful tips

It will be useful for you to learn the following points so that you become more skilled in talking to customers.

- If you do not know the name of the customer you should use the more impersonal forms, such as 'Good afternoon, sir/madam'.
- When you do find out the customer's surname then you can start to use it, but you should never use their Christian name, as this would be considered to be over familiarity.
- If the customer is a small child you should use their first name. This is because most children would be very puzzled to be addressed by their surname and to do so would not put them at their ease.
- It requires great tact and experience to know when a child is old enough to be addressed as an adult. Addressing a young person as a child when they consider that they are an adult may be seen by them as patronising and insulting.
- If the customer you are talking to is hard of hearing, or their English is not very good, speak slowly and clearly whilst looking directly at the customer.
- Check to see if any other member of staff speaks the appropriate language.
- If a customer does not understand what you say repeat yourself using other words and appropriate gestures. For instance if the customer does not understand when you ask them to take a seat, walk over to the seat and make a motion to sit down.
- Listen very carefully when the customer says something to you, and do not be afraid to ask them to repeat themselves if you did not understand the first time; accuracy in helping people is more important than short conversations.
- When speaking on the telephone you must be even more careful to be accurate in your communications, because you have no other method of double-checking that the information which you have given or received was correctly transmitted. For instance you cannot see a puzzled glance which might tell you something was wrong. As an example, if you are taking a booking it is always wise to repeat the information back to the customer for confirmation.

As noted before, if a second customer requires your attention while you are still dealing with the first, you should greet the second customer immediately and explain

> **MEMORY JOGGER**
>
> When a child asks you for a Coke, how should you respond?

Be helpful and attentive to customers

that you will attend to them as soon as you have finished with the first one. As long as the second customer knows that they have been seen, most people are happy to wait a few minutes. They will not be if you ignore them.

Bidding the customers farewell is as important as greeting them correctly, because this is often the last impression of the establishment that they will take away with them. It is also a good opportunity to try to encourage the customer to return in the future. It does not mean that you should ignore the customer for the rest of the time that they are in your restaurant. However, most customers do understand that you are busy, and will not expect individual attention throughout the visit, especially if the communications provided at the start were well done, efficient and accurate, and the service they required provided.

A simple farewell such as, 'Good-bye Mr/Mrs Johnson, I hope you enjoyed your meal with us and that we will see you again in the future' or to a regular guest, 'Good-bye Miss Easton, it was nice to see you again and I look forward to seeing you again next month', is sufficient. (Notice the use of the guest's name to make them feel like an individual not just part of the daily business). This should encourage the guests to pass any comments that they might have been wondering whether or not to make and it may also stimulate the customer to make their next booking there and then if they already know the date.

Specific individual needs

All the time that you are communicating with a customer you will need to consider them as a unique individual with their own special requirements. This is especially true if your customer has any impairments or disabilities. As mentioned previously if the customer is hard of hearing or does not speak English well, you will need to be very precise and clear in what you say. You might also use other methods to communicate. For instance you could show a customer who was deaf where the restaurant was within the establishment from a plan in the brochure, or direct them to signs. You could do the same with a customer who spoke little English, or find another member of staff who spoke the language. You may also find that there can be difficulties understanding very broad dialects. For instance a person with a strong Newcastle accent may find it difficult to communicate with locals when on holiday in Cornwall, and the same care will need to be taken in communicating with them as with someone who is not British.

MEMORY JOGGER

What information would a customer in a wheelchair need to have about your establishment?

If your customer has a speech impediment, perhaps a slight stammer, you must listen carefully to their request, and repeat it back to them to be sure that you have understood what they wanted. If they are unable to speak you can ask them to write down their requirements.

Those with physical disabilities will also need special attention. People in wheelchairs will need to know about access, lifts and toilet facilities. But even people less disabled, such as a person who has a broken leg and is on crutches, will need extra information, again often relating to access, where the lifts are, the shortest way to walk from one point to another, how to avoid stairs, etc.

People with learning difficulties, that is to say those who have great trouble in absorbing and retaining information, or have a very short attention span, can present other problems. If a customer who has learning difficulties approaches you to ask the way somewhere perhaps, it may be more sensible to take them there especially if the route is quite complicated. If they ask you to explain an item on the menu you must be careful not to appear patronising, but choose the simplest words that you can think of to explain, and speak slowly and clearly.

Do this

- Try to put yourself in the position of a customer. Next time you are in a shop observe and remember how quickly they served you and whether you felt happy with the service or not.
- Find out if your establishment has a particular way in which they would like you to address the customers.
- Practise becoming aware of people entering the food service area, and smiling a greeting to them as soon as they appear.
- Get one of your friends to put on a pair of ear muffs and try to explain something to them.
- Make a list of all the people who work in your area who speak a foreign language and list what languages they speak.
- Find out what your establishment feels is a suitable phrase for bidding a customer farewell.
- If applicable, make a list of the names of all the people who have reservations for tomorrow, then upon arrival and departure you will be suitably prepared to say goodbye to them all.

Case study

You have just taken the order for a group of Japanese customers. They seem very happy with what they have ordered, but you are not sure that their English was good enough for them to translate the menu accurately, especially as one customer has ordered goujons of sole for a starter and then Dover sole for a main course.
1 What action should you take?
2 What may happen if you take no action at all?
3 What can you do to make sure that this type of problem does not arise in the future?

What have you learned

1 How will your customers feel if you ignore them?
2 Why do your customers like to be remembered and recognised?
3 Why should you address children by their first names?
4 Why must you find out exactly what the customers want?
5 What should you do if you are unable to communicate accurately with one of your customers?
6 What alternative methods could you use to communicate with people who have difficulty in understanding you?
7 Why is bidding farewell to a customer so important?

Get ahead

1 Find out what legislation other than health and safety affects the way that you are able to work.
2 Find out how to check that large pieces of equipment, like tills, are working properly.
3 Find out which supplies take more than a day to arrive.
4 Make a point of actively asking each customer how they have enjoyed their visit, and make a note of their comments. You may want to discuss these with your supervisor later.
5 Find out what would be the difference between strawberry ice-cream and strawberry flavoured ice-cream under the Trades Descriptions Act.
6 Find out how many codes of practice your establishment has and how they relate to you and your job.
7 Write down all the formal communication routes within your establishment.
8 Find out what, if any, licensing laws relate to your place of work.
9 Find out what are the most common complaints that occur within your establishment, and why they occur.
10 List the nationalities and complaints of your customers over a period of time. Is there a correlation between the things people complain about and the culture they come from?
11 Make a list of all the types of incident that occur which require you to contact people outside your establishment, like the police. List those people that you would contact for each type of incident, and why.
12 When there is a serious problem, which you have to pass on to your supervisor, find out how your supervisor dealt with it, and why.
13 Find out the most common legal problems that occur if you do not handle an incident correctly.
14 See if it would be possible for you to learn another language, so that you could communicate with more people.
15 Some people have titles, like doctors and religious people. Find out how people with titles should be addressed.
16 Find out what are the most common mobility disabilities and what special facilities each type of disability needs to have provided.

Create and maintain effective working relationships

This chapter covers:

ELEMENT 1: **Establish and maintain working relationships with other members of staff**

ELEMENT 2: **Receive and assist visitors**

What you need to do

- Find out what your responsibilities are as an employee, in respect of health, safety, equal opportunities and confidentiality.
- Identify the working structures of your organisation so that you can seek and obtain advice and support in difficult or serious situations.
- Become familiar with the correct procedures and communication channels should an incident, breach of security or difficult situation occur

with customers.
- Recognise the importance of passing important information on promptly and accurately within acceptable time scales to establish and maintain constructive working relationships.
- Identify why it is important to receive customers in a polite and professional manner and promote the products and services available within your organisation.

What you need to know

- The company procedures for dealing with awkward or aggressive customers.
- How to adapt methods of communication to suit the person you are dealing with.
- What the products and services of your organisation are.
- What your own job responsibilities are.
- Why you should comply with equal opportunities.
- Where, when and from whom you should seek information.
- Why it is essential to be discreet when

handling confidential information.
- The most appropriate methods of communication when proposing change.
- What systems are in place for dealing with emergencies, incidents and breaches of security.
- Why it is important to operate paging systems effectively.
- Why you should receive guests in a polite and professional manner.
- Why it is important to ensure when using any form of communication that the information is complete and accurate.

INTRODUCTION

In a service industry one of the most important parts of your job will be dealing with people. You may work within the same organisation with these people or they may be external, for example, customers, suppliers, delivery people, maintenance personnel. The way that you deal with them will not only affect your relationship with them, but will also help them to form an impression of your company. Good 'people' skills are not just about relationships they are good for businesses too.

Dealing with people is a difficult skill because people are all individuals. You will need to develop many skills to deal with people. These skills relate to communication, team work and attitude as well as developing your knowledge about procedures, policies, legal requirements, structures, systems, products, services, and the facilities of your organisation.

In order to maintain relationships there is a need to pay constant attention to behaviour. This is often easier with external customers, because you are aware of the relationship that you have with them as being service or product related. However, we seldom consider what our colleagues or managers needs are. They are your customers too and they also need a product or a service from you as a team member. Teamwork is vital to the quality of the service and product being delivered by your organisation; everyone has a role to play.

ELEMENT 1: Establish and maintain working relationships with other members of staff

WORKING WITHIN THE COMPANY STRUCTURE

Understanding your own job role is of great importance and in a well-structured company usually a written job description is available. This normally contains the key tasks and duties that you should perform along with details of your responsibilities to your immediate supervisor and colleagues. In certain situations the details may not be written down and if that is the case it is important for you to have a discussion with your immediate supervisor to clarify your role and develop an agreed written job description.

Do this

- Obtain an organisational chart and identify your own job role within your restaurant.
- Obtain a copy of your job description.
- Using the same chart draw lines showing links that you have within your department.
- List the people that you have to deal with.
- Place all of the above in your portfolio of evidence.

TEAMWORK

What do you need from others to provide a service? What do others need from you to provide a product or a service? These questions are as vitally important as the relationships with external customers. In order to provide a quality product or service you will need the help of your colleagues. You must take the time to understand the pressures, priorities and schedules of other members of the staff.

For example a waiter and a chef are reliant on each other to deliver the service to the customer. The waiter must ensure that the tables are laid out well with clean cutlery, that the menu is explained and the order taken efficiently. The chef is then responsible for producing a meal to the desired quality and quantity within an acceptable time.

Other relationships within organisations are less apparent, such as the relationship between the housekeeping department and kitchen or the reception and kitchen. However, these links still exist. Every job role within any organisation is interdependent on other departments. This relationship is based upon communication, which is the life blood of every organisation. The channels of communication will

MEMORY JOGGER

There are two channels of communication. What are they?

vary from organisation to organisation, however they fall into two basic types: *formal* and *informal*.

Formal communication will take the form of standard operating procedures, organisational policy, legislative information, team briefings, memos, appraisal discussions, training sessions, coaching, telephone calls and letters. *Informal communication* usually occurs as one to one conversations, face to face or in a brief telephone conversation.

Whether communication is informal or formal the importance of a constructive exchange cannot be over emphasised. Some of the benefits that flow from effective communication are that it:
● helps you to improve the service
● strengthens the team effort
● informs both internal and external customers of the latest situations.

Good communication is the key to successful businesses. Everyone needs to be kept informed. Well informed people know what to expect and what is expected from them and understand what they can contribute to situations. Wherever you work good communication skills are necessary to achieve results. You need to know about appropriate communication channels, company structures, your role and the different situations that require contact with your line manager.

COMPANY STRUCTURES

Your own role and the role of others is formalised in the company structure. All companies, large or small, have some hierarchical structure. Within all organisations there are levels that relate to job responsibilities. They indicate a line of command, for example as a waiter your immediate line manager would be the restaurant supervisor; in the absence of the restaurant supervisor you would report to the next level in line – the Food and Beverage Manager. The line of command is important to you because it indicates who you should contact if there is a situation that you cannot resolve.

A simple example of a hierarchical structure for a department or an establishment might look like the following example.
● General Manager
● Departmental Manager
● Supervisors
● General staff

The example could be completed with other departments and the staff who work in them, as in the following example.
● General Manager
● Food and Beverages Manager; Restaurant Manager; Front of House Manager; Personnel/Trainee Manager
● Head Chef; Head Receptionist; Housekeeper; Secretary
● Sous Chefs; Supervisors; Receptionists
● Chefs; Food Service Staff; Room Attendants
● Kitchen Staff; Cleaning Staff; Porters

MEMORY JOGGER

All companies have hierarchical structures. What is the name of the most common form of this structure.

This structure when completed with all departments and names, forms a pyramid shape from the one, or few, general managers to the general staff, and is known as a pyramid structure.

However, companies today are beginning to take away the levels of management to produce a flatter structure, where the responsibilities are shared. In this type of organisation the communication channels are also likely to be easier because there are fewer levels involved and they may rely more on informal communication rather than on more formal memos and meetings.

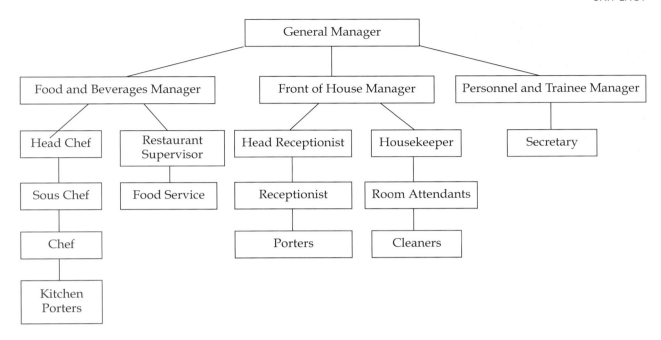

A typical pyramid structure of an organisation

Do this

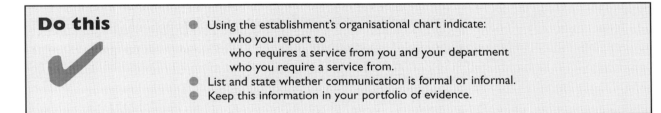

- Using the establishment's organisational chart indicate:
  who you report to
  who requires a service from you and your department
  who you require a service from.
- List and state whether communication is formal or informal.
- Keep this information in your portfolio of evidence.

YOUR OWN ROLE WITHIN THE ORGANISATION

You will have certain responsibilities wherever you work. Some of these you will be aware of, others, laid down in legislation, will affect you, possibly without you realising that they exist. The following list is intended to raise your awareness of some of the legislation affecting you. It is not exhaustive and much additional information will be found in the other units.

Common law rights and obligations

Common law rights and obligations affect both you and your employer. For the purpose of this unit a number of those that affect you have been identified:
- *a duty to serve*: which, in simple terms, requires you to be ready and willing to work to your contract.
- *a duty of competence* to carry out your job to a level expected within the organisation.
- *a duty of good faith*. The most important part of this relates to confidentiality. You must ensure that nothing is done to damage your employer's business. Information relating to the company's profits and/or its customers must not be divulged.

MEMORY JOGGER

You are affected by rights and obligations under common law. What are the three most significant?

Equal opportunities policies

You need to be aware of your responsibilities under equal opportunities legislation. All companies should operate an equal opportunities policy. This relates to the equal opportunity of every employee regardless of colour, gender, age, race, nationality, ethnic or national origin.

It is illegal for hotels and other similar establishments to discriminate against anyone with whom they do business. You will obviously be affected by this law and must serve people in these categories unless there are other reasons for not doing so, for example because they are drunk or pose a threat to others.

Legislation

You will also be affected by other legislation, covered in more detail in the units to which it relates, such as the following.

- Health and safety at work legislation indicates that you must take reasonable care of yourself and others and that you must co-operate with your employer, so far as it is necessary, to enable them to comply with any duty or requirements of the act or associated acts.
- Hygiene regulations relate to both personal hygiene and the wearing of appropriate clothing and to your working environment.
- COSHH regulations relate to the safe use and storage of hazardous material.
- Fire regulations.
- Reporting of accidents.
- Trade Descriptions Act.

To summarise: you need to be aware that your employer not only has a responsibility to you, but that you also have responsibilities to your employer and to internal and external customers.

Do this

Collect examples of the statutory law affecting you. Retain a copy of these documents in your portfolio.

COMMUNICATION SKILLS

People are the most important part of any business, whether they are internal colleagues, managers, external suppliers, visitors or customers. The way in which you communicate with them will make a difference to you, to them and to the business. It is important that when communicating with others you establish and build up a rapport.

The type of communication you use will depend upon who you are communicating with, what you need to communicate, why you need to communicate and the speed with which you need to communicate and whether it is immediate or can wait.

There are three general types of communication:
● **verbal** – face to face, one to one or within a group, or over the telephone
● **non-verbal** – one to one or within a group
● **written** – letters, notes, memos, fax or computer generated.

Face to face (verbal and non-verbal)

If communication is face to face, non-verbal communication will also play a part. First impressions are formed in the first few minutes of contact and are based largely upon non-verbal communication although stereotyping and prejudices will also play their part. Non-verbal communication is also known as body language and is more likely to convey attitudes than verbal communication which conveys information.

Body language accounts for nearly fifty-five per cent of the communication between two people, so it is easy to see why it is so important to understand body language but also why some people prefer face to face contact, rather than contact over the telephone, computer or fax machine.

Body language can convey messages that, without realising, we all send out. They are likely to be based upon:
● whether you like or think you might like the person you are dealing with
● how the person is reacting towards you
● the situation in which the meeting takes place
● other situations which may have conditioned you.

The whole of the body is used in non-verbal communication. The most expressive part of the body is the face, which can convey many different emotions and feelings. The head is used when nodding replaces the spoken yes or no. Facial expressions include the use of the eyes and mouth and will be linked to other body movements and gestures which will also need to be read. When reading body signals you must look at all of them to decide what they mean all together. Taking any one in isolation can be misleading.

MEMORY JOGGER

Body language conveys many messages. The way we act towards others is likely to be influenced by four reasons. What are they?

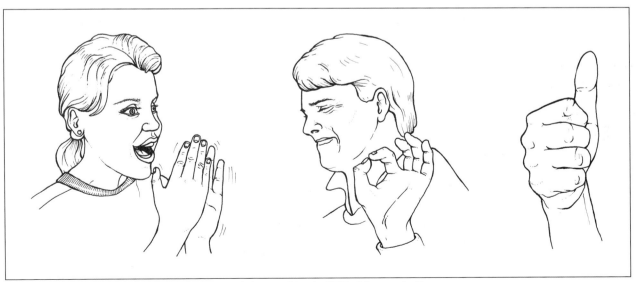

Face-to-face communication: 'Isn't it exciting!', 'Everything's OK!', 'No worries!'

95

Do this

Identify and list your own prejudices which may affect your body language and communication skills. (Recognising them will help to prevent using them).

Verbal communication by telephone contact

The use of the telephone as a means of communication is very common. It is immediate and often enables you to talk with the person that you need straight away. Care needs to be taken when using the telephone because calls can often be overheard by others, so if the information is confidential, the telephone may not be the best method of communication.

When you use the telephone as part of your job you need to make sure that:
● you speak clearly
● you establish who you are, who you are speaking to, and what the call is about
● you give clear information, taking notes if necessary
● you action any points that you agree during the conversation.

The organisation that you work for may also have a certain procedure to follow when using the telephone, for example, how many rings the telephone makes before being answered, how you should answer and what you should say, how you should record messages, and when and how you need to pass the call on.

Do this

● Find out if your organisation has any laid down procedures and if so, obtain a copy for your portfolio of evidence.
● If they do not, write down what procedures you use and include examples of messages as well as a summary of how, when and why this method of communication was chosen.

Verbal communication difficulties

Barriers to communicating may be encountered, the most common being language. Dialects, jargon and accents can cause difficulties. If you have to deal with people with language difficulties you will need to check that they have understood you and that you have understood them. This is achieved by using questions or gestures to confirm the level of understanding.

Emotions are conveyed in language by pitch, tone and volume. You will use a variety of skills to interpret and react to the person that you are dealing with. For example if you encounter someone who is annoyed or aggressive they will often use a raised voice. You must avoid shouting otherwise the situation is unlikely to be calmed down. You may also need to control your body language to avoid appearing threatening or aggressive in return.

Written communication

Written communication has many forms: letters, memos, notes, computer-generated information, facsimile messages and so on. When using writing as a means of communication you must ensure that:
● the style is appropriate to the audience
● it is clear who the communication is from and what it is about
● it is well worded, with accurate spelling, grammar and facts.

It is also vital that all written communication is circulated only to the intended audience. It is therefore important to establish whether it is the most suitable method of communication and ensure that anyone who needs to see it does.

Confidential information needs to be handled discreetly and may require a combination of communication methods to ensure confidentiality is maintained.

Do this

● Include in your portfolio some examples of written communication to a variety of people within your organisation.

EFFECTIVE WORKING RELATIONSHIPS

Communication is a tool used to establish and maintain relationships with internal and external customers within an organisation. It is important to keep other people around you informed about what is going on, what you need to deliver the product or service, and any problems you have encountered. By communicating effectively the quality of the product and/or service of your organisation can be maintained and improved. This is especially important when you work within a restaurant environment. Often the relationship between kitchen staff and restaurant staff is a difficult one, with restaurant staff thinking that they are invaluable and kitchen staff feeling the same about themselves. The reality is that each department is totally dependent upon the other. Each team member needs to understand the role of the other and more importantly appreciate the level of skill required to carry out the different roles.

Different organisations will use different methods of communication to achieve results. You need to demonstrate that you have taken appropriate opportunities to discuss work related matters using the correct communication channels. If there is a problem with food, for example, it is important not only to the customer, but also to the organisation and yourself that the problem is resolved. It is also important that the solution does not damage your internal relationships with other members of the team.

There are some simple rules that you need to follow in order to maintain effective working relationships.
● Always keep other people informed of the situation.
● Take care in selecting the method of communication, consider what you want to say, the best method of communicating it and how you phrase the communication.
● Always use the correct communication channels, based upon your organisation's structure.
● Always deliver whatever you have promised promptly.

MEMORY JOGGER

What action should be taken to ensure effective working relationships?

Case study

As in most hotel restaurants, you work different shifts and are expected to prepare the restaurant for breakfast service when you are on the evening shift. This sometimes requires staff to stay late to finish the work, and you always stay until the work is done. However, when you are on the breakfast shift the staff from the night before do not leave the restaurant fully prepared for breakfast service. This is not only annoying but also causes some problems with the quality of breakfast service.

You have spoken directly to the staff involved who have taken no notice. What should you do now? Who should you contact? What is the best method of communication? What action do you expect? How do you feel the situation could be resolved?

COMMITTING TO RESULTS

The success of any organisation is reliant on gaining the commitment of the people who work within it. Establishing the role of each person and appreciating how everyone fits together to form a team is vital. As part of a team your individual contribution to the organisation, to other team members and to customers is all of fundamental importance to achieving good results.

In addition to knowing your own job role, the role of others and the best methods of communication, you will also need to know about the products, services, standards of service and organisational policies of your organisation. In order to achieve this you will need to ensure that you obtain as much information as possible about the organisation where you work.

What have you learned

1 What is your role within the department and the organisation?
2 Who is your line manager?
3 What are the most appropriate methods of communication likely to be in:
   - handling a disagreement
   - handling a conflict
   - dealing with a problem?
4 What are your responsibilities under equal opportunities legislation?
5 What is the importance of consulting others about changes?
6 When and how should you consult other people about changes?
7 Why is it important to be discreet when handling confidential information?
8 What different methods of communication do you use and when is it appropriate to use them?
9 Why do you need to adapt and use different approaches in different situations?
10 What are the three methods of communication?
11 As a percentage how much does body language contribute to our communication with others?

ELEMENT 2: Receive and assist visitors

RECEIVING AND ASSISTING VISITORS

MEMORY JOGGER

Why is it important to create a good first impression when receiving and assisting visitors?

Receiving visitors is one of the most important duties that you will perform for your organisation. Whether they are internal, external, expected or unexpected it is essential that you should always maintain a degree of professionalism towards visitors to maintain standards and ensure security.

The visitors' impression of the organisation that you work for is created by the people as much as the environment. First impressions are considered to be the most important and creating a good first impression is vital. Many companies recognise the importance of creating a good impression and have developed detailed procedures for dealing with visitors.

Do this

Find out what procedures your organisation has in place for:
- dealing with visitors
- directing visitors to other departments
- dealing with emergencies, including aggressive customers.

Wherever you fit within the organisation you should be able and willing to deal with visitors. Disney recognised this when they created their theme parks. They found that the most likely people to be asked directions were the staff keeping the parks tidy so these staff were given the same amount of knowledge about the parks as the information staff. Other companies too have recognised the importance of 'people' skills.

In the restaurant the quality of the service is as important as the quality of the food; they go together. Most of the time the service we give and receive is adequate. If the service falls below expected norms a complaint may happen if you are lucky; from a complaint it is possible to learn a lot and improve the level of service. Compliments come from service that exceeds expectations, and must therefore be exceptional. Hence the fact that we are much more likely to receive letters of complaint than we are complimentary letters.

There are some simple rules that should always be followed to ensure that the service given to visitors fulfils both their needs and the needs of the organisation. These are as follows:

1   All visitors should be greeted promptly and in a friendly and courteous manner.
2   The nature of visitors' business should be established; if an opportunity exists to establish their name, find it out and, more importantly, use it.
3   All visitors should be directed to the appropriate people, products or services within the organisation promptly.
4   Any difficulties should be acknowledged and assistance sought from the most appropriate person.

There are different procedures for dealing with visitors that detail how you should greet customers and deal with them dependent upon where you work. An example of this might be whether, rather than simply giving directions to a customer, you should accompany any customer to their destination. This will help to maintain health, safety, security and confidentiality.

PROMOTING BUSINESS

It is important that you know about the products that your organisation offers. You should be aware of the products of each department, not just of your own. This offers you the opportunity to sell the products, services and facilities of your organisation, not simply your department. An example of this would be at reception where, ideally, the receptionist gives basic information about the facility and then offers the customer the opportunity to book a wake-up call, breakfast, papers and a meal in the restaurant. This opportunity exists for all staff, who should be able to promote the organisation's products and services. In order to do that you need to be able to describe what these products and services are. Equally important is the need to direct visitors or customers to the correct facility or person.

Essential knowledge

● You need to be familiar with your organisation's procedures
  You should be able to promote the facilities of the organisation, by knowing what it has to offer.
● You should have a reasonable knowledge about the local area; customers often ask food service staff more than what is on the menu.

Do this

Describe or obtain copies of the procedures your organisation has in place for the following
- Dealing with visitors.
- Routing visitors to other departments.
- Dealing with emergencies, including aggressive customers.
- Promoting the facilities of the organisation

Promoting the services and products is good for business. You should always recognise this when dealing with both internal and external customers because it is that business that keeps everyone in employment at all levels within the organisation. Knowing about the place where you work is good for business but it also has many benefits for you, the organisation and the customer:

For you:
- it makes you feel part of the organisation that you work in
- it allows you to act professionally
- it creates good team spirit.

For your organisation:
- it creates a good impression to customers
- it maintains security
- it is cost effective
- it promotes sales.

For the customer:
- it creates a good first impression
- the external customer is likely to return, and the internal customer likely to be more helpful towards you when you need some help, information or a product.
- they are likely to return or contact you again.

Do this

1 Write a description of the organisation's products and services. Include all departments.
2 Find out what the procedure is for evacuation of external customers if there is a fire where you work.

COMMUNICATION

Choosing the most appropriate method of communication is very important, when dealing with any person that you come into contact with. You need to choose the right method of communication, suited to the needs of that person. You will need to take into account:
- who they are
- what they require
- if they have any special needs, for example if they are foreign speaking, hearing impaired, or in a wheelchair where access could be a problem.

Routine enquiries

Most of the time the enquiries that you will be dealing with will be the routine enquiries that form most of your working contact with people. One example of this would be routing and directing people to other parts of the organisation. For this you will clearly need to know the lay out of your place of work, and the best way to reach different areas. You must also be aware of any routing policies that your organisation may have. For example, if someone asked if Mr Smith was in Room 36, what should you do? This particular example would also be affected by the need to protect confidential information and there is usually a company policy covering this. Confidentiality is very important; you must be careful not to divulge information. If in doubt you should always check.

Complex enquiries

You are likely to have to deal with people in many complex situations when they may be angry, upset, aggressive, drunk or distressed during an emergency. There may be procedures for dealing with problem situations such as aggressive customers or emergency situations. You need to check whether there are such procedures in place and what the procedure or policy states you should do. Where they do not exist the following should provide some guidance.

● Always try to stay calm.
● Try to move the angry customer away to a quiet area.
● If they are very angry, let them have their say, this time will allow you to think.
● Try to identify what the customer's needs are.
● Do not argue, and try to speak softly. This will have several effects: first it is likely to calm down the customer and second it is more difficult to argue with someone when they are speaking softly.
● Acknowledge your own difficulties as quickly as possible and seek help from the most appropriate person within the organisation.

Usually, the customer will eventually run out of steam. Trying to judge if you can deal with the customer or require assistance is important to establish early on, otherwise the customer will have to explain the situation all over again, which is likely to make them even more angry or distressed.

Dealing with emergencies requires some basic knowledge of the company procedures. In the case of emergencies, procedures and policies usually exist.

Do this

Find out if there are procedures for the following:
● fire
● suspicious packages
● bomb alert
● unknown visitors
● dealing with aggressive visitors.

Essential knowledge

You need to know what your own responsibilities are for the following examples:
● What to do if you find a package.
● What you must do if there is a fire or a fire alarm.
● Why you should challenge people that you might find wandering around your establishment.
● Who you should contact.
● When and how to contact someone else in a difficult situation.
● Your organisation's products and services.

PAGING SYSTEMS

Paging systems are used in many large organisations where people have to be contacted but there is no telephone extension near to where they are working. There are two types of paging systems used:

1   An electronic bleep that simply identifies that the person is required and should report back to a central point of contact, often reception.
2   An audible message transmitted using strategically placed speakers, usually used in reception areas of public rooms.

HEALTH, SAFETY AND SECURITY

Security is becoming an increasing problem for organisations. With fewer people employed large areas are left unattended. Wherever you work, because it is visited by numerous people, it is very difficult to control access. Many catering organisations such as hotels have a large number of exits, so the maintenance of security is compounded. It is therefore important that any person entering your place of work is challenged about why they are there and what they want.

You should make sure that you are familiar with any laid-down procedures, since in any of these circumstances you need to react quickly. Being familiar with the procedure helps because you do not have to think of a solution. Most of the time in these situations you will refer the matter to the appropriate line manager. However, there may be occasions when that person is not available. In this situation your knowledge of the company structure is vital, so that you can contact the next most appropriate person.

DEALING WITH EMERGENCIES

There are a few basic steps that you should try to follow in any emergency situation.

1   Do not panic, try to stay calm.
2   Try to think about the situation. If you feel it is beyond your control, contact someone who can help quickly, before the situation gets out of hand.
3   Always try to speak calmly, to avoid panic in others.
4   Try to use the procedures that your organisation have developed. They are there to help.

The best preparation is knowledge so you need to make sure that you know your job well and that you understand your role and how that fits with your responsibilities and other people's.

Case study

One evening while you are working in the restaurant a man arrives saying that he has come to repair the coffee machines. This surprises you because you did not realise there was a problem with the coffee machines. However, he explains that he will replace them immediately and says something about a contract. As you are busy laying up the restaurant for evening service you allow him to take the machines as he tells you he will be back shortly with the new machines. But he does not return.

1 What should you have done before allowing him to take the machines?
2 Who should you have contacted?
3 What can you learn from this situation?
4 What would you do if a similar situation happened where you worked?

What have you learned?

1 What systems for security are in place within your organisation?
2 What are the procedures for dealing with: a) aggressive visitors b) emergencies?
3 What are paging systems and when might you use them?
4 Why is it important to allocate roles and responsibilities clearly via the organisational structure?
5 What products and services does your organisation have available?
6 What are your responsibilities for dealing with visitors?
7 What are your responsibilities in complying with equal opportunities in relationship to visitors?
8 What systems in your establishment are in operation to maintain security?

Get ahead

1 Find out if there are other legislative laws affecting your job role.
2 Find out what legal problems could occur if you did not handle an incident correctly.
3 Look at the other units and see what evidence or additional material they could provide for this unit.
4 Find out the names of all the companies that carry out work for your establishment and make a list including the internal contact.

Prepare and clear areas for table service

This chapter covers:

ELEMENT 1: Prepare service areas and equipment for table service

ELEMENT 2: Prepare customer and dining areas for table service

ELEMENT 3: Clear dining and service areas after table service

What you need to do

- Plan and carry out your work to meet daily schedules in an organised and efficient manner taking into account priorities and laid-down procedures.
- Check that all service equipment, linen, and furniture is clean, free from damage, correctly prepared, stocked, stored and positioned ready for service.
- Switch on and check all electrical service equipment before service.
- Prepare, store and clear correctly, in accordance with food hygiene regulations, all food condiments and accompaniments.
- Make sure that tables are correctly laid and ready for service.
- Check that the environmental (e.g. temperature, lighting) systems are correctly set in accordance with laid-down procedures.
- Check all refuse and waste containers are clean and ready for service and that all waste is disposed of correctly after service.
- Deal with unexpected situations, within your responsibility, by taking appropriate action.
- Assemble all table items, service dishes and utensils used during food service for cleaning or storage.
- Ensure that the dining and service areas are left tidy ready for cleaning and that all service equipment is turned off or set in accordance to laid-down procedures.

What you need to know

- How to maintain an efficient service, promoting customer satisfaction.
- Why all table items and linen needs to be checked.
- Why a constant stock of food service items has to be maintained
- Why it is important to handle and dispose of waste correctly.
- Why it is important to check the menu before use.
- What factors affect room plans.
- Why dining and service areas have to be left tidy after service.
- Why certain electrical equipment should be switched on prior to service and switched off after service.
- How to prepare tables for table service.
- Why it is important to store food stuffs correctly.
- Where and from whom health and safety food hygiene information can be obtained.

INTRODUCTION

Restaurants need not only to attract potential customers but also to retain them as frequent customers. This can be done in a number of ways, such as through the type of menu, the name of the place or the atmosphere within the food service area.

The customers' first impressions of a restaurant are the most important, and these are largely determined by the professionalism of the service staff and their preparations prior to service. These pre-service preparations are known as *mise-en-place* and are vital in that they create the right environmental conditions by the setting and controlling of temperature, lighting and equipment.

ELEMENT 1:   Prepare service areas and equipment for table service

---

WHAT IS TABLE SERVICE?

The definition for table service is 'service where the customer is seated at a table, their order taken and the food brought to them and served'. There are several ways in which this can be done:
● silver service
● plated service
● family service
● French service
● Russian service
● guéridon service
● banquet service.

Banqueting is a term used to describe the service of special functions within an establishment, such as conferences, luncheons, wedding breakfasts and dinner dances. There is no real difference between restaurant table service or banquet service preparation other than the number of customers to be catered for at one time. For this reason, large establishments often have rooms set aside for these functions with a separate administration and staffing. Smaller establishments might use a room adjacent to the restaurant covered by the regular service staff and, perhaps, a couple of part-time staff.

Whatever the situation, each establishment has to consider these points:
● the type of clientele expected
● the restaurant's location
● the food and beverage service layout
● the type of service offered
● the funds available.

Once these are established the restaurant's environment can be decided, and considerations in turn given to:
1 service equipment
2 condiments and accompaniments
3 cover lay-ups
4 table items and table linen
5 environmental systems
6 food service areas
7 health and safety
8 establishment standards and procedures
9 food hygiene.

HEALTH, SAFETY AND HYGIENE

Before starting any sort of work, you need to be aware of the fact that all service staff are responsible for health, safety and hygiene standards within their working areas. The following list gives you some brief points to remember (additional information can be found in *Unit NG1*).

Hygiene points
● Cover all food to avoid contamination by dust, insects, coughing, etc.
● Refrigerate cold food stuffs until required at a temperature of 4°C (40°F).
● Remember that hotplates are for keeping hot food hot, not for heating it up.
● Serve food as soon as possible after preparation.
● Clean up any spillages immediately.
● Avoid cross-contamination: use a clean set of service equipment for each individual food item.
● Hold cutlery by the handles, crockery by the rim and glasses by the stem or base to prevent contamination.
● Never re-use food which has been served to customers and left uneaten (e.g. butter).
● Pay attention to personal hygiene; prevent food contamination in preparation and service areas by not spitting, smoking, etc. Always wash your hands after coughing, sneezing, going to the toilet, etc.

Safety points
Comply with all work procedures.
● Keep work areas clean and in a safe condition, i.e. remove any waste or dirty equipment.
● Report any faults or problems as soon possible to your supervisor.
● Report all incidents and accidents to your supervisor.

Preventing accidents

Most accidents can be avoided by practising some simple rules:
1 treat hotplates, gas or spirit lamps with care
2 keep any handles turned inward, away from people passing
3 use dry cloths to hold or carry hot items
4 keep floors clean and dry
5 remove potential hazards, e.g. trailing electrical wires
6 walk, never run
7 wear the correct clothing and footwear
8 take care when using knives
9 clear broken glass and crockery straight away: wrap it in paper, place it in a box and mark the box clearly; do not put it in a bin liner

The knives and forks protruding from this table are a potential hazard

10 when using electrical equipment make sure your hands are dry
11 switch off and unplug electrical equipment when not in use.

Unavoidable accidents and incidents
No matter what precautions have been taken, accidents sometimes happen. It is therefore wise to be prepared:
- learn the basic first-aid procedures
- make sure you know the name of your establishment's first aider and how to contact them
- be aware of all establishment procedures for dealing with accidents and incidents (including how to record them)
- be aware of fire procedures
- find out where the first aid box and fire extinguishers are kept
- be aware of your role in the event of an unexpected situation.

PLANNING YOUR WORK

In order to maintain efficiency and speed when preparing, using and clearing work areas, work needs to be planned and allocated to meet daily requirements. The restaurant supervisor is normally responsible for drawing up work plans to help the smooth running of service.

The order of preparation varies from one establishment to another and the tasks involved may be allocated under a rota system, where various tasks are completed by individual staff members in rotation. As there are so many different types and styles of food service establishments it is impossible to give a specific order of preparation or rota, but the following example may give a guide as to the principles of a work rota in a hotel restaurant.

Two week duty rota

Food Server	Sat	Sun	Mon	Tue	Wed	Thu	Fri	Sat	Sun	Mon	Tue	Wed	Thu	Fri
A	1	11	*	10	9	8	7	6	5	*	4	3	2	1
B	2	1	*	11	10	9	8	7	6	*	5	4	3	2
C	3	2	*	1	11	10	9	8	7	*	6	5	4	3
D	4	3	*	2	1	11	10	9	8	*	7	6	5	4
E	5	4	*	3	2	1	11	10	9	*	8	7	6	5
F	6	5	*	4	3	2	1	11	10	*	9	8	7	6
G	7	6	*	5	4	3	2	1	11	*	10	9	8	7
H	8	7	*	6	5	4	3	2	1	*	11	10	9	8
I	9	8	*	7	6	5	4	3	2	*	1	11	10	9
J	10	9	*	8	7	6	5	4	3	*	2	1	11	10
K	11	10	*	9	8	7	6	5	4	*	3	2	1	11

Key to tasks

1	Dusting	7	Accompaniments
2	Vacuuming	8	Silver cleaning
3	Polishing	9	Hotplate
4	Linen	10	Table and chair arranging
5	Stillroom	11	Miscellaneous
6	Sideboards and trolleys		

Whatever the size of establishment, the staff's approach to tasks will affect the overall standard of preparation, service and clearing. Consider ways in which you can save both time and effort while maintaining standards, such as those given below:
- make journeys worthwhile; never go empty-handed between wash-up and hotplate, or hotplate to restaurant
- stock sideboards with equipment that is polished ready for service and has been checked for chips and cracks

- always count the required cutlery, crockery, etc. needed for service; never try to guess
- while customers are eating one course, prepare the service equipment for the next
- avoid wastage by: turning off appliances when not in use; making small quantities only of perishables (e.g. mustards, butter and rolls) when the number of customers is unknown; return any leftover food items on trolleys to the kitchen as soon as service finishes.

Cleaning and preparing the service and dining area

The general 'light' cleaning of dining areas can be carried out by service staff, but the more 'heavy' cleaning is better done by trained specialist personnel. Light cleaning includes such tasks as the regular cleaning and polishing of restaurant chairs, tables, sideboards, mirrors, glassware, silverware, cruets and exposed surfaces.

Daily duties

Every day the restaurant supervisor checks the daily bookings for a restaurant, making out the seating plans, allocating 'stations', checking the menus and monitoring the carrying out of tasks. Each task area can be broken into daily duties, to be carried out by the restaurant team (*brigade*).

The following list gives an idea of how this may be carried out.

Everyday tasks
- vacuum carpet and brush surrounds
- clean and polish doors and glass
- empty waste bins.

Tasks on rota
- Tuesday: polish brasses
- Wednesday: brush and dust tables and chairs
- Thursday: clean and polish reception area
- Friday: clean and polish sideboards
- Saturday: clean window ledges and skirting.

THE SERVICE AREA

Most of the work of mise-en-place starts in the service area. In large establishments this area is found between the kitchen and the food service areas and is one of the busiest areas, especially at service time. The whole area can be broken down into five specific sections:
- silver (or *plate*) room
- wash-up
- stillroom
- hotplate
- spare linen room.

Throughout this unit we will make references to each of these areas and the work carried out within them.

Why is hygiene important?
It is important that all preparation and storage areas and equipment are kept clean and in a hygienic condition in order to:
- prevent any transfer of food poisoning
- comply with health and safety requirements
- maintain the highest standards of cleanliness
- prevent the risk of accidents or fire
- prevent a build up of waste and unpleasant odours which will then attract pest infestation.

THE SILVER (OR *PLATE*) ROOM

In very large establishments the silver and the plate room may be two separate units, but in the majority of places they are combined and in some cases, are a part of the wash-up.

The silver room holds the stock of silver required for the service of meals. The various types of silver are kept here on labelled shelves, with all the service flats of one size stacked together. Cutlery, flatware, hollowware and other smaller items are usually stored in drawers lined with baize, as this helps to reduce noise, slipping and scratching. Note that silver used for banquets may have a different design to the silver in everyday use.

For details on the silverware itself, see pages 116–118.

THE WASH-UP

At service time especially, the wash-up area is one of the busiest sections. It must be correctly sited to allow a smooth flow of work, promoting a fast and efficient service. There are two methods of washing:

● *the tank method*. Using this method, items of equipment are first washed in a sink of hot water containing detergent and then placed into racks and dipped into another sink. This second sink is known as a *sterilising tank*; the water temperature is very high, at approximately 75 °C (170 °F). The items need to be left in here for a few minutes then lifted out. As the water is so hot, the items, especially crockery, will air dry, making this a more hygienic method (no cloths are needed). The crockery can then be stacked and put away as required.

● *the machine method*. In principle the machine method is no different to the tank method except that the whole system is automated and therefore labour saving. It is essential here to follow the manufacturer's instructions.

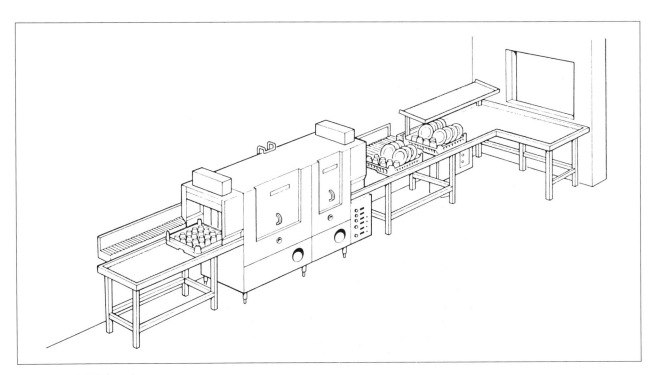

A commercial dishwasher

THE STILLROOM

The main function of the stillroom is to prepare and provide food items and equipment which are not catered for in any other department (such as the kitchen or larder). The actual daily work carried out in here will vary from one establishment to another according to the type of meals offered and the size of the establishment.

The stillroom has to produce a wide variety of food items, so it normally contains a considerable food stock as well as (possibly) a large amount of equipment for storage, preparation and presentation.

The equipment that may be found includes:
● bread slicing machine
● coffee grinding machines
● coffee machines
● general storage space, shelves and cupboards
● hot cupboard
● refrigerators for the storage of milk, cream, butter, cheese and fruit juices
● salamander
● sinks and washing machine
● steamer and hot water boiler.

Provisions from the stillroom
The list below gives the type of items that could be obtained from a stillroom:
● beverages such as: coffee, tea, horlicks, hot chocolate, etc.
● butter: pre-wrapped, curled or passed through a butter pat machine
● sliced and buttered bread (white, brown or malt) and toast
● rolls, croissants, brioches and breakfast toast
● Melba toast, gristicks and biscuits for cheese
● scones and tea-cakes
● sandwiches, assorted savouries and small cakes.

HOTPLATES AND HOT CUPBOARDS

MEMORY JOGGER

Why must you ensure that the correct temperature of the hot cupboard is maintained?

The hotplate is the contact point between the kitchen and the service staff. It is the point at which both areas must cooperate and communicate effectively so that the customer gets the quick and efficient service expected.

Hot cupboards can be used for either food or plates, but when you are using it for plates make sure the temperature is not too high or the plates will become too hot to handle, the glaze may be damaged and any food items placed onto the plates will burn.

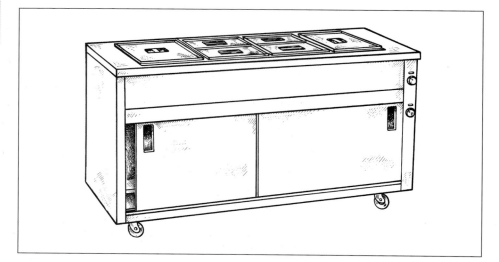

A bain-marie hot cupboard

Units as a whole are usually made up of a hot cupboard with sliding doors, topped by a heated serving surface. The top may also house containers acting as dry or wet heated bain-maries. *Dry-heat* keeps the food hot by electric elements or gas flame. The *wet-heat* method provides heat via an open tank of water, which itself is heated by gas-fired burners or by an electric immersion heater.

The hotplate or hot cupboard needs to be stocked with all the china and crockery needed for service, e.g. soup plates, fish plates, consommé cups, platters, soup cups, tea cups and demitasse.

OTHER HEATING/CHILLING EQUIPMENT

Plate warmers
This piece of equipment is specially designed to warm plates. Before loading the plates are checked to make sure they are clean and unchipped, then they are loaded into the top of the plate warmer and the machine turned on. The top section houses a spring which has been especially tensioned to carry plates; as plates are removed from the plate warmer the spring pushes the rest of the plates up, nearer to the top.

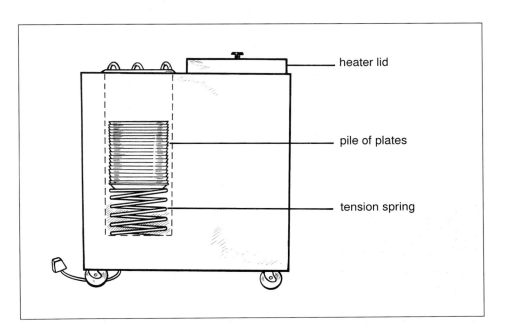

heater lid

pile of plates

tension spring

A plate warmer

Chiller cabinets
Chiller cabinets are used to keep food stuffs at a cool temperature. The items stored might include food items such as salads, sandwiches, sweets and beverages, all of which are generally displayed behind glass or perspex. Chiller cabinets may be situated in the restaurant or in the service preparation area. They can be mobile or static, and have either a motorised rotating display (which stops when the door is opened) or fixed, individually-chilled shelves.

Other refrigerated units such as a standard refrigerator may be used to store milk, cream and butter, etc. in the preparation area.

Temperature control
As refrigerated and heated units are used to store food items, they must be cleaned and turned on *before* service. This allows the units to reach the correct temperatures by service time. The following temperatures may be used as a guide:
● chiller cabinets should be at a temperature of approximately 4 °C (40 °F)

- hotplates are used for keeping food hot and the temperatures should be 75–88 °C (170–190 °F)
- plate warmers should be kept at 65 °C (150 °F).

Reporting of faults

Faults found, with any type of equipment, should be reported immediately to the manager or supervisor and the appropriate action and procedures followed.

SIDEBOARDS

Food service staff may work directly from the kitchen to dining room or use sideboards as a base from which to work within the dining area. Where a sideboard is used, it needs to fully stocked, containing items such as cutlery, crockery, linen and accompaniments in numbers adequate to service a number of tables. Having these items to hand helps maintain an efficient service and reduce service time.

Before any sideboard can be stocked it must be cleaned and prepared. Sideboard tops are generally heat resistant and may have a hotplate fitted; if so, take care when cleaning this, and always remove or disconnect the heat/power supply. Choose your cleaning materials carefully, as strong-smelling, lingering or scented cleaning and polishing agents should not be used; remember that cutlery, crockery and food items will be stored on and in the sideboard.

The actual layout of a sideboard depends on its construction and the establishment requirements. Whatever the type or style of sideboard, all sideboards within an establishment should be stocked the same way so that any food server can approach any sideboard knowing the position of particular items. This saves time and therefore provides the customer with an efficient and speedy service.

Always store cutlery carefully into drawers or racks placing the handles in the same direction; this will make handling safer and more hygienic. Sideboard shelves may be lined with clean cloths on which to store crockery.

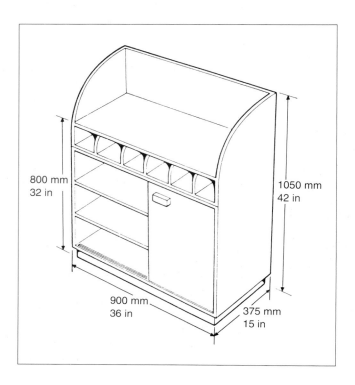

A typical sideboard

How a sideboard may be stocked

Left to right in the drawer section:	First shelf:	Lower shelf:	Side cupboard:
● Service spoons and forks	● Joint plates	● Service salvers	● Clean linen (tablecloths and napkins etc.)
● Dessert spoons and forks	● Fish plates	● Spirit or electric heaters	
● Tea and coffee spoons	● Side plates	● Bread/roll baskets	
● Fish knives and forks	● Sweet plates	● Check pads, service cloths, menus	
● Joint knives	● Coffee saucers		
● Side knives and soup spoons		● Service plates	

Do this

● Find out where your establishment uses sideboards.
● Check whether they are all stocked in the same way. If not, ask your supervisor to explain why they differ.
● Draw up a plan to show how one of your sideboards is stocked.

DRINK DISPENSERS

There is a wide range of drink dispensing machines for both hot and cold drinks; the one chosen by your establishment will depend on the type of service offered. The main types include: pour and serve, espresso, bulk systems, water boilers, Cona systems and cold drink dispensers.

Pour and serve
Here cold water is poured into a machine which brings the water to the boil before filtering it through coffee into a jug. The coffee can then be kept hot on the machine hotplate until needed.

Espresso
This is where a machine uses an internal pressure boiler to force steam through a small amount of coffee to make one or two strong cups of coffee. Other hot drinks can also be made this way.

Bulk systems
In this system the water is boiled in the centre of a machine and then fed into two containers (urns) either side by a swinging arm tap. The water passes through a filter which may contain either tea or coffee and the temperature of the container is then controlled by thermostat. To dispense the beverage, each urn has a tap to release the hot liquid; one cup or a pot can be poured depending on the selection button pressed.

A Cona coffee maker

Water boilers
Water boilers allow service staff to make drinks to customers' individual requirements. The boiler can be a single kettle, a wall mounted unit or a large bulk boiler or pressure boiler.

Cona system
This method of making coffee is often considered eye-catching. The system consists of two containers (a bottom flask and a top bowl) connected by a glass tube holding both the coffee and a filter. The bottom flask is heated, and as the water heats it passes up through the connecting tube, infusing the coffee, and fills the top bowl. As the liquid cools slightly it falls back through the connecting tube via the filter and into the bottom flask ready for service.

Cold drink dispensers
Most cold drink dispensers use either liquid or powder concentrates. There are two main types: pre-mix and post-mix dispensers. *Pre-mix dispensers* contain ready-

prepared drinks, e.g. still orange. *Post-mix dispensers* mix concentrates with water at the point of service; the water can be carbonated if the unit is fixed up to a carbon dioxide cylinder, so making for example, lemonade.

Milk can be bought in bulk (one gallon boxes), with a plastic inner which is placed within a refrigerated unit then connected to a tap or lever via a plastic pipe. Fruit juices can be dispensed in much the same way although fresh juices can also be bought frozen, fresh or dehydrated, canned or bottled. Juices can also be served by lines, much like draught Coke or beers. Care must be taken however, in the monitoring of storage and rotation. The majority of bulk juices have been through a form of preservation process, the most common being pasteurisation.

Key points to remember

1 Follow the manufacturer's instructions carefully for all types of dispensers. This relates especially to mixing preparations, the quantity and dispense settings and operational procedures. Following instructions correctly will:
   ● reduce waste
   ● prevent accidents
   ● maintain speed and efficiency in service, so maintaining customer satisfaction.
2 Do not overload electrical circuits by putting two appliances on the same plug.
3 Keep all equipment spotlessly clean.
4 Report faulty electrical equipment and have it removed immediately so that it cannot be used until repaired. This will prevent further damage to equipment or injury to staff or customers.

SERVICE EQUIPMENT

Trays

Trays used for food service are normally rectangular and flat with only a slight lip. They should ideally be:
● heat resistant
● easily cleaned (with few or no mouldings)
● lightweight yet strong
● non-slip
● stackable.

They are useful in the service of cold food, breakfast and afternoon teas, or where food needs to be quickly transferred from the kitchen to the service area. The smaller trays can be used in restaurants at the tables, but the larger ones tend to be used only to transport food stuffs from the kitchen to sideboard and for clearing dirty equipment from the sideboard to the washing area.

Salvers are a particular type of tray used for the service of drinks and the removal of dirty glasses as well as being a general service aid. If trays and salvers are used then they should be covered with a clean tray cloth or napkin. This will soften noise, reduce the risk of sliding and give a better presentation.

Trolleys

Trolleys provide an opportunity for either the chef and/or service staff to show off their skills. Display trolleys can be used to show customers a selection of foods from the menu such as hors d'oeuvres, cold meats and salads, sweets and cheeses.

Care should be taken when preparing, loading and using trolleys:
● do not over-load them
● check that the wheels run freely

- check that the trolley is stocked with the correct, clean and unchipped plates
- have clean service equipment ready to serve food items, and check that each food item has its own service utensils; this minimises any risk of cross-contamination or spoilage
- wherever possible cover all food items
- refrigerate highly perishable items such as cream products and make sure that they are kept at the correct temperature
- hold any hot food at the correct temperature and keep it covered.

Trolley types

Hors d'oeuvres trolley
This holds hors d'oeuvres dressed in glass bowls, china dishes or plates. The trolley may have rotating shelves, allowing the customer to view the selection (see p. 146 for illustration).

Sweet trolley
Owing to the length of time it is in the restaurant, the warmth of the room and the amount of people within a restaurant the sweet trolley must be covered and ideally refrigerated to prevent any risk of food poisoning. This trolley can be quite large in some establishments, carrying such items as gâteaux, flans, fruit salad, crême caramels, trifles, fresh cream, etc.

A refrigerated dessert trolley

Carving trolley
This trolley is a specialist, expensive piece of equipment and great care should therefore be taken in its handling. The trolley consists of a main carving top with containers at the side for gravy and sauces and an adjacent plate rest. The top of the trolley is covered by a silver or electroplated nickel silver (EPNS) dome which needs to be cleaned and polished regularly. Carving trolleys are heated, in most cases by methylated spirit lamps heating a container of water. This heating method requires certain safety factors to be noted:
- ensure the lamps are filled to cover the service period
- check that the wicks are trimmed and that the lamp is functioning properly
- check that there is sufficient water in the water container
- check that all safety valves and retaining screws are set correctly.

Besides these safety checks other items need to be prepared:
- carving board and knives
- service spoons and forks
- sauce ladles
- service plates for dirty cutlery
- spare serviettes and service cloths.

A carving trolley

Cheese trolley

This trolley holds a selection of cheeses, and possibly fresh fruit and a cheese biscuit selection. The cheese in this case is usually covered by a roll top see-through lid. When using a cheese trolley, make sure that each cheese has its own service equipment.

Cutlery trolley

This trolley has deep-moulded, individual compartments for storing cutlery and flatware. As these items are washed they should be placed in their compartments on the trolley and later wheeled in to the food service area for laying up or for restocking the sideboard during preparation time.

Trolleys in non-luxury restaurants

Trolleys are also used for the service and clearing of food and drinks on airlines, trains and in situations where the food is served on sites far removed from the preparation and cooking area. For instance, hospitals use heated trolleys to serve food on wards, and trolleys are commonly used to serve working lunches in conference and board rooms.

Do this

- Look around your food service area and see what trolleys are used.
- Draw up a list for each trolley giving the preparation requirements.

SILVERWARE

Silverware is a general term used to describe metal cutlery, flatware and hollowware. Most silverware items made now are stainless steel, as this is cheaper and more hard-wearing; however, silver items are still used in many establishments, and these are in most cases made of electroplated nickel silver (EPNS).

The silverware used in a restaurant depends on:
- the type and amount of business done
- the menu
- the type and style of service.

A good guide to the amount of cutlery needed for table service can be calculated by multiplying the restaurant capacity by three times.

Types of silverware

The term *flatware* includes all forms of spoons and forks, while *cutlery* is used to refer to knives and other cutting equipment. Any other item made from silver or stainless steel (e.g. tea/coffee pots and milk/cream jugs) is referred to as *hollowware*.

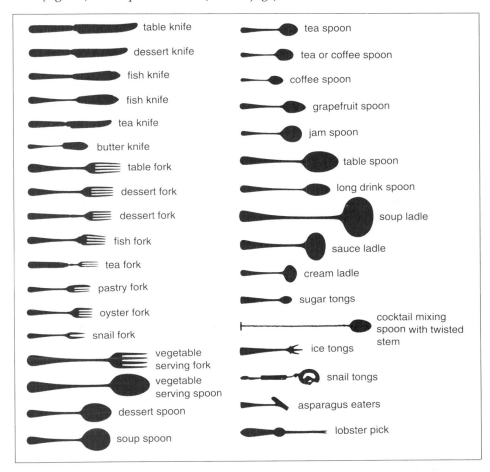

Cutlery and flatware guide

The table given below shows various types of equipment that may be found in your work areas.

Silverware for table service

Table silver
Soup spoons, fish knives and forks, meat knives and forks, dessert/sweet spoons and forks, small fruit knives and forks, small/side knives, teaspoons, sundae spoons, coffee spoons, service spoons and forks

Silver for serving food
Soup tureens, oval/round vegetable dishes and covers, soup bowls, oval/round entrée dishes, oval flats and covers, sauce boats and plates, oval/round under-dishes, soufflé dishes

Stillroom silver
Coffee pots, teapots, hot water jugs, hot/cold milk jugs, toast racks, cream jugs

Speciality items
Gâteau slices, pepper and salt mills, ice cream coupes, grape scissors, fingerbowls, pastry forks, asparagus tongs, soup and sauce ladles, sugar tongs

Cleaning and polishing silverware

In large establishments the cleaning and polishing of silverware is the responsibility of the plate room staff, but in smaller establishments the service staff generally look after their own silverware.

Silverware can be cleaned and polished by a number of methods:
● by using a burnishing machine
● by using the polivit method
● by using plate powder
● by using silver dip
● by using other pastes, powders and cleaning materials sold under trade names.

All service equipment needs to be washed after each service period although need not be polished as often. If your establishment uses silver, a rota for dipping, burnishing, etc. needs to be set out. An example of a polishing schedule for silverware is given below:

Tuesday:	knives, flats, coffee pots, milk jugs
Wednesday:	forks, small coffee pots, small flats
Thursday:	vegetable dishes and lids, spoons
Friday:	soup tureens, other small specialist service equipment
Saturday:	spirit and flare lamps
Sunday:	any other items within the restaurant.

Safety precautions
● It is important to wear protective clothing, aprons and gloves, as some of these cleaners and polishing agents can cause damage, e.g. bleaching clothing and causing skin irritations.
● Always thoroughly wash silver after using any polish and cleaners; cleaning chemicals can cause food poisoning.

Do this
● From the list of cleaners and polishes mentioned find out how each is used and note which items are best cleaned by which method.
● Identify the silver items in your chosen service area and make out a cleaning and polishing rota; include the appropriate cleaner and polisher to use.

GLASSWARE

Glasses on restaurant tables contribute towards the table presentation and vary in shape and size depending on what drink is to be served. The majority of restaurants use plain, clear glasses although certain high-class restaurants use cut glass and traditional glasses for particular wines (e.g. hock wine glasses with brown stems and Moselle wine glasses with green stems). Whatever type or style of glass is used, glasses must be washed correctly (either by hand or machine), rinsed and dried then checked that they are not smeared, cracked or chipped.

Cleaning and polishing glasses

Ideally, glasses should be washed in a glass washing machine. If you are operating one of these, read the machine manufacturer's instructions carefully; it is important to carry out the correct operating procedures and set the machine to the right temperature. Remember to empty the machine at the end of service periods and do not wash any items other than glass as this is likely to leave smears on the glasses.

The polishing of glassware is very important. Dirty or smeared glasses are unhygienic and will spoil the customer's enjoyment of the drink.

To polish glasses:

1 assemble the necessary equipment, i.e. a jug or pot of boiling water and a clean, dry glass cloth
2 holding the base of the glass, upturn it over the pot of boiling water and rotate it in the steam, allowing the steam to enter and circle the glass. Take care not to scald yourself
3 remove the glass from the steam
4 hold the base of the glass in one hand with a corner of the cloth then fill the bowl of the glass with the opposite corner of the cloth
5 place the thumb of your free hand inside the bowl with your fingers on the outside of the glass, making sure the cloth is in between
6 holding the glass firmly yet gently, use the hand holding the base to rotate the glass slowly so that the cloth is drawn around the bowl
7 check that the glass is polished and sparkling clean by holding it up to the light and looking through it. If it still appears to be smeared or dull do not breathe on it; return it to be washed again.

Carrying empty glasses

When carrying glasses, such as during mise-en-place or when transferring glasses from one point to another, carry stemmed glasses upside down between your fingers. Upturn your hand and pick up the glasses by their stems, lacing the stems between alternate fingers. Do not try to carry too many. Alternatively, carry them upside down on a tray or salver.

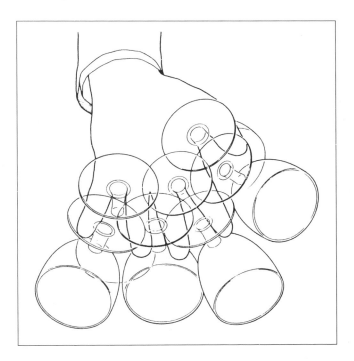

Carrying glasses

Types of glasses

The list below gives some of the more common types:

- brandy balloon   a large balloon-shaped bowl on a small stem
- burgundy balloon   a large distinguished glass for fine burgundy wines
- champagne coupe   a wide shallow glass
- champagne tulip   a tall slender glass
- claret glass   175 ml (6 fl oz)
- fruit juice glass   125 ml (5 fl oz)
- general glass   250 ml (9 fl oz)
- lager glass   285 ml ($\frac{1}{2}$ pt)

- liqueur glass   a small single-measure glass
- port glass   100 ml (4 fl oz)
- sherry glass   75–100 ml (3–4 fl oz)
- water or wine goblet   225 ml (8 fl oz)

The number and type of glasses used in an establishment will vary but as a guide to quantity, the number of glasses required is approximately one and a half times the number of restaurant seats.

Do this

- Using the ratio suggested above, calculate how many glasses of one type your restaurant would require.
- Compare the cost of buying this number of glasses in a plain design of glass to that of buying a cut glass design.

CHINA OR CROCKERY

China is a term used for crockery whether bone china (i.e. fine and expensive), earthenware (opaque and cheaper) or vitrified (metallised). Most catering crockery used these days tends to be vitrified earthenware, which is very durable, having been strengthened. Crockery is also usually given rolled edges to make it more chip resistant.

One fairly recent development is the use of stackable crockery, including cups and even tea and coffee pots (sunken knobs on lids allow stacking). All the lids for the pots are the same size and are therefore interchangeable. Another development is in ovenproof ware, which has in many cases replaced silver serving dishes. This type of crockery consists of enamelled, cast-iron, ovenproof dishes such as casserole and cocotte dishes which allow food to be brought straight from the oven to the table.

Stackable crockery

Whatever quality of crockery or china is used, the most important thing to ensure is that it is washed, rinsed and dried correctly to ensure that no dirt, stains or streaks appear. Never use chipped or cracked crockery: chipped and cracked items harbour germs and should therefore be disposed of carefully.

Plates

Plates come in a variety of shapes, sizes and designs depending on the type and style of service offered.

Plate types: their sizes and uses

Cereal plate	19 cm ($7\frac{1}{2}$ in)	deep plate used for all cereals and porridge, also for compôtes and milk puddings, etc.
Entrée plate	21.5 cm ($8\frac{1}{2}$ in)	hors d'oeuvres, fish/entrees when not the main course, underliners, cover/service plates
Meat/fish plate	25.5 cm (10 in)	main course service
Salad plate		crescent/half moon shaped
Side plate	17.5 cm (7 in)	cheese and bread rolls
Soup plate	23 cm (9 in)	thick soups, mussels, oysters, goulash and Irish stews
Sweet plate	21.5 cm ($8\frac{1}{2}$ in)	sweets and puddings
Tea plate	19 cm ($7\frac{1}{2}$ in)	bread and butter, cakes

Cups

Cups, like plates, come in various shapes and sizes but there are four main types used:
- soup cup   300 ml ($\frac{1}{2}$ pt)
- breakfast cup   300 ml ($\frac{1}{2}$ pt)
- tea cup   150 ml (5–6 fl oz)
- coffee cup   75 or 125 ml (3 or 5 fl oz).

Storing crockery

In the mise-en-place period you need to place crockery into various storage places ready for service such as:
- on sideboards
- in/on hot cupboards and plate warmers
- on trolleys
- in chiller units
- on a service point (as underplates).

Handling crockery hygienically

For reasons of hygiene the following points need to be remembered when handling crockery:
- always hold cutlery by the handles
- hold glasses by the stem
- hold crockery by the rim
- always use a clean service cloth or disposable towels to polish glasses and cutlery.

Do this

- Look through your restaurant crockery stock and identify the types of plates and cups stored.
- Check with your supervisor which pieces of crockery are needed for today's menu and find out where and how it is to be stored ready for service.

TABLE LINEN

The term *linen* is used to describe tablecloths, napkins and any other cloth or textile items used in the presentation of tables whether made from linen or not. Actual linen could be used, but it is expensive and difficult to launder. Table linen today is generally recognised as being made up of cotton, man-made fibres, mixed linen and cotton, or any combination of these. White tablecloths and napkins are the most commonly used, although various pastel colours and even, in some theme restaurants, bolder colours may now be used.

Not all restaurants use tablecloths. They may choose instead to place mats on polished, marble or finely-textured tables. However, where cloths are used, the tables underneath are often baized or felt-topped to help soften the noise of the plates, crockery and cutlery being placed on the table. This type of table also prevents the cloth from slipping and provides the customer with a softer support for their wrists. Tablecloths also provide a background for crockery, cutlery and glassware, while at the same time showing up dirt: this ensures the frequent changing of cloths, so enforcing high standards of hygiene.

Supplies of linen and laundering can be done by three means. An establishment may:
- buy all its own linen, then launder and iron it itself on site
- buy its own linen and then send it to a company to launder and iron
- hire linen from a company who will supply, launder and iron it as required.

Types of table linen

The list below shows some standard sizes of linen:

Square tablecloths	137 3 137 cm (54 3 54 in)
	183 3 183 cm (72 3 72 in)
	285 3 285 cm (90 3 90 in)
	(All square cloths can be used on round tables)
Rectangular tablecloths	137 3 183 cm (54 3 72 in)
	137 3 274 cm (54 3 108 in)
	183 3 244 cm (72 3 96 in)
Buffet cloths	2 3 4 m (6 3 12 ft) is the minimum size to cover a buffet table
Napkins	Vary in size: tea napkins 30 cm (12 in) square, dinner napkins 46–50 cm (18–20 in) square
Slip cloths	Designed to be laid over the main tablecloth to protect it from spoilages – cheaper to launder due to its size, at least 1 m (3 ft) to 122 cm (48 in) square
Tea and glass cloths	Best made of linen and cotton. Nowadays being replaced by paper disposable towels and by the use of glass-washing machines which also dry. Tea and glass towels can be unhygienic if not spotlessly clean
Trolley and sideboard cloths	Often made up from tablecloths which may have been repaired or cut down to fit their purpose

Linen storage

Cloths should be stored neatly stacked on shelves or in a cupboard lined with paper or old, worn, clean tablecloths. They should be stacked in sizes with the central fold outwards to aid counting and handling, then covered with paper or cloths. The requisition of linen differs from one place to another, but in larger establishments where a housekeeping department exists, a system of exchanging dirty for clean is an effective means of control. Under this system the food server counts out the dirty laundry, enters it into a duplicate book, and has this checked by the housekeeper. The housekeeper is then able to issue clean laundry, sign the book and retain the top copy leaving the second copy in the book. The system is sometimes known as *one for one* or *clean for dirty*.

The spare linen room
This refers to a cupboard or room near to the service area where a supply of linen is kept. It is kept locked and the linen used for emergencies only. The day-to-day linen supply is always drawn from the housekeeping department.

Handling linen

Linen needs to be handled correctly or the items become creased and dirty, so increasing laundry costs. There are several ways you can prevent unnecessary costs:
● make sure all surfaces are clean before placing linen on them
● dust and vacuum before laying tablecloths
● check you have the right size of tablecloth before you unfold it
● wash and dry your hands before handling linen; this will keep the cloth visibly clean and reduce the risk of cross-contamination.

See also page 129 on laying a tablecloth.

Disposable cloths

A combination of linen and disposable cloths are often used. Disposable cloths come in all the regular sizes or can be purchased in long rolls and cut to the required length. Paper napkins and slip cloths can also be purchased in many different qualities of paper, from thin single-ply to three and four-ply, some napkins having a linen feel to them. All of these disposables can be printed with the establishment's logo or advertisement.

There are some advantages to using disposable cloths and linen:
● the cost generally works out to be less than laundry or hire costs
● there is a large range of colours and designs to suit different occasions
● labour time is saved, as there is no need to sort and bundle laundry
● disposables are more hygienic, as dirty laundry does not accumulate in service or preparation areas (disposables are thrown away when dirty).

SERVICE CLOTHS

A service cloth is a very important part of service equipment as well as being part of the food server's uniform. It must be kept clean and ironed at all times and only used as a service cloth for certain activities, such as:
● carrying hot plates
● final polishing of plates
● wiping small spills
● brushing crumbs onto a service plate
● wiping the undersides of plates before placing plates on the table.

CONDIMENTS AND ACCOMPANIMENTS

A cruet set

The term *accompaniments* includes a range of sauces, seasoning and breads which are offered with certain dishes. The term *condiments* refers to any spice or sauce such as salt, pepper, or mustard which may be offered at the table. Accompaniments and condiments are offered so that the customer can alter the flavour or counteract the richness of dishes to suit their personal taste or to provide a contrast of texture. They can be dry, fresh, preserved, or reconstituted prior to service (e.g. mustard), and they may be served hot or cold.

Accompaniments are served with all kinds of dishes throughout the menu, including savouries, sweets, desserts and cheeses.

Preparing accompaniments and condiments

Some accompaniments are prepared in the kitchen and sent to the restaurant with the dish they accompany. Others, especially dry and cold types, may be prepared by the service staff. Accompaniments can be served in sauce boats, in small bowls, on plates or from jars and bottles.

The same accompaniment may be served differently in different establishments, for example:
● salad dressings may be made to order at the table or served made-up in bottles or jars
● sauce may be offered from a sauce boat on a doily covered plate or from a jar
● toast may have the crusts removed and then be arranged in a toast rack on a doily covered plate or wrapped in a linen napkin.

Always use clean utensils for each item being prepared, store food items correctly (see below) and thoroughly clean down and dispose of waste carefully when finished. This will reduce the risks of contamination, fire, accidents, pest infestation and unpleasant odours.

Storing accompaniments

If accompaniments are prepared some time before service they will need to be stored correctly. The storage of hot accompaniments is normally undertaken by the kitchen staff, but any cold and dry types may be the server's responsibility. If you are responsible for this, store cold accompaniments in a refrigerator and cover them to prevent transfer of smell and taste onto other stored food items. Store dry ones by covering them and keeping them in a cool, dry place until needed. Avoid waste: make only small quantities if the numbers for the meal are unknown.

<table>
<tr><td colspan="2">**MEMORY JOGGER**</td></tr>
<tr><td colspan="2">To comply with hygiene regulations how should cold accompaniments be stored?</td></tr>
</table>

Standard accompaniments

Hors d'oeuvres/appetisers	Hors d'oeuvres variés: oil and vinegar
	Grapefruit: caster sugar
	Melon: caster sugar and ground ginger
	Tomato juice: Worcester sauce
	Prawns: mayonnaise, brown bread and butter
	Pâté: hot toast
Soups	Minestrone soup: Parmesan, grilled cheese flutes
	Cream of tomato soup: croutons
Pasta	Spaghetti: Parmesan
Fish	Whitebait: cayenne pepper, peppermill, segments of lemon, brown bread and butter
	Poached salmon, hot: hollandaise, cold: mayonnaise
	Fish fried in batter: tomato sauce
	Fish fried in breadcrumbs: sauce tartare
	Grilled fish: segments of lemon and cold sauce, e.g. tartare, remoulade, Gribiche or hot sauce, e.g. bearnaise or tyrolienne
Meat and poultry	Curry: poppadums, Bombay duck, mango chutney, chopped apple, sultanas, sliced bananas and desiccated coconut etc.
	Roast beef: horseradish sauce, Yorkshire pudding, English and French mustard
	Roast lamb: mint sauce
	Roast pork: apple sauce, sage and onion stuffing
	Roast chicken: bread sauce, bacon rolls, game chips, stuffing and watercress

Do this

- Check the menu or find out from your restaurant supervisor what cruets and accompaniments will be required for service.
- Empty, clean, polish and refill: any cruets, peppermills and cayenne pepper pots, oil and vinegar sets. sugar basins and dredgers required.
- Prepare any other accompaniments, putting them into their appropriate dishes or dispensers.
- Distribute cruets to the tables and accompaniments to the sideboards or store as otherwise required.
- Check different types of menus and find out which accompaniments would be served with them. List them under the following headings according to how they are served: dry, cold, hot, reconstituted.

DISPOSING OF WASTE

To prevent the risks of accidents, fire, contamination, pest infestation and unpleasant odours:
- do not let waste build up within your work area
- clean up as you work
- make sure that waste is disposed of cleanly and efficiently
- keep all storage areas clean and tidy
- dispose of broken or chipped glass and crockery carefully; if possible wrap in paper or place in a box and mark the package clearly.

Essential knowledge

Waste must be handled and disposed of correctly in order to:
- prevent accidents
- prevent risk of fire
- prevent contamination of food and food areas
- prevent pest infestation and unpleasant odours from arising
- comply with the law
- comply with establishment procedures.

Case study

A member of your brigade is working within the stillroom area. All the electrical equipment has been turned on by someone else, except for the hot cupboard. He assumed that this unit had been forgotten and therefore switched it on. An electrical shock is received, but luckily not lethal. It is found that the person who had first switched on the equipment heard a sparking noise, left it off and had gone to tell the supervisor.

1. *Although the fault was being reported, what immediate action should have been taken?*
2. *Who, in this situation, is liable under the Health and Safety Act? (Refer to Unit NG1: Element 3.)*
3. *If this situation were to happen in your working environment what procedures should be followed?*

ELEMENT 2: Prepare customer and dining areas for table service

PLANNING YOUR TIME

Consideration of the following points will help to make preparation time short, efficient and effective:
- identify the task
- know how it is to be done
- collect all the equipment needed before you start
- complete your work tasks to meet the required schedules
- work as a team.

HEALTH, SAFETY AND HYGIENE

As with any kind of work involving food, contamination can occur if national and establishment standards are not met. Remember:
- keep all work areas and surfaces clear of rubbish, waste and other obstructions
- use protective clothing as required
- store all food items correctly
- practise good personal hygiene
- comply with all health and safety regulations.

To prevent the risks of accidents. fire or injury to yourself and others:
- always follow safety procedures when using machinery and electrical appliances
- do not carry lighted candles, oil, spirit or gas lamps
- if refilling oil, gas or spirit lamps, do so in a well-ventilated area away from food items and naked flames
- dispose of all waste and empty fuel canisters carefully.

THE RESTAURANT ENVIRONMENT

Arranging the furniture

The way in which furniture is arranged in a food service area influences the atmosphere and mood. For instance, soft, luxurious seating relaxes customers and produces a leisurely dining mood; round tables are associated with sociability and communication. In contrast, if you were to seat customers in large parties at long narrow tables you would only generate communication between people sitting side by side or opposite one another. It is also worth noting that rows of rectangular tables give an image of authority, conjuring up school meals, etc.

Tables which are packed closely together can make customers feel uncomfortable;

they may feel that other tables can overhear their conversations. This arrangement also increases the likelihood of service staff knocking customers when passing.

Table plans

The organisation of table plans depends on a number of factors and could include some of the following:
● organisers' requests
● the type of meal or occasion
● the size and shape of the room
● the number of people being catered for.

For banqueting, either 'U' or 'T'-shaped table plans can be used or a top table could be flanked by several round or rectangular tables. Banqueting requires very careful use of space; as a guide the minimum space between *sprigs* (rows) is 2 m/6 ft (table edge to table edge), and between two chairs 46 cm (18 in) with a gangway of 1 m (3 ft). A table to wall space would therefore be 1.4 m (4 ft 6 in), i.e. one chair with a 1 m (3 ft) gangway. The space required for each cover width is 50–60 cm (20–24 in) depending on the type of cover to be laid.

In normal restaurant situations it is not unusual to find a mixture of table sizes, shapes and positioning. The space between tables should be enough to allow customer privacy and ease of movement for staff, with room for trolleys to pass between tables. A mixture of round and square tables may be used to allow maximum flexibility: people like to sit in rounds with their friends, but square tables are more economical as they can be used for small parties yet easily pushed together to accommodate larger parties. Some designs of tables are inter-locking or adaptable with various extensions to suit requirements.

You may work in a restaurant that uses fixed seating. Here, tables and chairs either come fixed together, or the tables might be free while the seating is fixed (e.g. to the wall). Where chairs and tables are fixed together they are usually also fixed to the floor, and are therefore static.

Chair positions

The position of the chair at a table is quite important. So as not to discomfort customers, chairs should be placed between table legs. This is relatively easy to achieve on rectangular tables, but can become a problem when seating more than four people on round ones. The standard round table has four legs although occasionally one centre leg may be found. In the case of four legs the following options can be adopted:

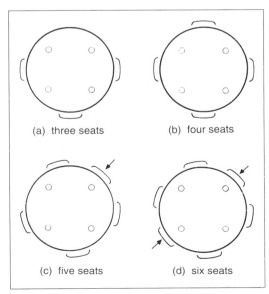

(a) three seats   (b) four seats

(c) five seats   (d) six seats

Arranging seats at round tables

Arranging furniture safely
- Remove and report any faulty or damaged furniture immediately; this will prevent any unnecessary accidents or injuries to staff or customers.
- Take care not to block any fire exit doors or escape routes with tables, chairs, spare furniture, laundry, other equipment or rubbish and waste.

Ventilation and temperature

It is important to keep the dining room free of stale smells (i.e. of food and tobacco) from any previous meals. This can be done by the use of extractor fans, by opening windows or with air conditioning systems. Ideally, the temperature should be comfortable for customers (who are sitting still) as well as for the staff (who are moving about). The generally accepted temperature is 18 °C (65 °F). This can be set on timers or thermostats; it is worth noting that the temperature will start to rise once service starts and fall as it comes to an end, so the flexibility of a thermostat may be more efficient. Air conditioning systems can be set to monitor the air quality and temperatures in a room and adjust themselves accordingly.

Lighting

Before opening the restaurant to customers, always check that all light bulbs are in working order; all candlesticks are clean and candles renewed; and all oil lamps are cleaned, refilled and have trimmed wicks. As a general rule, lunches need to be well lit with as much natural light as possible, while evening meals need a more subdued, soft lighting. Consideration also needs to be given to the fact that coloured lighting reflects onto food items.

Music

Check that where music is provided, the equipment is in working order and that the selection of music is appropriate. The volume should be such that it does not interfere with the customers' conversations while at the same time provides background ambience.

LAYING TABLES

The tablecloth

Tablecloths provide an excellent backdrop to a lay-up although not all restaurants use them (see page 122). Where cloths are used they may be changed every service session or at least once every day. In order to prolong the life of tablecloths some establishments use slip cloths. These are slightly smaller than tablecloths (so are cheaper to launder), and can be placed over the top of slight blemishes.

When placing a tablecloth on a table, make sure the centre of the cloth is in the centre of the table with the corner points hanging down the table legs. The correct way of laying a cloth is as follows:
1 stand between two legs of the table
2 open the cloth so that the edges of the tablecloth are underneath the folded centre of the cloth
3 hold the top loose edge between your first finger and thumb, and the second edge between your first and second finger
4 lift the cloth across to the far edge of the table and let the lower edge drop
5 as you bring the cloth back towards you, release the centre crease covering the table as you come back
6 check the cloth is clean, in good repair, has an even drop all round and that the corners of the cloth drop down the table legs

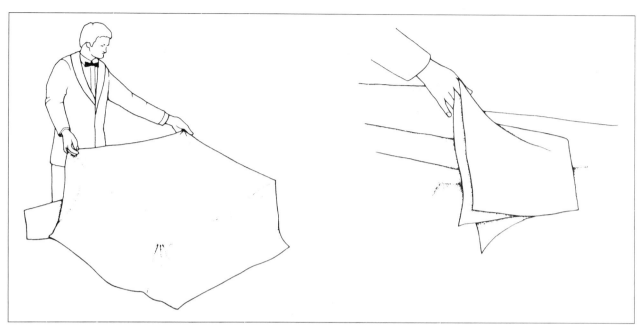

Laying a tablecloth

7 if more than one cloth is used on a table, make sure that the overlaps run away from the entrance door and that all the main creases run together.

The term used to describe a lay-up on a table is a *cover*, although it does have two meanings:
1 the number of customers expected
2 a place setting on the table.

Types of lay-up

There are two basic lay-ups:
● *table d'hôte*; used for a fixed price menu of three or more courses with limited choice on each course
● *à la carte*; used for a menu with a selection of individually priced dishes.

The cover for each type of menu differs as given below:
● *table d'hôte*: joint fork, joint knife, fish fork, fish knife, soup spoon, side plate, side knife, napkin, dessert spoon, dessert fork, wine glass
● *à la carte*: cover plate (if used), napkin, fish knife, fish fork (or meat knife, meat fork), side plate, side knife, wine glass.

Laying up procedures

The items laid on a cover may differ slightly depending on menu requirements and establishment standards, but the basic procedures are the same whenever laying up on tablecloths, place mats or other surfaces:
● collect all the equipment needed (e.g. cutlery, crockery) from either the sideboard or cutlery and flatware trolleys
● collect a service cloth
● place a cover plate or a napkin in the centre position of the cover space (where the customer will be seated)
● lay the cover from the inside out. This will help you to achieve even spacing and prevent over-handling, which can leave finger marks. Start with the items which

MEMORY JOGGER

What are the names given to the two basic table lay-ups?

the customer will need last, so that when the cover is fully laid the items to be used first are on the outside of the cover
- place the side plate to the left of the place setting
- place a side knife on the side plate
- place a folded napkin either on the cover plate (if used), in the glass or under the side knife depending on your establishment standard
- lay all cutlery and flatware so that the base of each item is 1.25 cm ($\frac{1}{2}$ in) away from the table edge; this will prevent the items of equipment being knocked when the customer sits down
- if the equipment has a badge or logo on it, make sure this is face up
- place any glasses at the top of the cover (above the joint knife) and upside down until just before service starts (if this is your establishment standard). This will prevent dust or other contaminating items from falling into the glasses. It is especially used where tables are set several hours before service
- give all equipment to be laid on the table a final check and polish with your service cloth
- lastly, place any condiments (e.g. butter) onto the table.

A basic table d'hôte cover. Note the position of the wine/water glass at the top of the meat knife

---

Do this

- Find out how the temperature is controlled in your restaurant.
- Note the furniture used. If possible, find out why this type and arrangement was chosen.
- Collect the equipment needed for one à la carte and one table d'hôte cover, or the cover used in your establishment, and practise the laying up procedure for each.

Laying up functions (e.g. banquets)

The procedures used are generally as given above, the only difference being that there is likely to be more cutlery, flatware and glassware to lay per cover (this will be determined by the establishment standard, the menu and the wines chosen).

If there are a number of service staff laying-up it is not unusual for one to lay a particular piece of equipment throughout the room while another staff member follows, laying another item. If a long function table is used and the equipment is laid clean, systematically and symmetrically, the room can be checked by looking down the table and seeing that all the glasses, cruets and napkins, etc. are in a line.

On smaller tables laid for an even number of covers (e.g. for two or four people) the accompaniments should be placed centrally; while tables laid for an uneven number (e.g. three people) should have them placed in such a way as to make them accessible yet balance the table. As a guide, place one set of cruets per four place settings.

Placing glasses on the table

If the wine has been ordered in advance, the number of glasses required will be known and can be placed on the table prior to service. If the choice is unknown, then one or two glasses can be placed on the table, one for water and the other for wine. They should be highly polished and arranged neatly to the right of each cover.

Napkins

Napkins are usually folded into decorative shapes, but it must be remembered that the same rules apply to the handling of napkins as to other linen (see page 123). When deciding on a napkin fold, consideration should also be given to the amount of handling, as over-handling and folding is unhygienic and time-consuming and may leave the eventual open napkin creased; simple folds reduce these problems.

ADDITIONAL TABLE ITEMS

Accompaniments

Table accompaniments are usually the same for both à la carte or table d'hôte menus, although they may vary from one establishment to another. In most cases, the additional items would be as follows:
- cruet (salt, pepper, mustard and mustard spoon)
- ashtray
- decoration: e.g. flowers (fresh or dry), candles, lamp (spirit or oil)
- table number.

Extras on sideboard or near to hand, may include:
- roll basket
- Melba toast
- gristicks
- peppermill
- cayenne pepper
- butter.

Other accompaniments are stored in the refrigerator or on the sideboard and they accompany specific dishes when served.

Table decorations

Table decorations such as a vase of flowers, a candle stick or a lamp can give an attractive finish to a well-laid table. The following needs to be noted:
- each decoration should be in keeping with the theme and not interfere with the meal presentation
- no decoration should be so large that it obstructs the customer's view
- any candles and lamps (spirit or oil) should be odourless and smokeless
- flowers need to be checked for insects (which must be removed), and the strength of their perfume (it must not be too strong).

Table items

It is commonplace these days to find that ashtrays are not put on the tables, but kept on the sideboard or near to hand until it is apparent that a customer requires one.

Throughout the process of laying a table it must be remembered that the customer will sit at the table for some time looking at the whole room, and nowhere more closely than the actual table they are sitting at. It is, therefore, very important that every tablecloth is in good order, clean, and positioned correctly; that all crockery, cutlery and glassware is spotlessly clean, polished, and in the correct position as well

MEMORY JOGGER

Why is it essential to check table linen and table items before service?

as being the correct cover for the dishes on the menu. If any problems are identified prior to service they must be brought to the attention of the supervisor or manager to be resolved. If, on the other hand, a problem occurs during service then the situation must be dealt with by you immediately or the customer informed of your intentions to resolve the situation. It may well be said that the chef creates the picture on the plate, but the scene is set first by the table.

Menus

Menus are one of the most important items in a restaurant. As well as showing the dishes available, they are the link between restaurant and kitchen, and in a way determine the order of work. They are also a link between the customer and restaurant, showing the standard and skills of the establishment. They must be checked prior to service to ensure that:

- the correct type and number of service items are prepared
- the appropriate accompaniments can be prepared
- the menu is the correct one on offer for that day
- they are clean and presentable with no misleading information
- there are enough for that day's service
- any promotional information is included and correct.

Legal requirements for menus

There are certain legal requirements that need to be observed when using menus:

- under the *Price Marking Order (Food and Drink on Premises) 1979*, a restaurant must display their menu where it can be easily read by prospective customers
- the displayed menu must show and state the prices charged (inclusive of VAT), whether a service or cover charge will be added, and what, if any, is the minimum charge.

MEMORY JOGGER

Describe two legal requirements that must be observed when putting a menu on display?

An example menu

However, there are some exceptions:
- restaurants with large menus and wine lists need not show all items, but must give a fair selection. This 'fair' selection is clearly defined in the *Price Marking Order (Food and Drink on Premises)* 1979
- establishments that only serve their members, e.g. clubs, schools, office canteens and colleges are exempt
- pubs, wine bars and other establishments offering food and drink from a self service counter must have their menus visible to customers before they make their selection. If the menu and prices are behind the counter, but cannot be seen from the service entrance, they must be displayed there as well.

Essential knowledge

Menus should be checked before use in order to:
- ensure that the information is correct and clear, to prevent the customer from being misled
- ensure menus are clean and presentable
- ensure that the correct quantity are ready for use
- ensure that the table lay-up is correct
- comply with the law.

FINAL PREPARATIONS FOR SERVICE

Certain mise-en-place tasks can be left until just before service, as dictated by establishment procedures. Butter, Melba toast and other bread items may be brought into the dining area, along with sugars, accompaniments and display trolleys.

If display trolleys or cabinets are to be used, they should be switched on in time to achieve the correct temperature before the items are placed on or in them.

Case study

You work in a restaurant which offers different dishes on the menu each day and as part of your job role you have to prepare the accompaniments and cutlery for the sideboards. The establishment's lay up consists of a traditional à la carte cover. On the menu today the following choices are included: Demi Pamplemousse, Omelette au Fromage, Spaghetti Bolognaise.
1 *What accompaniments are needed?*
2 *How, where and why should the accompaniments be stored?*
3 *What cover/equipment may be needed for each of these dishes and how would the cover be laid?*

What have you learned

1 How can you create a relaxed, leisurely dining area when table planning?
2 What factors contribute to table planning?
3 Why should menus be checked before use?
4 What procedures should be followed for faulty or damaged furniture?
5 How can hygiene and appearance problems be reduced in napkin folding?
6 What five points need to be observed when using table decorations?
7 What legal requirements have to be observed concerning menu presentation?
8 How can ventilation and temperature be controlled in a service area?

ELEMENT 3: Clear dining and service areas after table service

WHY IS CLEARING IMPORTANT?

People who work within the food industry have a legal and moral responsibility to their colleagues and customers, so it is up to you to prevent outbreaks of food poisoning. This can be achieved by:
- complying with the law
- removing food debris on which bacteria can grow
- removing food which may attract pests
- clearing and storing items correctly.

Working efficiently and safely
At the end of service all food items which have not been served to customers must be returned to the kitchen or service preparation areas for refrigeration or other hygienic storage. Do not re-use food items which have been returned from customers' tables.

In order to ensure that the clearing procedure is effective and efficient, you need to consider the possible methods of working and select the most appropriate, where clearing can be done in a methodical and systematic way. The clearing procedures must also at all times follow health, safety and hygiene regulations (see *Unit NG1*).

Essential knowledge

Dining and service areas should be left clean after service in order to:
- prevent accidents
- maintain establishment standards
- prevent pest infestation
- prevent unpleasant odours developing
- provide a clean and organised environment for staff on the following shift
- comply with the law
- maintain customer satisfaction and expectations.

HEATING, VENTILATION, MUSIC AND LIGHTING

If the heating system is on a control timer it should be self regulating, although it is wise to check that it has turned itself off at the correct time. Ventilation is important as the smells of the last meal need to be cleared before they go stale; either open windows or (where appropriate) check that the air conditioning system is working correctly. Music needs to be turned off and the system unplugged if possible. Clear under full lighting, but make sure all lighting is turned off once clearing is finished (except any security lighting).

CLEARING ELECTRICAL OR HEATING EQUIPMENT

Before clearing or cleaning any electrical or heating equipment:
- turn it off and disconnect it from its power source
- allow it to cool.

Doing this will prevent the risk of injury or fire.

HOTPLATES, BAIN-MARIES AND PLATE WARMERS

1　Turn off or disconnect the power supply; if wet, drain.
2　Allow to cool.
3　Remove any extra equipment and food debris.
4　Clean with detergent and a damp cloth.
5　If cleaning a wet bain-marie, clean out with detergent then rinse thoroughly and refill.

REFRIGERATION UNITS

1　Switch off and disconnect.
2　Return unused food items to the kitchen.
3　Clean with detergent and disinfectants which do not taint food then rinse well with hot water.

HOT AND COLD BEVERAGE DISPENSERS

All types of drink dispensers need to be switched off and disconnected, with the exception of certain types of chilled drink dispensers. Whichever type of dispenser is used, check the manufacturer's instructions to find out what procedures need to be followed once service has finished; this prevents damage to equipment or products.

Essential knowledge

Certain types of electrical equipment should be turned off after service in order to:
● prevent injury to yourself, colleagues and customers
● eliminate risk of fire
● be resourceful and economical.

CLEARING SIDEBOARDS

Sideboards can either be emptied at the end of service or restocked ready for the next service period. In both cases:
● if a hot plate is fitted, switch it off and unplug from the mains
● empty any stock still held in the sideboard and return any food items to the kitchen
● using a damp cloth lightly impregnated with an anti-bacterial cleaner, wipe out the cutlery drawers; make sure the cloth is not too wet (this would damage any baize lining)
● remove and exchange any shelf cloths then wipe each shelf with a damp cloth
● clean the hotplate once it has cooled.

CLEARING TROLLEYS

Before cleaning a trolley, switch off the heat or power supply and return any unserved food items to the kitchen then:
● remove any service equipment and crockery
● remove any cloths
● wash/wipe down with an anti-bacterial cleaner
● return the trolley to its normal storage area.

Do this

- Make a list of the clearing and cleaning tasks that need to be carried out in your service area and ask your supervisor to explain the establishment procedures for completing them.
- Check the manufacturer's instructions for the beverage dispensers in your establishment.
- Ask your supervisor to show you the establishment procedures for laundry supplies. If you do not use laundry, arrange a visit to a hotel nearby which uses linen, asking to study their laundry system.

CLEARING TABLES

Tables need to be cleared of all food debris and equipment. Depending on the establishment procedure, tablecloths can either be taken off and sent to the laundry or base cloths left on and the slip cloths changed.

If the tables are polished or texture-finished, they need to be wiped down with a damp cloth impregnated with an anti-bacterial cleaner. If the tables were used for a function they may need careful storing or stacking (this also applies to any side tables).

Linen
The methods of laundering in establishments will vary, but the main principle of exchange must occur. The method of laundering depends on the system used by the establishment (see *Table linen* on pages 122–123). To make the exchange easier and quicker, the tablecloths can be bundled into fives or tens, depending on size, while napkins can be bundled into tens or twenties.

Cutlery and crockery
All dirty crockery and cutlery needs to be sent through to the wash-up area where food debris should be cleared off and the crockery and cutlery stacked for cleaning. The clean equipment should be returned to its original storage area or set for the next service session (depending on establishment procedures).

MEMORY JOGGER

Why must particular attention be paid to the disposal of broken glass, crockery and the emptying of ashtrays?

Silverware
Care needs to be taken with silverware. If it is not cleaned, washed and dried immediately after use its appearance will be damaged. It should also be stored very carefully; items which are only used for special occasions and then returned to storage need to be polished and ideally wrapped for protection.

Ashtrays
Empty ashtrays with great care: a smouldering cigarette can easily be missed when clearing, but if thrown into a waste bin along with flammable materials (such as paper), a fire can easily start. Ideally, ashtrays should be emptied into metal bins or containers with lids and left until there is no risk of fire.

Wash ashtrays separately to all other items then return to storage area.

Glassware
Glasses are best washed in glass-washing machines as they are time-saving and hygienic. If you are using a glass-washing machine, read the manufacturer's instructions carefully; it is important to use the correct operating procedures and temperatures.

If washing by hand, wash the glasses in hot water with a detergent, then rinse in hot water (82 °C/180 °F), dry and store upside-down on shelves lined with glass storage matting.

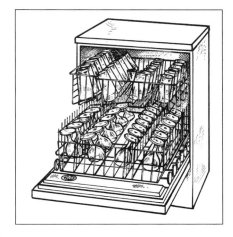

A glass washer

Menus and holders
Collect all the menus and wipe down any folders. If new menus are to be used for the next service period, make sure that all of this period's menus are removed.

Table decorations
All table decorations need to be collected together, checked, and stored according to requirements. If they include lamps or candles, extinguish these and allow to cool before moving.

Condiments and accompaniments
As with food items, return to the kitchen or service preparation area, where those items which have not been used can be stored and used again or disposed of.

DEALING WITH WASTE

All food waste must be disposed of carefully, either through waste disposal units or into containers with tight fitting lids. When handling waste:
● empty bins regularly
● do not allow bins to become full or over-full
● wash the bins, lids and surrounding areas thoroughly with detergent or disinfectant before or after every service session or whenever they become full
● wash your hands after handling rubbish bins
● store waste in designated areas away from fire exits, preparation areas and corridors.

Essential knowledge

Waste must be handled and disposed of correctly in order to:
● prevent accidents
● prevent the risk of fire
● prevent the contamination of service and preparation areas
● prevent pest infestation and unpleasant odours from arising
● comply with the law and all establishment procedures.

Case study

*At the end of service you are asked to clear away the refrigerated sweet trolley. The establishment procedure at the end of service is to return all **usable** food items to the kitchen. On closer inspection you notice that an eight-portion bowl of trifle, with only two portions removed, is cracked and chipped in a couple of places.*

Because you are unsure as to when and how the bowl was damaged:
1 How is this particular dessert to be disposed of?
2 What other procedures need to be followed with this incident and why?
3 How should the sweet trolley be left at the end of service?

<table>
<tr><td>

What have you learned

</td><td>

1 Why should all dining and service areas be left clean after service?
2 What should be done with left-over food at the end of service?
3 Why should certain types of electrical equipment be turned off after service?
4 What two points of safety need to be observed before clearing heated and electrical equipment?
5 Why must waste be handled and disposed of correctly?
6 Why must care be taken when emptying ashtrays?

</td></tr>
</table>

<table>
<tr><td>

Get ahead

</td><td>

1 Study the work carried out within your food service and dining areas to see if any tasks or service procedures can be improved to provide a more efficient service.
2 Look through a catering supplier's equipment brochure to see if there are any pieces of equipment which would help with these improvements. Be prepared to justify the purchases of these pieces of equipment.
3 Design a long-term maintenance programme for your restaurant, to include redecoration, furnishing and equipment replacement.

</td></tr>
</table>

UNIT 2NC2

Provide a table service

This chapter covers:

ELEMENT 1:   **Greet customers and take orders**
ELEMENT 2:   **Serve customers' orders**
ELEMENT 3:   **Maintain dining and service areas**

What you need to do

- Deal with customers in a polite and welcoming manner at all times.
- Identify customer requirements and check booking records.
- Escort customers to an appropriate table or waiting area and assist with coats and bags as required.
- Deal with unexpected situations.
- Provide customers with the correct table items.
- Serve the correct type, quality and quantity of food in accordance with laid-down procedures.
- Clear customer's tables of soiled and unrequired table items at appropriate times.
- Remove soiled table linen, left-over food items and accompaniments throughout service.
- Carry out all work, causing minimum disturbance to customers.
- Present the correct menus and translate them where appropriate, giving customers accurate information on individual dishes.
- Guide customers to an appropriate menu choice, then identify and record customer orders.
- Work in an organised manner, planning your time to meet daily schedules.

What you need to know

- Why menus should be checked before use.
- Why information given to customers should be accurate.
- Which condiments and/or accompaniments complement which menu dishes.
- Why care has to be taken to serve and arrange food correctly.
- Why waste should be handled and disposed of correctly.
- Why a constant stock of linen, table items and accompaniments must be maintained.
- Why dining and service areas must be kept tidy and free from rubbish and food debris.
- How to deal with spillages and breakages in an appropriate manner.
- How to deal correctly with left-over food items.
- How to deal with unexpected situations.

INTRODUCTION

The term *table service* applies to any situation where the food is served at a table, e.g. Little Chefs, Beefeaters, ethnic restaurants, five-star hotels. This type of service gives food service staff the opportunity to use their knowledge and skills to help provide an enjoyable and satisfying meal experience for customers, who come to a restaurant for relaxation and pleasure as well as nourishment. A professional waiter or waitress providing a table service therefore requires not only technical expertise, but also sales and social skills to fulfil his or her role as a representative of the establishment in direct contact with the customer.

139

Professional table service leads to satisfied customers

The term *banquet service* applies to the service of large groups – all of whom should be served at the same time. This involves serving in a similar way to table service but with the waiting staff watching for the head waiter to give the go-ahead to proceed with the service or clearing of each course.

ELEMENT 1:   Greet customers and take orders

Greeting customers is often the job of the receptionist, head waiter or supervisor, but in smaller establishments it could be the responsibility of anyone, so it is important that all restaurant staff know how to greet customers in an appropriate manner since this can determine their first impressions of the restaurant. It is important for all restaurant staff to develop a sound knowledge of dishes on the menu so that they can offer assistance to the customer as necessary, while taking orders in an organised and efficient manner.

It must be noted that practices and policies may vary in different establishments. The practices described here are those generally accepted, but remember that different styles of restaurant, e.g. a Beefeater, a Little Chef or an Italian restaurant, will adopt different procedures and standards, so you should use the following text in conjunction with the methods used in your own establishment.

GREETING CUSTOMERS

<table>
<tr><td>

MEMORY JOGGER

Why is it important that customers are dealt with in a polite and helpful manner at all times?

</td></tr>
</table>

As a member of staff involved in food service, you will come into regular contact with customers. This is an important link; if you are able to ensure that customers leave with pleasant memories of the restaurant, they are more likely to make a return visit. Establishments are often judged by the standards of service and staff as well as the quality of food served, so professional personal appearance and presentation are important.

● As customers arrive at the restaurant, greet them in a polite but friendly way, by addressing them either as 'Sir' or 'Madam' or, preferably, by their name if known. This has the effect of making them feel more welcome. Children should be warmly welcomed and spoken to in a manner appropriate to their age.
● Offer your assistance in removing their coats, hats, etc. to the cloakroom.
● Check if the party has a booking; if not, find out whether there is a suitable table available.
● Many restaurants seat guests in a bar area when they first arrive, where they may

be offered an aperitif. However, if the customers' table is ready you may offer them an alternative of going straight to their table.

● Customers' needs vary greatly: some may need extra attention and assistance from the staff, for instance, if they are suffering from mobility or communication difficulties. Be aware of your customers' special requirements and offer assistance in a polite but unobtrusive way.

● Most importantly, remember that during this time it is essential that a welcoming and efficient image is conveyed to the guests.

SEATING GUESTS

Identifying the host

As the head waiter or supervisor approaches the table with the guests, the waiter should greet them and identify the host of the party. This can be done in a number of ways:

● the head waiter may tell the waiter which member of the party is the host
● the name the table is booked in is usually that of the host
● the host generally takes control when guests are sitting down or deciding what to order
● the host may enquire about the special dish of the day or ask for the wine list.

Assisting the guests in seating

As a waiter, you will need to assist guests in taking their seats.

1 Pull out each chair slightly, then push it in again carefully as the guest sits down. Offer this assistance to female guests first, followed by male guests and lastly, the host.

2 While seating the guests, engage them in light conversation, creating a friendly atmosphere. It is important to ensure that each table has the correct number of place settings and that if applicable, these have been arranged in accordance with any special customer requirements.

3 In a traditional restaurant, the station waiter may unfold each guest's serviette or napkin and place it on their lap once the customers are seated (this is known as *breaking the serviette*). The station waiter may then also turn the glasses up the right way if this has not been done beforehand.

4 At this point it is appropriate for the waiter or wine waiter (*sommelier*) to approach the table and offer an aperitif to the customers.

5 In some restaurants it may be necessary for the waiter to offer the guests bread rolls and/or Melba toast, followed by water (some establishments place jugs of iced water on the table for guests to help themselves).

6 If the menu is not already on the table, it should now be presented to the guests. Give them information on any special dishes of the day and be ready to answer any enquiries about dishes suitable for specific dietary requirements, e.g. vegetarian. Allow a short time for guests to make their choice.

Essential knowledge

Menus should be checked before use in order to:
● ensure accuracy of ingredients, availability and pricing
● ensure the inclusion of promotional items.

Do this

● Ask your supervisor who is responsible for greeting customers when they first arrive in your restaurant.
● Find out how bookings are taken in your establishment.
● Check that you know where customers can leave their hats and coats.
● Find out the procedures for seating guests in your establishment.

TAKING THE ORDER

1. The waiter normally takes the order for the entire table through the host. Stand to the host's left and be ready to offer suggestions, advice and explanations of dishes on the menu. You may need to translate the foreign names of certain dishes. This point represents an ideal opportunity to promote sales.

2. Food checks (written copies of the order) should be written in the language of the menu and orders are usually taken up to and including the main course. It is a good idea at this stage to establish a permanent point for yourself at the table, i.e. a point at which you will always stand when approaching the table for the rest of the meal. If you list the dishes ordered in a clockwise direction around the table from this point, you will be able to deliver the correct dish to the correct guest when serving the order without having to ask the guests what they ordered. This creates a more professional impression.

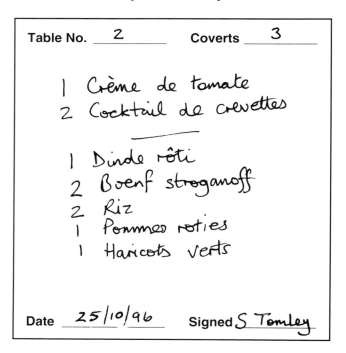

A check written out for the first two courses of a meal

3. Record all the dishes ordered accurately and clearly on the food check, together with any additional information necessary, e.g. the degree of cooking required for a steak.

4. Record any other important information on the food check. Most restaurants would require you to record:
   - the date
   - the table number
   - the number of covers
   - the waiter's initials

Essential knowledge

Information given to customers should be accurate in order to:
- ensure an efficient service is maintained
- ensure customer satisfaction.

Case study

It is a very busy lunch time in your restaurant and a party of six have made their own way to a table, they have been given the wrong menu and an order has been taken by a new member of staff who is trying hard to help out.
1   *Why has this problem arisen? What is the correct procedure for customers when entering your restaurant?*
2   *What immediate actions should be taken?*

METHODS OF TAKING ORDERS

There are two traditional methods for taking orders, as given below.

1 Triplicate checking system
This is a control system used in many medium-sized and large establishments. Here the food check consists of three copies, which are divided as follows:
● the top copy goes to the kitchen and is handed to a member of the kitchen brigade at the hotplate
● the duplicate (bottom) copy goes to the cashier who will make out the guests' bill
● the flimsy (middle) copy is kept by the waiter as a means of reference (you may need to hold this copy against a white background to make it easier to read)

2 Duplicate checking system
This control system is more likely to be used in a smaller establishment. It is generally used where a table d'hôte menu is in operation. Here the food check consists of two copies, which are divided as follows:
● the top copy goes to the kitchen
● the second copy is used for service and billing purposes (the waiter may carry out the billing)

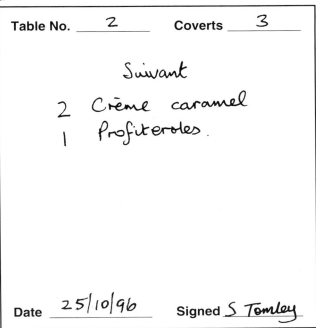

An example check for an additional order

Other points to note

● Additional checks may be written out later for sweets and coffees.
● If an à la carte menu is in use, record the time the order was taken and the individual dish prices on the check. Abbreviations may be used when taking orders

as long as they are understood by everyone and cannot be misinterpreted by the kitchen, causing subsequent delay in service.
● Even the most sophisticated electronic system is based on the duplicate or triplicate system, even though the actual checks may not be written but communicated electronically to VDUs or print-out machines.

Do this

● Find out what system is used for taking orders in your establishment.
● Check with your supervisor what type of menus are used.
● Ask your supervisor who is responsible for taking orders.

What have you learned

1 Why is it important that customers are greeted correctly?
2 Why should menus be checked before use?
3 In what order should you assist guests to sit down?
4 How may you be able to identify the host of a party?
5 Why must information given to guests always be accurate?
6 What information should be recorded on a food check?
7 When using the triplicate system, where do the three copies go?

ELEMENT 2:   Serve customers' orders

TYPES OF FOOD SERVICE

There are a variety of styles of food service; the type used in any establishment will depend on a number of factors:
● the policy of the establishment
● the type, size and site of the establishment
● the time available
● the type and number of customers
● the type of menu and its cost.

For most types of food service customers are seated at a laid table and served by one (or a combination) of the service methods listed in the table below.

Service methods

Silver/English	The waiting staff present and serve food to the customer from a flat or dish (see *Unit 2NC5: Provide a silver service*).
Family	Main courses are plated with dishes of vegetables placed on the table for customers to help themselves, e.g. ethnic restaurants
Plate/American	This type of service is found in a wide variety of catering establishments and is probably the most common style of food service. Food is pre-plated and served to the customers, sometimes under cloche/plate covers which are removed in front of the guests. The advantages of this type of service include the maintenance of food presentation and portions, and the possibility of a faster turnover of customers.
Butler/French	Food service staff present the food on dishes or flats to each customer and they help themselves.
Russian	The table is laid with food and the customers help themselves.
Guéridon	Food is served onto the customer's plate from a side table or trolley. This style of service can also include the preparation of salads and their dressing, the filleting of fish, carving, cooking and *flambage* (flaming of dishes at the table).

SERVING THE CUSTOMER

After you have taken the customers' orders you will probably need to change the cover according to the dishes ordered. If this is the case, carry the cutlery to and from the table on a salver or plate with a serviette on it to help deaden the noise. If a table d'hôte menu is in operation the covers are usually changed up to and including the main course. If an à la carte menu is in operation the cutlery for each course should be placed on the table before the service of each course. Any accompaniments may also be placed on the table at this time.

In order to comply with current food safety and trade description legislation, it is important to ensure that the food served is of good quality and meets the customers' expectations.

GENERAL ACCOMPANIMENTS AND COVERS

Covers

Many items on the menu will require alternative cutlery to that which is already on the table, and you may also need extra service equipment. Make sure that these items are kept on the sideboard for easy access.

Accompaniments

Accompaniments are often highly flavoured seasonings of various kinds offered with certain dishes to improve the flavour of the food or to counteract its richness. There are standard accompaniments for some dishes and it is important for you to have a thorough knowledge of these, so that you can automatically offer the correct accompaniments.

Although there are traditional accompaniments for specific dishes, in certain parts of the country alternative accompaniments may be acceptable. Note also that if a customer requests an unusual accompaniment to be served with a specific dish this should be undertaken without question.

All accompaniments for the menu should be placed on the sideboard or on a service table ready for service.

Hors d'oeuvres

The first part of a meal can consist of either an hors d'oeuvres variés or a single hors d'oeuvres.

Hors d'oeuvres variés
This usually consists of a selection of foods and salads which are either plated in the kitchen or served from a table, trolley or tray so that customers may select for themselves. If served in the restaurant, the salads are usually presented in dishes called *raviers* with a clean spoon and fork for each variety.

When serving from a trolley: place the trolley between the table and yourself and rotate it away from the guest so that he or she can see everything on the trolley and so make a choice.

When serving from a tray: rotate the tray on your hand so that the item being served is in the ravier closest to the customer's plate.

Single hors d'oeuvres
This consists of one item or dish such as avocado pear, melon, fruit cocktail, pâté, smoked salmon or oysters.

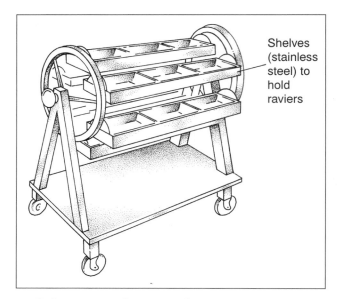

Shelves (stainless steel) to hold raviers

An hors d'oeuvres trolley

Hors d'oeuvres: their accompaniments and covers

Dish	Cover	Accompaniments
Potted shrimps	Fish knife and fork; cold fish plate	Cayenne pepper; pepper mill; lemon segment; hot toast or brown bread and butter
Smoked eel/trout/ mackerel	Fish knife and fork; cold fish plate	Cayenne pepper; pepper mill; lemon segment; brown bread and butter; horseradish sauce
Fresh prawns	Prawns are placed over the rim of a wine goblet filled with crushed ice on an underplate with doiley Fish knife and fork; cold fish plate (for debris); finger bowl (with warm water and a slice of lemon, placed at the head of the cover); spare serviette	Brown bread and butter; mayonnaise
Gulls' eggs	Small knife and fork; cold fish plate; fingerbowl; spare serviette; sideplate for shell	Brown bread and butter; Oriental salt (4 parts salt to 1 part cayenne pepper)
Hors d'oeuvres variés	Fish plate; fish knife and fork	Brown bread and butter; oil and vinegar
Grapefruit cocktail	Coupe or goblet on sideplate with doiley; grapefruit spoon or teaspoon	Caster sugar
Fruit juices (orange, pineapple or grapefruit)	Coupe or goblet on a side plate with doiley	None
Chilled melon (melon frappé)	Dessert spoon and fork; cold fish plate	Ground ginger, caster sugar
Pâté maison	Side knife and dessert fork; cold fish plate	Hot toast without crust, cut into triangles and served on a sideplate
Corn on the cob	Hot fish plate; corn-on-the-cob holders either inserted into each end of the cob or placed on a sideplate ahead of the cover	Melted butter

Essential knowledge	Care must be taken to serve and arrange food correctly in order to: ● comply with costing considerations ● maintain a professional appearance ● maintain customer satisfaction

Do this

- Find out what service methods are used in your establishment.
- Ask your supervisor what hors d'oeuvres are usually offered in your restaurant and check what covers and accompaniments are usually used.
- Find out what covers and accompaniments are standard for the following dishes:
  - Avocado pear
  - Asparagus
  - Escargots
  - Smoked salmon
  - Seafood cocktail
  - Oysters
  - Globe artichoke

Soups

Soup may either be served as the first course or the second, following the hors d'oeuvres. It may be plated in the kitchen or served from a tureen. Most thick soups, purees, creams and broths are served in soup plates on underplates. Clear soups (consommés) are served into a consommé cup on a saucer and underplate. These are usually eaten with a dessert spoon.

Soups: their accompaniments and covers

Dish	Cover	Accompaniments
Purée or ungarnished soups	Soup plate; underplate; soup spoon	Croutons
Minestrone	Soup plate; underplate; soup spoon	Grated Parmesan cheese; toasted flute
French onion soup	Soup plate; underplate; soup spoon	Grated Parmesan cheese; toasted flute
Petite marmite	Special earthenware dish called a *petite marmite*; underplate and doiley	Grated Parmesan cheese; toasted flute

Fish

Fish can be served as a course on its own or as a main course with vegetables and potatoes. The accompaniments are the same in both cases and the cutlery is normally a fish knife and fork. Some fish can be filleted at the table (e.g. Dover sole) while other fish (e.g. trout) should have the head and tail removed by the waiter. Fillets of fish may be served by using two service forks or two fish knives: these are fanned out and slid under the fish to be served.

When fish is served as a main course it should always be served on a hot joint plate. However, some establishments serve fish on an oval platter.

Serving fish

Fish dishes: their accompaniments and covers

Dish	Cover	Accompaniments
Deep fried scampi	Fish knife and fork; hot fish plate	Tartare sauce; lemon segment
Cold lobster	Fish knife and fork; lobster pick; debris plate; fingerbowl; spare serviette	Mayonnaise; lemon segment
Fish fried in batter	Fish knife and fork; hot fish plate	Tomato sauce; lemon segment;
Fried fish in breadcrumbs	Fish knife and fork; hot fish plate	Tartare sauce; lemon segment
Blue trout	Fish knife and fork; hot fish plate	Hollandaise sauce; lemon segment; melted butter

Do this

- Ask your supervisor how soups are served in your establishment.
- Find out what accompaniments are standard for: bouillabaisse (Mediterranean fish stew); borsch; consommé.
- Find out what covers and accompaniments are standard for: whitebait; hot poached salmon; grilled herring; mussels; cold salmon.

Farinaceous dishes

This category includes all pasta (e.g. spaghetti, macaroni and ravioli), rice dishes (e.g. pilaf and risotto) and gnocchi (little dumplings) when served as a course on their own. All of these dishes except spaghetti are served on a fish plate and eaten with a dessert spoon and fork. Spaghetti is served into a soup plate with an underplate and a dessert spoon and joint fork.

Farinaceous dishes: their accompaniments and covers

Dish	Cover	Accompaniments
Spaghetti	Joint fork (on the right); dessert spoon (on left); hot soup plate on underplate	Parmesan cheese
Others	Dessert spoon (on the right); dessert fork (on left); hot fish plate	Parmesan cheese

Egg dishes

These can be served as various courses during a meal, i.e. as a starter, main course, intermediate course or dessert.

Egg dishes: their accompaniments and covers

Dish	Cover	Accompaniments
Oeuf sur le plat	Sur le plat; underplate and doiley; dessert spoon and fork; (small knife depending on garnish)	
Oeuf en cocotte	Cocotte dish on underplate and doiley; teaspoon	
Omelettes	Hot fish plate; joint fork (on the right)	
Main course omelettes	Hot joint plate; joint knife and fork	
Sweet omelette	Hot fish plate; dessert spoon and fork	

Meat, poultry and game

These dishes are usually served as main courses. When you are serving meat dishes, particularly joints of meat, offer their traditional accompaniments.

Meat, poultry and game dishes: their accompaniments and covers

Dish	Cover	Accompaniments
Roast beef	Hot joint plate; joint knife and fork	Roast gravy; French and English mustard; horseradish sauce; Yorkshire pudding
Roast lamb	Hot joint plate; joint knife and fork	Roast gravy; mint sauce
Boiled mutton	Hot joint plate; joint knife and fork	Caper sauce
Boiled fresh beef	Hot joint plate; joint knife and fork	Rock salt; grated horseradish; gherkins
Grilled steak, mixed grill	Hot joint plate; joint knife and fork	French and English mustard; parsley butter
Roast chicken	Hot joint plate; joint knife and fork	Roast gravy; bread sauce; parsley and thyme stuffing; bacon rolls, game chips; watercress
Roast duck	Hot joint plate; joint knife and fork	Roast gravy; sage and onion stuffing; apple sauce
Hare	Hot joint plate; joint knife and fork	Heart-shaped crouton; redcurrant jelly

Do this

- Find out what *sur le plat* and *cocotte* dishes are.
- Find an example of a sweet omelette.
- Ask your supervisor whether accompaniments are ever served with omelettes.
- Find out what covers and accompaniments are standard for the following dishes:
    - Curry
    - Roast pork
    - Irish stew
    - Roast mutton
    - Lancashire hotpot
    - Roast goose
    - Roast game birds
    - Boiled salt beef
- Ask your supervisor to tell you of any speciality meat dishes that are served in your establishment and find out what covers and accompaniments are used.

Vegetables and salads

Some vegetables are served as a course on their own (such as asparagus and corn on the cob); these have already been mentioned in the hors d'oeuvres section. Many other vegetables are served with sauces which form part of the actual dish.

Case study

Here is a food check (from a table d'hôte menu) for four customers dining at your restaurant

RIVERSIDE RESTAURANT

Table No. 2   (Covers 4)

2 x prawn cocktails
2 x minestrone

3 x goujons of plaice
1 x roast beef
3 x vegetables
1 x salad

2 x bavarois
2 x cheese

Date 30·3·96 Initials B P

1   Why must their cutlery be checked?
2   Indicate any cutlery changes which may be necessary.
3   Which accompaniments will be needed for the dishes ordered?
4   When the time comes, how should you serve the cheese?

Vegetables and salads: their accompaniments and covers

Dish	Cover	Accompaniments
Baked (jacket) potato	Hot sideplate; dessert fork (on side-plate, placed at top left of cover)	Butter pat; pepper mill
Side salad	Salad crescent, sideplate or bowl; dessert fork (placed on crescent at top left of cover)	Vinaigrette or other salad dressing

Cheese

The cheese course is normally offered towards the end of a meal, as an alternative or an extra to the sweet. Some restaurants may adopt the continental custom, where the cheese is offered before the sweet. A restaurant will usually offer a selection of cheese from a trolley or cheeseboard; the cheeses should be arranged attractively. Make sure you are familiar with all the cheeses offered so you are able to help the customers with their choices.

When serving a cheese course, lay the cover first. This consists of a sideplate, side knife and sometimes a small fork. Present the cheeseboard or trolley to the customer and offer assistance or information as required. Once the customers have made their choice, cut a portion of each cheese chosen (using a clean knife for each variety) and place the portion on a sideplate. Two factors are particularly important when cutting cheese: make sure you cut the correct portion size and take care to maintain the attractive appearance on the cheeseboard.

Note that Stilton should no longer be served in the traditional manner of scooping out (which creates a large amount of wastage), but by cutting out thin wedges across the surface of the cheese.

After the cheese has been served, you may offer any of the following accompaniments:
- cruet (salt, pepper and mustard)
- butter (in a dish on an underplate with doiley, with a butter knife)
- celery (served in a celery glass half-filled with either crushed ice or cold water)
- radishes when in season (placed in a glass bowl on an underplate with a teaspoon)

From left: two ways of cutting hard cheese; portioning soft cheese; an economical way to cut Stilton

● caster sugar (for cream cheeses)
● apples, grapes and pickles
● assorted cheese biscuits.

Sweets

Restaurants may offer their customers either a sweet menu or a sweet trolley, or a combination of both, since some sweets are unsuitable for serving from a trolley.

When using a trolley, make sure that sweets are attractively presented and arranged at all times so that customers have a clear view when making their choice. Once a sweet has been selected, hold the plate or bowl in your left hand and serve the sweet using a spoon and fork or a gateau slice (in your right hand). Offer cream as an accompaniment.

Most sweets are usually served onto a plate or into a pudding bowl on an underplate. Bowls are usually used when a sauce is served with the sweet (e.g. custard). Certain sweets, such as mousses, fruit fools and syllabubs may be served in a glass or coupe on an underplate. Most ice cream sweets are served in coupes.

Sweets are generally eaten with a dessert spoon and fork, although some ice creams and mousses may be eaten with a teaspoon or sundae spoon. Note that sorbets are often served as a sweet but occasionally they are served in the middle of a large banquet to cleanse the palate for the next course.

Do this

● Find out which cheeses are normally offered in your establishment.
● Check which service methods and accompaniments are used when serving the cheese course in your establishment.
● Find out what type of dishes sundaes and banana splits are normally served in.

Fresh fruit and nuts

These may be served as an alternative to a sweet or as an extra course at the end of a meal. Lay the cover as follows:
● dessert plate
● dessert knife and fork
● spare sideplate for shell or peel
● spare serviette
● fingerbowl
● nut crackers and grape scissors (to be placed on the fruit basket).

MEMORY JOGGER

Which service equipment is appropriate for the service of grapes?

If nuts are chosen, place some nutcrackers on the table next to the dessert knife or on a sideplate at the head of the cover. If grapes are chosen, cut off the selected portion of grapes using the grape scissors.

Accompaniments would consist of caster sugar (in a holder on a sideplate) and salt (for nuts). You may offer cream to accompany fruit; it may be served in a cream jug placed on the table, or from a sauceboat and offered to the guest, using a sauce ladle or dessert spoon.

Savouries

Savouries may be served at the end of a meal either as well as or as an alternative to a sweet; items such as hot canapés or croûtes, bouchées, savoury soufflés or fritters may be offered.

The cover for savouries consists of a hot fish plate and a small knife and fork. Savoury soufflés may be eaten from an individual soufflé dish presented on an underplate with a teaspoon, dessert fork or fish fork. Set the following accompaniments:
- cruet to be replaced
- cayenne pepper (placed on a sideplate on the table)
- pepper mill (on a sideplate on the table)
- Worcester sauce (placed on a sideplate on the table but only offered with a meat savoury).

Serving coffee

Coffee is normally served from the right. Place coffee cups, saucers and spoons on the table for each customer with the handle on the right and the spoon underneath.

There are many ways of serving coffee, including silver service. Other methods include:
- cups of coffee taken straight to the table
- jugs of coffee, cream or hot/cold milk placed on the table for guests to help themselves
- service of milk or cream and coffee from pots, one held in either of the waiter's hands. The sugar is placed on the table for customers to help themselves.

GENERAL FOOD SERVICE POINTS

- Always use a waiter's cloth when carrying hot plates to help protect against burns and scalds.
- Serve cold foods before hot foods. This ensures that when the hot food is served, the customer may eat it immediately without having to wait for other food to be served to the table.
- In general, food should always be served from the left. However, this may vary according to establishment practices; check with your supervisor on whether this applies to your establishment.
- Serve guests in the following order: female guests, male guests, host.
- When carrying items to and from the table, place them on a salver, underflat or service plate.
- Always ensure that sufficient accompaniments, bread items and seasonings are available to customers throughout their meal.
- Make sure that all crockery and cutlery used is clean, polished and free from damage in order to maintain customer satisfaction.

Finally, remember that the practices and methods given in this element are those generally accepted within the catering trade, but these may vary depending on establishment style and customer requirements.

Presenting the bill

At the end of the meal, usually when the customer requests, you will need to collect the bill from the cashier. When doing this, fold the bill to conceal the figures and then present it to the host on a sideplate. When payment has been made, take it to the cashier and then return the receipt and change to the customer on the sideplate.

Guest departure

When customers are ready to leave, be ready to assist them with chairs, hats and coats making sure that nothing has been left behind. You may then thank the customers and say goodbye.

What have you learned

1 Name three different service methods and describe them.
2 Why must care be taken to serve and arrange food correctly?
3 Why is it important to ensure that food served is of a good quality and meets customer expectations?
4 What are the cover and accompaniments for French onion soup?
5 What are the possible accompaniments for cheese?

ELEMENT 3: Maintain dining and service areas

MEMORY JOGGER

Why must dining and service areas be kept tidy and free from rubbish and food debris?

CLEARING TABLES

Clearing should only begin when all the guests at the table have finished eating. It is important to learn how to clear tables correctly for a number of reasons:
- it ensures speed and efficiency
- it avoids the possibility of accidents
- it creates minimum disturbance to the guests
- it allows dirty dishes to be stacked neatly and correctly on the sideboard with minimum delay
- more can be cleared, in less time and in fewer journeys between sideboard and table. This helps to speed up the eating process, allowing for greater turnover.

Essential knowledge

Dining and service areas must be kept tidy and free from rubbish and food debris in order to:
- prevent contamination of food and food areas
- prevent accidents
- maintain customer satisfaction
- comply with the law

Clearing techniques

All clearing techniques stem from two main hand positions but also depend on what is being cleared from the table. The following principles should be maintained whenever possible.
1 Clear plates from the right-hand side of the customer.
2 Position yourself so that you are standing sideways-on to the table.
3 Collect any plates with your right hand and then transfer them to your left. Remember to turn away from the guests while you clear the plates.

4 Hold a joint plate by placing your thumb on top of the plate and your first two fingers underneath; the remaining two fingers should stand upright to help balance and support further plates.

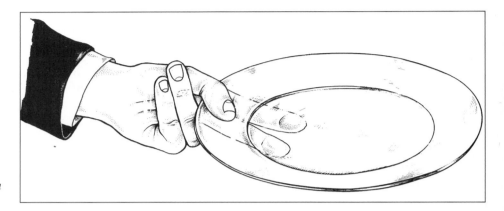

Holding the first plate when clearing

5 Secure the fork under your thumb and slide the knife underneath the fork. This prevents the cutlery sliding about or falling to the floor.
6 Balance the next plate on your left forearm, thumb and two upright fingers.
7 Scrape any food debris from the second to the first plate and place the dirty cutlery onto the first plate.
8 Continue to clear the remaining plates following this method.
9 If clearing the main course, remove the sideplates, butter dish and cruet.

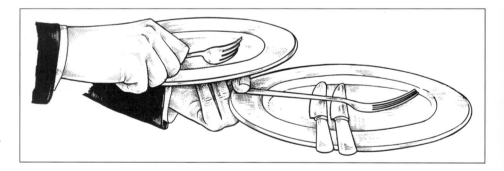

Clearing the debris from the second plate

Clearing soup plates

1 Collect the first bowl and underplate, positioning the underplate as for a joint plate.
2 Collect the second bowl and underplate, positioning it on the forearm, thumb and fingers of your left hand.
3 Transfer the spoons from the first bowl to the second bowl.
4 Place the second bowl into the first bowl, so that a clear underplate remains, allowing you to continue the process.

Clearing accompaniments

Cruets should be removed after the main course but should remain available nearby for service with cheese if required. Mustards, sauces, dressings, etc. should be cleared away at the end of each appropriate course.

Clearing soup plates

Crumbing down

Crumbing down usually takes place after the main course has been cleared and before the sweet order is taken. The process is carried out to remove any crumbs or debris left on the tablecloth. If a table d'hôte cover has been laid, the dessert spoon and fork will normally have been laid at the head of the cover (see steps 2 and 3 below); if an à la carte menu has been laid there should not be any cutlery remaining on the table when you come to crumb down (the cutlery is not laid until after the dessert order has been taken).

Crumbing down

1 Working from the left-hand side of the customer, place a service plate just slightly beneath the edge of the table. Brush any crumbs towards the plate using a neatly folded napkin or waiter's cloth.
2 Move the dessert fork (where necessary) from the head of the cover to the left-hand side.
3 Move around to the right-hand side of the same guest and complete the crumbing down procedure for that place setting. Then move the dessert spoon from the head of the cover to the right-hand side.

4 After completing the crumbing down for that place setting, you are now in the correct position for crumbing down the next place setting.

Essential knowledge	A constant stock of linen, table items and accompaniments must be maintained in order to maintain: ● speed and efficiency of service ● customer expectations and satisfaction

MEMORY JOGGER

Why must a stock of linen, table items and accompaniments be maintained?

Changing an ashtray

This may be carried out at any stage of the meal if necessary.
1 Carry two clean ashtrays to the table; place one onto the table for use and place the second upside down over the dirty ashtray already on the table.
2 Remove the covered, dirty ashtray from the table, preventing any cigarette ash from being blown onto the tablecloth.

Clearing glasses

Used, dirty glasses need to be cleared at regular intervals throughout the meal (preferably at the end of each course). Place them on a napkin-covered salver and return them to the bar or wash-up area. Clear any water glasses at the end of the main course unless the customer requests otherwise.

Carrying dirty glasses from a cleared table

Do this

● Ask your supervisor what your establishment's policy is on smoking in the restaurant.
● Practise clearing plates from a table (when the restaurant is empty).

AN EXAMPLE ORDER OF SERVICE FOR A FOUR-COURSE À LA CARTE MEAL

The following order of service should be read as an example only. Note that practices and policies may vary in different establishments; the procedures listed below are the generally accepted procedures for restaurant table service.

1 The guests enter and are greeted and seated.
2 The station waiter unfolds each serviette and places it over the guest's lap.
3 Apéritifs may be offered by the *sommelier* (wine waiter).
4 Bread rolls/Melba toast and water are served.
5 Menus are presented, allowing time for guests to make their choice.
6 The station waiter takes the food order through the host.
7 The sommelier takes the wine order.
8 Covers are changed for the first course and any accompaniments are placed on the table.
9 The first course is served.
10 Once all the guests have finished the plates are cleared.
11 The cover is laid for the fish course and all accompaniments are placed on the table.
12 The fish course is served.
13 Once all the guests have finished the plates are cleared.
14 The cover is laid for the main course and all accompaniments are placed on the table.
15 The main course is served. The meat should be served first on that part of the plate which is nearest the guest or at the bottom of the cover. This should be followed by potatoes, vegetables and any hot sauces and accompaniments which have to be offered.
16 The station waiter may offer more rolls, Melba toast and butter if required.
17 When all the guests have finished, the main course plates, sideplates, sideknives, cruets, butter dishes and any accompaniments are cleared.
18 Each place setting is crumbed down and any ashtrays changed if necessary.
19 The sweet menu is offered and the order taken.
20 The sweet covers are laid and any accompaniments brought to the table.
21 The sweet course is served.
22 Once the sweet course is finished, the plates are cleared when all guests have finished.
23 The coffee order is taken.
24 The *sommelier* may then offer liqueurs.
25 Coffee cups are placed on the table and coffee is served. More coffee is served as required.
26 The bill is presented to the host.
27 Payment is taken from the host to the cashier; then receipt and change returned to the host.
28 The station waiter sees the guests out of the restaurant.
29 The table is cleared down and re-laid if necessary.

Essential knowledge	Waste must be handled and disposed of correctly in order to:
	● prevent accidents
	● prevent the risk of fire
	● prevent contamination of food and food areas
	● prevent pest infestation
	● avoid pollution of the environment
	● comply with the law

UNEXPECTED SITUATIONS

When an unforeseen incident occurs it should be dealt with promptly and efficiently, causing the minimum of disturbance to any of the guests. Quick action will often soothe an irate customer and ensure a return visit to your establishment.

In the case of accidents or spillages, a report of the incident must be kept and signed by those involved, and your supervisor must always be informed of the incident.

Case study

As a member of the restaurant brigade you have had a new commis waiter assigned to you. A party of eight guests have just finished their main course and the table is about to be cleared. In order to show the commis the correct procedure:

1   What items should be cleared from the table at this stage?
2   In what order and what methods would you use to clear them?
3   Describe how you would crumb down

Dealing with spillages

Slight spillages

If the accident involves a slight spillage on the table, the following procedure is generally acceptable.

1   Check to make sure that none of the spillage has fallen on the guest being served. Apologise to the guest.
2   Remove any items of equipment which may have been soiled or are in the way of cleaning up the spillage.
3   Clean the spillage with either a clean, damp cloth or a knife onto a service plate.
4   If tablecloths are being used, place an old menu card under and over the spillage to prevent marking the table and the clean cloth.
5   Unfold a clean serviette over the soiled area.
6   Replace any items as necessary.
7   Return any meals to the table that had been taken to the hotplate.

More serious spillages

More serious spillages may require the table to be completely cleared and re-laid.

1   If possible re-seat the customers at another table. If there are no tables available, follow Steps 2–6 below.
2   Clear all items from the table using a salver. Hot food should be placed on the hotplate.
3   Seat the customers slightly back from the table so you have more room to work.
4   Mop up as much spillage as possible with a clean absorbent cloth.
5   Change the tablecloth without showing the table top:
   ● place the partly unfolded clean cloth across the table
   ● drop the bottom fold of the clean cloth over the far edge of the table
   ● take hold of the soiled cloth and lay the clean cloth, while at the same time drawing the soiled cloth towards you
   ● the table will now be covered with the clean cloth and the soiled cloth can be taken away.
6   Re-lay the table and return the customers' food to the table from the hotplate.

Spillages onto guests

If some spillage falls onto a guest's clothing it will need to be dealt with immediately to avoid staining. Apologise to the guest and check that he or she has not been burned or scalded. Provide the guest with a clean, damp cloth to remove the worst of the spillage.

If the guest has to retire to the cloakroom, remove his or her meal to the hotplate. Depending on the nature of the spillage, the establishment may offer to have the garment concerned cleaned.

Changing a tablecloth

What have you learned

1 Why must a constant stock of linen be maintained?
2 Why must the dining and service areas be kept tidy and free from rubbish at all times?
3 Describe how to *crumb down*.
4 Why must waste be handled and disposed of correctly?
5 Describe how you would deal with a small spillage.

Get ahead

1 Visit other establishments and investigate the different methods of service used.
2 Carry out some research into table service for banquets, breakfasts and afternoon teas.
3 Find out more about guéridon service; what techniques and equipment are used? What sort of dishes are often served this way?
4 Find out how to carve certain meat dishes and fillet fish dishes at the table. Watch this being carried out.

UNIT 2NC3 (INCORPORATING UNIT 1NC10)

Prepare and serve bottled wines

This chapter covers:

ELEMENT 1:   **(2NC3) Prepare service areas, equipment and stock for wine service; (1NC10) Prepare bottled wine for service**

ELEMENT 2:   **(2NC3) Determine customer requirements for wines; (1NC10) Serve bottled wines**

ELEMENT 3:   **(2NC3) Present and serve wines; (1NC10) Serve bottled wines**

Note to candidates of Serving Food and Drink: Function.

This chapter has been prepared to cover all the performance criteria, range statements and underpinning knowledge requirements of the two-element unit 1NC10 (Prepare and serve bottled wines).

What you need to do

- Prepare the wine service area according to operational requirements.
- Perform a range of pre-service checks to ensure that you have sufficient stocks of clean linen, table items and service equipment.
- Check that all wine lists/menus are clean, undamaged and ready for service.
- Check the stock of wine that is available to ensure that there is a sufficient supply to meet possible service needs.
- Check that sufficient stocks of wine are stored at the correct temperature to meet possible service needs.
- Amend the wine list/menu if some wines are no longer available.
- Deal with customers in a polite, helpful and welcoming manner at all times.
- Identify the host and present the wine list at the appropriate time.
- Provide the customer with accurate information about the wines on the

list, if requested to do so.
- Establish an effective and professional relationship with the customer and maintain it throughout the service.
- Respond politely, promptly and accurately to customers' enquiries and refer any enquiries that you cannot deal with to the appropriate person.
- Write down customers' orders clearly and accurately and deal with them according to your establishment's procedures and the service operation.
- Correctly prepare the beverage service areas, service equipment and wine for service.
- Serve customers in a polite and helpful manner at all times.
- Handle and present the wine to the customer in the style appropriate to the type of product.
- Serve wine only to permitted customers at the correct temperature

using the correct service equipment.
- Identify any faults with the wine and deal with the situation in line with the customers' requirements and following organisational procedures.
- Regularly refill customers' glasses in line with customer requirements.

- Deal effectively with unexpected situations and inform the appropriate people where necessary.
- Carry out your work in an organised and efficient manner taking account of priorities, organisational procedures and legal requirements.

What you need to know

- What activities you should undertake to prepare the wine service area.
- What checks you should make to ensure that you have sufficient stocks of clean service items and equipment and what actions you can take if you have any problems.
- How to check that you have a sufficient supply of wines to meet possible service needs and what actions you can take if you meet any problems.
- What the correct storage methods and temperatures are for wines which are being prepared for service.
- How to greet customers and deal with them in a polite and helpful manner.
- How to identify the host in a party of customers.
- When to present the wine list and promote wines to customers.
- How to read and interpret the label of a wine bottle.
- How to describe the characteristics of wines to customers.

- What factors you should consider when advising customers on the wine to choose.
- Who you are permitted to take orders from for bottled wines.
- How to record customers' orders.
- How to prepare the service area, your equipment and the wine ready for service
- Why customers must be dealt with and served in a polite and helpful manner at all times.
- How to handle a range of wines and present them to the customer.
- How to serve wine at the correct temperature using the correct service equipment and who you should not serve.
- How to identify faults with wine and what action you can take to resolve any difficulties.
- When to refill customers' glasses.
- How to deal effectively with unexpected situations.
- How to carry out your duties in an organised and efficient manner.

INTRODUCTION

Many food outlets now offer wine with their meals. The wines on offer may range from a small number of house wines to extensive lists which range from basic red and white wines to some of the most famous wines of the world. It is often only the most expensive restaurants and hotels that employ a specialist wine waiter, known as a *sommelier*. Occasionally a member of the waiting staff may be allocated this role, leaving other staff to concentrate on serving food. More commonly, however, it is the duty of each station waiter or waitress to promote and serve wines.

The aim of this unit is to introduce you to the knowledge and skills you will need to be able to provide an efficient and professional service to your customers.

ELEMENT 1: **(2NC3) Prepare service areas, equipment and stock for wine service; (1NC10) Prepare bottled wine for service**

PREPARING THE WINE SERVICE AREA

The activities that you have to undertake in preparing for wine service will depend on the type of establishment that you work in, such as a hotel, restaurant, bistro or bar, and the type of facilities that your establishment offers, such as à la carte or table d'hôte menus and whether or not you cater for large functions like weddings and banquets.

However, regardless of the type of establishment or the facilities it offers, you should be able to organise the area in which wine is to be served to meet the type of service operation that is to take place. In order to be able to do this, there are two essential activities that you must perform:

1 You must perform a range of pre-service checks to ensure that you have an adequate supply of all the equipment that you will need during the service session and that it is clean and ready for use.
2 You must check that you have a sufficient supply of undamaged wine stock available and stored at the correct temperature to meet possible service needs.

Planning your time

In order to use your time efficiently and effectively when preparing for wine service, it is important that you should:
- identify and prioritise the tasks you have to perform or follow any work plan given to you by your supervisor
- know how each task is done and how long it takes
- collect any equipment such as irons or cleaning materials before you start
- complete all work tasks to meet the required time schedule and establishment standards.

Do not be tempted to take short cuts, to leave tasks undone or not finish them as these will only generate problems at a later stage.

PREPARING SERVICE ITEMS AND EQUIPMENT

In order to serve wines professionally, you will need to ensure that you have all the service items and equipment that you need to promote, present and serve them to your customers. Some specialised items of equipment are required, but the types of equipment available will depend upon your establishment and its procedures. As wine is classed as a food under the *Food Safety* and *Food Safety (General Food Hygiene) Acts*, it is extremely important that any item that comes into contact with the bottle or the wine must be clean and sterile.

Check your service linen

An important part of the service etiquette (method, procedure) for bottled wines is the use of service cloths. There are many points during service where you will need to use them including:
- when presenting the wine
- when uncorking the wine
- when lifting a bottle from an ice bucket

- when pouring the wine
- when leaving a wine either on the table or in an ice bucket after the first glasses have been poured.

As the service cloth will come into contact with the rim of the bottle on several occasions, it is vital that any cloth used should be clean and sterile. There should be an adequate supply available to meet your needs.

- Check the reservation book for the number of tables and covers expected to be filled during the service session. Allow an extra two tables for walk-in customers if you are not fully booked.
- Assume that each table of four to six covers will order two bottles of wine, possibly a red and a white.
- Estimate your requirement for service cloths by multiplying the number of tables by two (e.g. twelve tables by two cloths equals twenty-four).
- Where large parties are concerned, allow two cloths for each six covers.

If you are not in charge of the whole service area, but of a number of tables, you can adjust the calculation as necessary.

Once you have roughly estimated the supply of clean service cloths required, you should draw the necessary amount from the linen stock along with a supply of napkins. Follow your establishment's procedure for drawing linen.

- Service cloths and napkins should be clean and pressed.
- Check each cloth carefully and reject those which show signs of damage or staining. Iron any cloths that are unpressed or have to be re-folded.
- Depending on how your food service area operates and whether side tables or sideboards are used, place the service cloths as required ready for use after the food service area has been cleaned and polished.
- Make sure that any surface you place service linen on is clean and dust-free.
- Report any problems or deficiencies to your supervisor.

Check your table items

Side plates
When a red wine is served, the bottle is normally placed on a covered side plate to the right of the host's cover. Occasionally, an ice bucket may be left in this position if there is an inadequate supply of stands and no side tables.

- Make sure there is an adequate supply of side plates available, allowing one or two per table, to meet your service needs. Place them in the sideboard or on side tables.

Promotional materials
When specific wines are on promotion in an establishment, tent cards or other forms of promotional literature are often placed on the table to advertise the wines.

- Check that an adequate supply is available and that they are clean and free from damage. Place one on each table as required.

Check your glassware

Wine glasses
As wine is appreciated through the eyes and nose as well as the mouth, it is important that you use the correct glasses for their service.

Size and number
The size and number of glasses that you will need will depend upon your establishment's procedures. Table settings may range from a single stemmed glass like a Paris goblet in the basic table d'hôte setting to a range of glasses of increasing size for white wine, red wine and water or even full banquet settings with five or six glasses depending on the types and styles of wines to be served.

General

- Wine glasses should be stemmed and clear in colour. The exceptions are the brown and green stemmed Hock glasses traditionally used to serve white wines from the German wine-producing regions of the Rhine and Mosel respectively.
- The rim of the wine glass should taper in from the bowl to enclose the bouquet of the wine.
- A larger size of glass is used for red wines than for white. This is to allow the wine to be swirled in the glass to release its bouquet. See the section on filling glasses in *Element 2NC3.3.*
- Champagne and other sparkling wines are served in tall, narrow 'flûtes' which hold the bubbles for a longer period and show the wine more attractively.
- The smaller white wine glass is normally set closest to the customer's right hand. The larger red wine glass is set above and to the left of the white wine glass. Set glasses in the order they will be used.

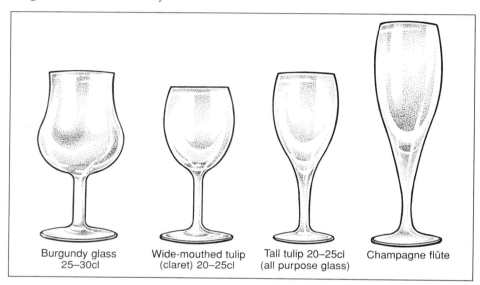

| Burgundy glass 25–30cl | Wide-mouthed tulip (claret) 20–25cl | Tall tulip 20–25cl (all purpose glass) | Champagne flûte |

Wine glasses

Even though it may be the responsibility of other staff to set glasses on the tables, it is advisable that you make a more thorough check and examine each glass carefully for lipstick, smears, fingerprints, chips from the rim or base and cracks.

- Always handle glasses by the stem when lifting and placing them.
- Holding each glass against a good background light, turn it completely to check the bowl for faults or smears.
- Reject and replace any glass which is chipped or cracked.
- Clean and polish any glass that is not clean and sparkling. Re-read the section on glassware in *Element 2NC1.1* for details of cleaning and polishing.
- If wine is served by the glass from a dispense bar, it is also advisable to check that there is a sufficient supply of clean glasses available behind the bar.

Carafes and decanters

As red wines develop and mature when they age in their bottle, a sediment gathers. It is important that this is not disturbed and mixed into the wine when it is being served. Aged or mature red wines are sometimes decanted into a carafe or decanter before being served. The procedure is described in *Element 2NC3.3.*

Some establishments also sell their house wines in carafes. House wines are often bought in large 1.5 litre bottles or 2 to 3 litre bag-in-a-box containers and transferred to carafes for service.

- Wine in carafes must be sold in quantities of 25 cl, 50 cl, 75 cl (standard bottle size), or one litre.

- A carafe may have a line showing the correct fill height and should be shaped so that all the wine is poured out when the neck of the carafe is tilted about 30 degrees downwards.
- The quantities of wine sold in carafes must be clearly stated on the wine list.
- Check that any carafes or decanters that you may need to use are completely drained with no off-odours and are clean and polished.

Check your trays or salvers

Trays or salvers are made of various materials and used for the service of drinks in glasses and for clearing dirty or unused glasses from tables. The trays for drink service are round and are usually found in a range of sizes. The smaller sizes are used to serve a small order of drinks such as dry sherry before a meal: the larger sizes are used for large amounts, such as wines or Champagne by the glass at functions, or for clearing tables. The rim of the tray is usually raised or lipped.

All trays and salvers should be cleaned and polished.
- Stainless steel trays should be washed in warm water and a detergent-sterilant and polished with a clean, dry glass cloth.
- Silver salvers should be cleaned either with plate powder or an appropriate silver-cleaning product at regular intervals.
- Wooden or plastic trays should be wiped with a damp cloth soaked in a detergent-sterilant and polished with a clean, dry cloth.

After cleaning, trays should be covered with a linen or paper napkin according to your organisation's policy. This prevents glasses slipping on the polished surface of the tray and will absorb any spillages.

- After checking that there is a sufficient supply, trays or salvers can be stored either at the dispense bar or on a sideboard.

A wine cradle

Check your wine cradles or decanting baskets

Most customers prefer their wine to be served from the bottle, rather than decanted into a carafe. This can create problems with mature red wines which throw a sediment. These have to be transported from the cellar or rack to the table without any change in position unless they have been stored upright for a short while prior to service. To do this, a decanting basket or cradle is often used. The bottle is removed from the rack, kept in an almost horizontal position and carefully placed in the basket or cradle which has been lined with a napkin.

● Check that all baskets and cradles are clean and undamaged. Polish metal or silver cradles with an appropriate cleaning agent.

Check your ice buckets and stands

Ice buckets

Wine is normally stored in the cellar at around 13 °C (55 °F). However, the service temperature for white, rosé and sparkling wines is usually lower as they are often served chilled. Ice buckets are used either:
● to maintain the temperature of a lightly chilled wine, or
● to lower the temperature of a wine from its storage temperature when a customer prefers it to be more chilled.

As the ice bucket is going to be highly visible, being either placed in a stand to the right of the host or placed on a napkin-covered plate on the table or side table, it is important that it is cleaned and polished. Most ice buckets are made of either stainless steel or silver-plated and should be cleaned and polished using the methods described for trays and salvers in the section above.

Stands

Various types of stand to hold ice buckets are available. It is important to check that they are sufficiently firm and that there are no missing fittings, such as nuts or bolts, especially on the types that fold away for convenient storage.
● Just before service starts prepare several ice buckets by filling them with a mixture of ice and water to a height which will reach the shoulder of a wine bottle placed in the bucket.

Note that a mixture of ice and water is more effective than ice alone as more of the bottle is in contact with the cold liquid.
● Place the prepared buckets in their stands close to the service points so that they can be brought into service as soon as necessary.

Check your wine chillers and coolers

As an alternative to using ice buckets, some establishments use wine chillers or coolers. There are several varieties available, some of which contain a type of freezing gel; others are insulated, in a similar way to double-glazing in windows, and will keep wine cool for about forty-five minutes. Some types require to be placed in a freezer or refrigerator for several hours before being used.

Before service starts:
● make sure that any chillers or coolers are clean and undamaged
● place them in the appropriate temperature environment (fridge, freezer) for the correct length of time
● if your establishment uses an electrically operated rapid chiller, check that it is in good working order.

Check your corkscrews and bottle openers

There are several methods available for opening wine bottles, ranging from the simple 'T'-shaped corkscrew to systems where nitrogen gas is injected into the bottle to push out the cork. The type available will vary with the establishment.

The three most common types are the 'Waiter's Friend', the winged or 'butterfly' corkscrew and the screwpull. The most common type is the Waiter's Friend which contains three elements: a short blade for cutting the capsule, a corkscrew and a lever arm, which doubles as a bottle opener.

Whichever type of corkscrew is used in your establishment, you should:
● check that a sufficient number is available for staff and that they have not been

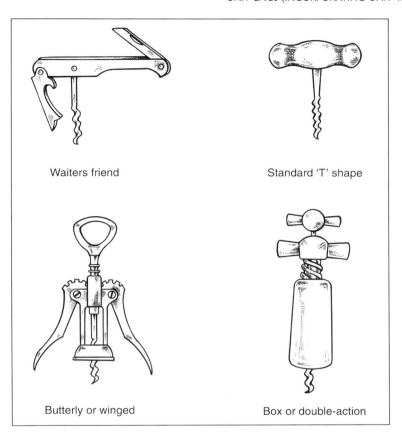

Waiters friend

Standard 'T' shape

Butterly or winged

Box or double-action

Four types of corkscrew

removed to other areas or misplaced
● check that they are clean and have not been damaged during a previous service session.

Other items

Also check that you have any other small items of equipment that may be required during service. These might include items such as:
● a foil cutter
● a three-pronged cork extractor
● pincers/pliers for removing difficult corks from sparkling wines
● a sealing cap or stopper for bottles of sparkling wine
● equipment for decanting port and mature red wines such as a decanting funnel or strainer or muslin cloth.

Check your wine lists or wine menu

The wines available in your establishment may be:
● listed in a separate typed section with the food menu
● separate from the food menu and contained in their own cover
● in the form of a pre-printed folder or card
● written daily on a blackboard alongside the dishes of the day.

Whichever form the list takes, you must check that it is accurate, clean and free from stains or damage. As the wine list is a type of sales material used to promote your establishment's products, it is important that it is as clean and attractive as possible.
● Remove any wine lists that are damaged or stained and store them where other staff will not pick them up and use them.

- Report damaged wine lists to your supervisor or arrange to have the pages typed out again or photocopied.
- If wine orders are to be taken by food service staff, wine lists should be placed either at each service station or on the sideboards.

Do this

1. Find out your establishment's procedure for drawing fresh service linen (service cloths, napkins) from stock.
2. Ask your supervisor to show you which types of wine glasses you should use for the wines on your list. Make a note of them.
3. Ask your supervisor to demonstrate the table settings for wine glasses that the establishment uses for *table d'hôte*, *à la carte* and banquet/function settings.
4. Find out if carafes or decanters are used in your establishment. If so, ask your supervisor or *sommelier* what equipment is used. Find out if wine cradles or decanting baskets are used.
5. Find out what equipment is available (buckets, chillers, coolers) to cool wine down to service temperature or to hold chilled wine at the table.

Essential knowledge (2NC3)

In order to be able to serve a range of wines correctly, you will require:
- a selection of wine glasses including a white wine glass, a red wine glass and a Champagne flûte
- a small knife or foil cutter, a corkscrew or bottle opener, pincers or pliers for difficult corks and a bottle stopper for sparkling wines
- ice buckets and stands or wine coolers/chillers for white, rosé and sparkling wines
- side plates for placing red wine and, possibly, ice buckets or coolers on the table or side table
- service cloths and napkins for the presentation and service of all wines and as tray coverings when placing and clearing glassware
- a number of trays or salvers
- carafes, decanters and wine cradles/decanting baskets for the decanting of mature red wines and the service of house wines.

PREPARING WINES FOR SERVICE

MEMORY JOGGER

How can you estimate how much wine you will need during service and what checks should you make?

The amount of wine required during a service session will depend on a number of factors such as the type of service operation (open restaurant, function), the number of different wines on offer, the number of guests and the occasion as in the following examples:
- A function where guests are only offered a choice between one red and one white wine will require a large stock of both wines to be available.
- If six glasses are obtained from a 75cl bottle, you will have to allow ten bottles for each sixty guests.
- A wedding breakfast may require a large stock of sparkling or semi-sparkling wine to be prepared.
- An open restaurant service operation may require two or three bottles of each wine on the wine list to be ready for service at all times.

Obviously, it is important to check what type of service operation you will be engaged in before drawing and preparing stock. Once you have roughly established the amount of stock you require, you have to check that:
- an adequate supply is available to meet possible service needs
- the stock is undamaged and fit for service
- the wines are stored under the right conditions to make them ready for service on demand.

THE STORAGE OF WINES

Storage in the cellar

The correct storage of wine is extremely important. Wine is a 'living' product containing bacteria and organisms which enable it to continue to develop and mature in the bottle. Wines such as vintage port and the high quality wines of several countries take many years to reach their peak of maturity. However, even the best quality wines will deteriorate if they are stored in the wrong conditions.

General storage conditions
There are ideal conditions under which wines should be stored in the cellar.

Temperature
The ideal storage temperature is around 13 °C (55 °F) for both red and white wines. The temperature should be kept as constant as possible and the storage area should be free from draughts which can cause the temperature to fluctuate. Wines should not be stored close to any heat sources, like radiators or high-wattage light bulbs, as too much heat will lead to rapid deterioration of the wine.

Humidity
The storage area should be clean and dry. Damp conditions will encourage moulds to form or ink to fade, both of which can damage the labels on bottles and can also encourage insect pests to thrive.

Lighting
The storage area should be kept as dark as possible. Strong light such as sunlight or high-wattage electric light bulbs can make wine age more quickly and cause white wines to darken in colour.

Vibration
Vibration from traffic and machinery can also cause wine to deteriorate as it will disturb the sediments in some wines.

Position
Bottles should be kept lying on their sides. The ideal angle is where the neck is slightly above the horizontal so that the wine is partly in contact with the cork. They should be stored with the label uppermost so that bottles do not have to be disturbed for the wine to be identified.

Bottles stored in an upright position for long periods may become damaged if the cork is allowed to dry out.
● As a cork dries, it may shrink and allow air and bacteria into the wine causing it to go off.
● A dry cork is one of the commonest reasons for the cork breaking when it is being extracted.
● A dry cork may crumble into the wine when you attempt to extract it, making the wine unfit for service.

Wine stored in a completely horizontal position may eventually begin to seep through the cork and leak from the bottle.

THE SERVICE TEMPERATURE OF WINES

The temperature at which wine is served is a major factor in the customers' appreciation of its qualities. There are no hard and fast rules about ideal service temperature as the temperature that a wine is eventually served at will be largely a matter of customer preference.

In general, a red wine should be drunk at a temperature which is warm enough to allow its bouquet and flavour to be appreciated fully. A white wine should be served

---

MEMORY JOGGER

What are the appropriate service temperatures for red and white wines?

---

at a temperature which is cool enough for it to be refreshing, but also allow its more delicate bouquet and flavour to be appreciated.

Essential knowledge (1NC10)	It is important to maintain wine at a suitable temperature. In storage: ● because wine is a 'living' product which needs to be stored at an appropriate temperature to develop and mature in the bottle or retain its flavours and condition ● because constant changes of temperature or storage in too hot or too cold an environment will cause them to deteriorate and eventually be unfit to drink. In the service area: ● so that it can be served as soon as possible at the temperature the customer requires ● so that the customer can enjoy the wine and appreciate its full flavour and bouquet ● to ensure customer satisfaction with the wine and its service.

Broadly, the ideal temperatures that wine should be held at to be ready for service are given in the table below.

Ideal service temperatures for wines

Wine style	Examples	Service temperature
Full-bodied red wines	Barolo, Chianti Riserva Brunello di Montalcino Burgundy, Rhône	Between 17 and 19 °C (around 65 °F)
Medium-bodied red wines	Claret, New Zealand Cabernet Sauvignon, Rioja	Between 15 and 17 °C (around 60 °F)
Light-bodied red wines/Full-bodied white wines	Loire reds, Beaujolais, white Burgundy, Australian or Californian Chardonnay	Between 11 and 13 °C (around 55 °F)
Medium-bodied/ Sweet/Semi-sweet white wines	German *Spätlese, Auslese* Alsace *Vendange Tardive* Sauternes, Barsac	Between 8 and 10 °C (47 to 50 °F)
Light-bodied white, Rosé, Sparkling wines	German QbA wines, Frascati, Anjou Rosé, Champagne	Between 6 and 8 °C (43 to 47 °F)

It would not be possible in most establishments to hold a complete stock of wines at the variety of temperatures required. This would require several storage locations being kept at different controlled temperatures. Most establishments would tend to hold the bulk of their wine stock, both red, white and rosé, at cellar temperature, 13 °C (55 °F) and hold those wines which were to be used for service at a point close to their service temperatures.

Some establishments will keep a stock of white wines either in a Cold Room or chill cabinet at around 10 to 11 °C (50 to 52 °F) and a stock of red wines at a dispense bar or in a wine cabinet at room temperature, 18 °C (64 °F).

Key points
It can take several hours to lower the temperature of a white wine or raise the temperature of a red wine.

● Always bring new stock from the cellar or storage area to the service area as soon as possible. This will allow the wines to be brought close to their service temperatures.
● Do not bring out more stock than you require. Extended chilling can damage white wines and over-heating can damage red wines.
● Once a red wine has been *chambré* (warmed up to drinking temperature), it should not be returned to a cold cellar. Frequent heating and cooling will damage most wines.
● It is better to serve a wine too cool than too hot. A wine will warm up gradually, but can be badly damaged if it is allowed to become too hot.

Essential knowledge (2NC3)	Wines should be stored and maintained at the appropriate temperatures in both the cellar/storage area and at the service point.

● All wines in the cellar or storage area should be stored at a temperature between 10 and 14 °C (50 and 57 °F).

At the service point
● White, rosé, and sparkling wines should be stored in a chill cabinet, Cold Room, or wine refrigerator at a temperature between 8 and 10 °C (46 and 50 °F).
● Light-bodied red wines should be held at a temperature close to cellar temperature at around 13 °C (55 °F).
● Medium-and full-bodied red wines should be stored at room temperature i.e. approximately 18 °C (64 °F).

DRAWING AND EXAMINING STOCK

Once you have checked the reservation book or established the type of service operation that will take place, check that you have sufficient stock of each type of wine to meet possible demand.

Check:
● if you have a sufficient number of bottles of each type of wine at the service point
● if the wines you have are undamaged and fit for service

Essentially, this requires you to complete several quantity and quality checks.

Quantity checks

MEMORY JOGGER

How should you draw and check replacement wine stock?

In the normal restaurant situation, the simplest method of checking that you have a sufficient quantity of stock is to use the wine list or wine menu. Most establishments will operate on a 'par stock' system whereby they will maintain a constant level of wine stock at a service point like a dispense bar. An example of a par stock system would be to hold two bottles of each red wine and three bottles of each white wine on the wine list ready at the service point.
● After each service session, new stock is drawn from the cellar to replace the stock sold to maintain a constant level.
● By checking the quantities at the service point against each item on the wine list, you can find out what stock you need to replace.

Obviously, an establishment with a limited wine list of two or three red and white wines would keep a larger par stock of each wine at the service point. One with an extensive wine list of sixty or seventy items would keep a smaller supply of each wine at the dispense point, but might keep a larger supply of the most popular wines. The stock level will vary between establishments.

Drawing new stock

Having established your service needs or what stock was sold during the last service session, you should draw whatever new or additional stock you require. The procedures for doing this will depend on your establishment and its stock control procedures. Normally, a written requisition signed by the Restaurant Manager is required. Follow your establishment's procedure.

Update/amend the wine list

When checking the stock at the service point and drawing additional or replacement stock, you may find that you have a low stock of a particular wine or have run out of a wine advertised on your list.
● Report low levels of stock to your supervisor so that replacement stock can be ordered.

If you have run out of stock of a particular wine:
● Inform your supervisor that you have run out of stock.
● Amend the wine list, if this is possible, by writing 'Out of Stock' against the particular wine.
● If other waiting staff are involved in promoting and serving wine, tell them which items are out of stock so that they can inform customers when they present the wine list.

Some wine lists are printed professionally and these should not be written on or changed unless it is certain that the wine concerned cannot be re-ordered. Check with your supervisor before attempting to alter this type of wine list.

Wine lists typed or produced on a word processor inside your establishment can usually be changed quite quickly. If this is possible, ask your supervisor to have the wine list amended.

Breakages and spillages

Take care when drawing, transporting and storing wine stock.
● If wines are stored in layers on a shelf rather than on racks, do not withdraw bottles from lower layers first.
● Do not attempt to carry too many bottles at one time. Use empty wine cartons to transport wines and use a kitchen trolley, if necessary.
● Store wine securely at the service point and do not overload racks or shelving.

Any breakages or spillages should be cleaned up immediately.
● Brush up any broken glass. Avoid using your fingers to gather glass as small splinters can enter your skin.
● Wrap broken glass in thick paper. Carry the wrapped glass on a tray, not in your hands. Dispose of it in a rigid metal or plastic bin, ideally outside the premises.
● Wash floors immediately to prevent the wine forming a sticky deposit and place a 'Wet Floor' sign, if necessary.

You should report breakages and spillages to your supervisor as soon as possible.

Essential knowledge (1NC10)

If breakages occur during the issuing, transporting or storage of wines, you should retain the broken bottle(s) and inform your supervisor or employer:
● so that your supervisor can witness that stock was broken and prevent staff being wrongly accused of dishonesty
● because breakages may have to be noted in records of cellar stock
● so that your employer can claim the cost against tax and V.A.T.
● because it may be necessary to re-order or replace quickly any stock which has been broken

Quality checks

As well as checking that you have a sufficient number of bottles for service, you should also check that the wine is of sufficient quality for service. You should check for signs of superficial damage to bottles and for obvious problems with the wines in their bottles.

Superficial damage
Some types of damage to bottles may make the wine unfit for presentation and service. These include:
● torn, missing or faded labels which would make it either difficult to establish the authenticity and/or origin of the wine or unsuitable for presentation to the customer
● cut or missing capsules which could suggest to the customer that the bottle had been opened previously and may not contain the correct wine. (It is possible to remove a cork without piercing it.)
● leakages from beneath the capsule which leave the neck of the bottle sticky and could mean that there is less than the advertised quantity in the bottle and/or that the wine is infected.

Faults with wine
It is not easy to detect faults with wine in unopened bottles, but you should inform your supervisor if you notice any of the following.
● Cloudiness or a haze in red or white wines. It may only be the sediment that has been disturbed in a red wine, but cloudiness can also be a sign of wine being faulty or having been stored in too hot an environment.
● White wines with a brown colour. This may indicate that the wine has oxidised and is unfit to serve.
● Crystals in white or red wines. These are harmless, but customers often believe that there is 'glass' in the bottle.
● Bubbles in still wines. Again these may be harmless such as in Muscadet 'sur lie', but can also indicate that the wine will be infected or off.

Essential knowledge (1NC10)

It is important that you should check wine bottles for damage before service:
● to ensure that you will have a sufficient supply to meet your service needs
● so that customers' requirements can be met during service
● so that customers will not be served a wine which is faulty or defective
● so that damaged stock can be removed from sale and replacement stock ordered
You should always inform your supervisor about damaged or faulty stock so that the appropriate action can be taken.

Cleaning wine stock

In the past, wine cellars were not subject to food safety and food hygiene legislation. Bottles which had been stored for some years were often brought to the table and presented covered with dust and cobwebs. This was done to show that the wine was of the correct age and maturity.

As wine and other beverages are classed as food under the terms of the *Food Safety Act* and the *Food Safety (General Food Hygiene) Act*, it is no longer acceptable to bring bottles of wine in this condition into a food service environment.

Clean all bottles brought from the cellar or storage area with a damp cloth. Dry them with a clean, dry glass cloth before storing them at the dispense point prior to service.

Essential knowledge (1NC10)

When preparing the wine service area, it is important that you should use safe and hygienic working practices.
- Ensure that all equipment that will be needed during service is clean and free from damage.
- Handle all glasses by the stem or base not by the bowl or rim. Check each glass for lipstick, smears, fingerprints, chipping and cracks.
- Clean up any spillages immediately and place 'Wet Floor' signs to alert other staff, if necessary.
- Keep all preparation areas clean, tidy and free from obstructions.
- Take care when dealing with broken glass and dispose of it safely in a rigid bin outside the premises.

Do this

1 Find out the storage temperature for the following wines in your establishment.
(a) All types in the cellar or other storage area
(b) White, rosé and sparkling wines being held ready for service
(c) Red wines being held ready for service
2 Find out your establishment's procedures for drawing stock from the cellar or storage area.
(a) Do you have to complete a written requisition?
(b) Do you have to sign out keys for the storage area?
(c) Must your supervisor be present when stock is withdrawn from storage?
3 Find out if your establishment operates on a par stock system and if and when the amount of stock available for service is increased.
4 What records should you keep of breakages and spillages? Is a wastage book kept?
5 Find out how your establishment disposes of wine stock which has only superficial damage, but is unfit for presentation and service.

Case study

A private party of twenty-four guests had booked the restaurant for a business lunch. The Restaurant Manager told one of the waiters to prepare four bottles each of fairly expensive red and white wines for service. The arrangement was that the host would pay for each bottle opened and used. During the meal, the Restaurant Manager noted that the party only drank sparingly. The majority of guests took either water or a soft drink with their meal. At the end of the lunch, when he was asked to make up the bill, he went to the dispense bar to find out about the amount of wine served and the bar bill. When he went behind the bar, he found that the waiter had cut the capsule and drawn the cork on all of the eight bottles he had been told to prepare. The customers had only used one bottle of the white and two bottles of the red.

1 How do you think the Restaurant Manager reacted to this discovery?
2 What had the waiter done incorrectly?
3 How should the waiter have dealt with the service task?

1 What equipment is necessary for the service of
   (a) a red wine?
   (b) a white wine?
   (c) Champagne or sparkling wine?
2 At what points during service will you need a service cloth?
3 What type of glass would you use to serve
   (a) Champagne or a sparkling wine?
   (b) A German hock from the Rhine?
4 What are the general conditions under which wine should be stored?
5 What are the suggested service temperatures for
   (a) Full-bodied red wines?
   (b) Full-bodied white wines?
   (c) Sweet or semi-sweet white wines?
   (d) Rosé and sparkling wines?
6 Why is it important to store wines at the correct temperatures in the service area?
7 What should you do if you run out of stock of a particular wine?
8 Why should you inform your supervisor about any breakages that occur?
9 What types of superficial damage to a wine bottle would make it unfit for presentation to the customer?
10 What signs would indicate that there was a fault with wine?
11 Why should you check wine bottles for damage before service?
12 Why should you follow safe and hygienic working practices when preparing the wine service area and equipment ready for service?

ELEMENT 2: (2NC3) Determine customer requirements for wines; (INC10) Serve bottled wines

GREETING AND DEALING WITH CUSTOMERS

Greeting customers on arrival is often the job of the Restaurant or Function Manager or the Head Waiter. However, all restaurant staff should know how to greet customers and make them feel welcome. A customer's first impressions of your establishment are important. A favourable impression is created by smiling, friendly staff when customers arrive and this helps them to relax and feel comfortable. Customers do not only pay for food and drink. They pay for the 'total experience', which includes a good standard of service and a pleasant and relaxing environment as well as the quality of any food and drink they consume.

- Address customers you have not met before as 'Sir' or 'Madam'.
- If you are aware of their family name, greet them as Mr or Mrs.

Customers like to be recognised and feel more important and welcome if they are greeted this way. Try to make your customers feel special.

Read the appropriate section in *Element 2NC2.1* for more detail on greeting customers.

When dealing with customers, it is important to remember that you should be helpful and avoid behaviour which can embarrass customers.

Appropriate and inappropriate behaviour

Helpful behaviour
- Only giving advice when asked for it.
- Suggesting appropriate wines and guiding customers in their choice, if they are uncertain.
- Suggesting suitable alternatives if customers ask for brands or wines which are not available.

Embarrassing behaviour
- Hovering around tables and staring at customers.
- Standing over customers to make them hurry with their order.
- Being pompous or superior when giving advice to customers.
- Correcting customers in front of their guests if they pronounce a wine's name wrongly or make an incorrect choice.

Problem customers

While providing a table service, you will probably meet several types of problem customers. Some of the main types and how you should deal with them are given in the following table.

Dealing with problem customers

Type of customer	Actions to be taken
Grumblers	• Treat with calmness, good humour and courtesy. • Pay particular attention to providing quick and efficient service. • Do not respond to or agree with any criticisms that are made.
Over-familiar or flirtatious (male or female)	• Do not respond in kind as this may encourage them further. • Provide quick service or ask a different member of staff to serve them. • Report serious difficulties (propositions, touching) to your supervisor.
Drunks, eccentrics and trouble-makers	• Be tactful, avoid getting into conversation. • If there are any signs of trouble, bad language or unacceptable behaviour, report them to your supervisor immediately. • It is unlawful to serve alcohol to a drunken person or anyone behaving in a violent or disorderly manner. (See the later section *Licensing law and wine service*).
Children running/playing	• Be tactful. Explain courteously to parents the reasons why they should keep children close to them. • Refer continuing problems to your supervisor or a senior member of staff.

Do this

1 Ask an experienced waiter or waitress about how they address their customers. Find out:
    (a) which customers they greet formally using 'Sir' or 'Madam'.
    (b) which customers they greet using their title such as 'Mr Smith' and 'Mrs Jones'.
2 Ask an experienced member of staff how they would deal with the following types of problem customer:
    (a) Rude and argumentative customers.
    (b) Regular customers who demand immediate service when other customers are waiting.
    (c) Customers who constantly criticise or find fault with the wines they have been served.
    (d) A customer who keeps changing their mind about which wine to order.

IDENTIFYING THE HOST

Before you offer the wine list, it is important that you should find out who is the host of the party. It is the host who will usually place the order for the wines which will be served. For methods of identifying the host, see the following *Essential knowledge* .

Essential knowledge (2NC3)

There are several ways in which you can identify the host of a party:
- by checking the reservation book as the name in which the table is booked is usually that of the host
- by watching the guests when they are being seated as the host often takes control when guests are sitting down
- the host may ask the guests if they would like pre-dinner drinks and give the order
- the host may ask for the wine list or respond if you ask the guests if they would like to see it

If you have any doubts, consult your supervisor or Head Waiter.

PRESENTING THE WINE LIST

In the traditional form of restaurant service, there are several steps which may be taken before the waiter or *sommelier* offers the wine list. After the customers are seated:
- the station waiter may unfold each guest's serviette and place it on their lap
- the station or wine waiter might approach the table and ask the guests if they would like a drink before their meal
- the guests may be offered bread rolls and water
- the menu is presented and guests given a short time to make their choice.

As the choice of wines may depend on the dishes chosen, the wine list can be offered by the station waiter or *sommelier*:
- immediately after the menus have been presented
- after the guests have had time to consider the menu, but before the food order has been taken
- immediately after the food order has been taken.

The wine list should be open when presented to the customer. Present it from the right-hand side, if possible. When presenting the wine list, the waiter should inform the customer of
- any promotions or special offers which are available
- any wines on the list which are unavailable or of which there is a low level of stock.

Most customers would be annoyed if, after studying a wine list and making a choice, they were told that the establishment was out of stock. If you have only one bottle of a wine left, you should inform the customer if they enquire about it in case they would wish to order a second bottle later.

PROMOTING WINES

There are several aspects to consider when promoting wines to your customers.
- Your establishment may have some wine stock it is anxious to promote and sell. These may be slow-selling wines which it wishes to dispose of or new wines which are being specially promoted to establish them with customers.
- Some types of wine are appropriate at certain stages of a meal and with certain dishes.
- Some wines are appropriate on special occasions or with certain types of customer.

Promotions and special offers

- Check with your Restaurant Manager or Head Waiter before service starts if any wines are to be promoted or are on special offer such as 'end-of-bin' wines.
- Draw your customers' attention to any promotional literature either in the menu, on the wine list or placed on the table. Inform them of any special offers, reduced prices, free gifts or samples and any prizes that are available.

Promoting wines at appropriate stages

Some wines are traditionally associated with certain stages of a meal and with certain dishes. You can promote:
- dry sparkling wines like a Brut Champagne as an apéritif before a meal
- Fino or Manzanilla sherry with clear soups like beef consommé
- white, red and rosé wines with main courses of fish, poultry, meat or game
- sweet and semi-sweet white wines with desserts containing fruit such as peaches, pears and strawberries
- vintage port as a *digestif* after a meal or with strongly-flavoured cheeses like Stilton.

Obviously, the time of day and the nature of the function or service operation will affect your opportunity to promote wines. However, you should be aware of what is happening at each table and be alert for opportunities to promote your establishment's products.

Special occasions and groups

Occasions
Special occasions such as weddings, engagements and anniversaries create the opportunity for you to either promote sparkling wines like Champagne or to suggest more expensive wines from your list. Special menus, featuring seasonal dishes like game, spring lamb or fresh salmon, offer you the opportunity to promote appropriate wines to accompany them. See the section on food complements later in this element.

The time of year may also provide opportunities to promote certain wines. Beaujolais Nouveau is often heavily promoted when it is released around the second week in November. Sparkling wines are appropriate at celebrations like New Year's Eve.

Groups
You should also be aware that some customers may enjoy the taste of wine with their meal, but are not allowed to consume alcohol by their religion. Other customers may choose not to drink alcohol or to restrict the amount they consume.
- Strict Muslims, high-caste Hindus and devout Buddhists are forbidden to consume or do not drink alcohol.
- Some Christians in Lent and members of Temperance groups choose not to consume alcohol.
- Some customers for health or social reasons may either abstain from alcohol or consume only small amounts.

Be alert for opportunities to promote non- and low-alcohol wines to customers. However, take care you do not insult or embarrass customers accidentally when promoting wines. You should also take care not to force customers into spending more than they wish to or can afford. When promoting wines, you should always use the 'soft sell' approach.

Essential knowledge (2NC3)	You should know the difference between non-alcoholic wines and wines which are low in alcohol or have reduced amounts of alcohol.
	● An alcohol free wine will contain between 0 and 0.05% of alcohol by volume.
	● A de-alcoholised wine will contain between 0.05 and 0.5% of alcohol by volume.
	● A low alcohol wine will contain between 0.5 and 1.2% of alcohol by volume.
	● A reduced alcohol wine will contain between 1.2 and 5.5% of alcohol by volume.
	It would be impossible to drink sufficient non-alcoholic wine to be over the drink-drive limit. However, it would be possible to drink sufficient low or reduced alcohol wine to be over the limit.

Do this

1 Find out what methods are used to promote wines in your establishment. Find out about
   (a) tent cards
   (b) menu inserts
   (c) Wine of the Day/Week/Month promotions
   (d) wine tastings and free samples.
2 Ask your supervisor if there are any groups or customers who use your establishment and do not consume alcohol either because of their religion or by choice

PROVIDING CUSTOMERS WITH INFORMATION

The *Trade Descriptions Act* requires you to provide customers with accurate information about any product you sell, including details of the quantity, ingredients and price. This can sometimes create problems for staff serving wines, especially if they have not had the opportunity to taste the wines. However, waiting staff can gain some indication about the wines they serve by recognising the traditional shapes of bottles and, more importantly, understanding the label information.

Traditional bottle shapes

Some French, German and Italian wines have traditionally been sold in bottles which have distinctive shapes:
● Bordeaux wines are sold in square-shouldered bottles.
● Burgundy wines are sold in bottles with sloping shoulders.
● The wines of Alsace, the Rhine and the Mosel are bottled in 'flûtes'. Brown glass is used for Rhine wines and green glass for Mosel wines.
● Chianti was traditionally bottled in a circular flask which was bound in woven straw and Verdicchio dei Castelli di Jesi bottled in a green amphora-shaped bottle.

Some of these bottle types are now widely used throughout the world. However, you should not assume that the wine bottled in another country will have the same characteristics as a French or German wine because it is bottled in one of these traditional shapes. For example, it is possible to find widely different wines such as a Vinho Verde from Portugal and a late-harvested Muscat from Australia both sold in a flûte-shaped bottle.

Label information

Three types of label can be found on wine bottles: a front label, a neck label and a back label. The most important of these is the front label which has been described

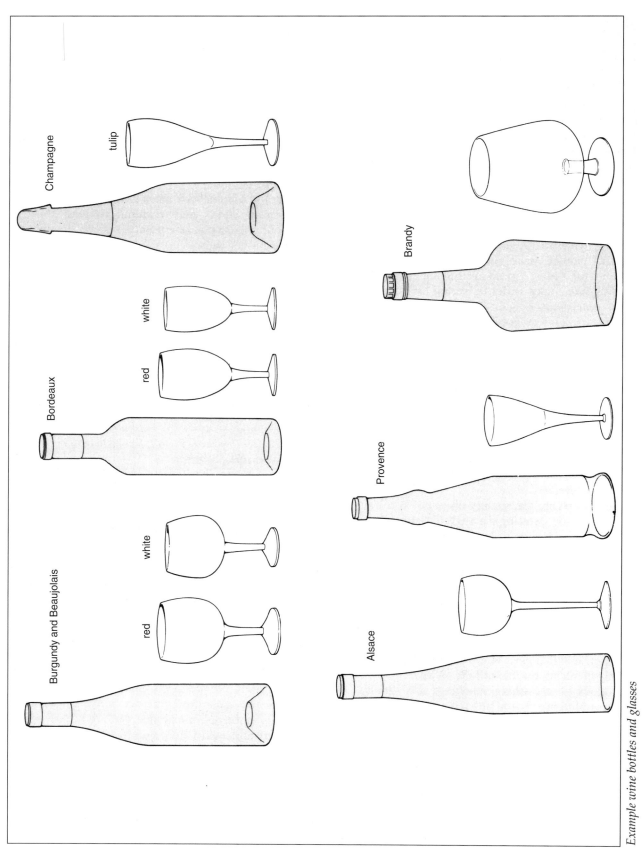

Example wine bottles and glasses

as the wine's 'birth certificate'. The back label often gives additional information about the wine or the company that produced it. It may also give information about a recommended service temperature and food complements.

The labels on any wine produced in the European Union (EU) or imported into the EU from another country must contain certain information:
● the region of origin
● the country of origin
● the name and address of the bottler or supplier
● the quantity of wine contained in the bottle
● the alcoholic strength as a percentage of the volume

In addition EU wines must give an indication of the quality of the wine. Most wines will also have a name which can be a brand name, the name of the area in which it was produced and/or the grape variety used to make the wine.

Other information which is optional, but which is often found on labels includes:
● the year of the harvest or vintage
● the colour of the wine
● a description of sweetness/dryness
● an indication of its style such as sparkling or semi-sparkling
● where the wine was bottled such as château or estate bottled.

Common label terms

English	French	German	Italian	Spanish	Portuguese
Dry	Sec	Trocken	Secco	Seco	Seco
Medium	Moelleux	Lieblich	Amabile	Semi-dulce	–
Sweet	Doux	Suss	Dolce	Dulce	Doce
Sparkling	Mousseux	Schaumwein	Spumante	Espumoso	Espumante
Lightly sparkling	Pétillant	Spritzig	Frizzante	Petillant	–
White wine	Vin blanc	Weisswein	Vino bianco	Vino blanco	Vihno branco
Red wine	Vin rouge	Rotwein	Vino rosso	Vino tinto	Vihno tinto
Rosé wine	Vin rosé	Schillerwein	Vino rosato	Vino rosado	Vihno rosado
Vintage	Vendange	Hauptlese	Vendemmia	Vendimia	Colheita

QUALITY LEVELS OF SOME EU WINES

As part of the information described above, the labels of wines from EU countries carry information about the quality level that the wine belongs to. When you study your wine list, you will notice that some wines from the same country are more expensive than others. One of the reasons for this will be the quality level of the wine.
● **Table wine** is the lowest level of quality and it can be produced anywhere in the country and be a blend of wines from several different regions. It is the everyday drinking wine of the country.
● **Table wine with a geographical description** is a slightly higher level. It must be produced in specific wine-producing areas to a slightly higher standard than table wine.
● **Quality wine produced in a specific region (QWPSR)** must be made from grapes grown in a specified region in the EU. These wines are made under stricter quality controls and in smaller quantities than table wines.

Some countries have more than one level of quality wine.
● France bases the higher quality levels of its wines on specific communes (parishes) or vineyard sites called 'growths' or *crus*. Wines from these sites will have a phrase on their label such as Premier Cru or Grand Cru.
● Italy and Spain base their higher level on the fact that some regions produce better quality wines than others.

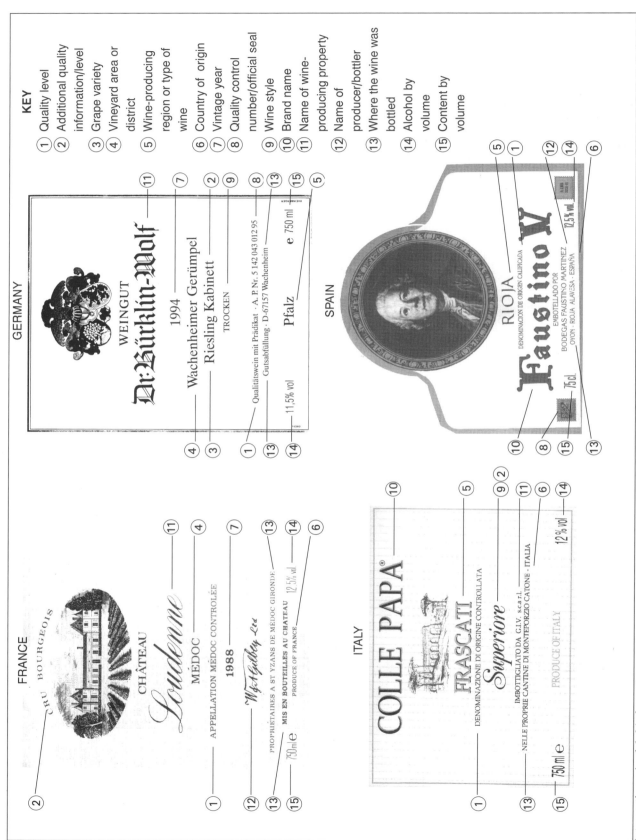

KEY

① Quality level
② Additional quality information/level
③ Grape variety
④ Vineyard area or district
⑤ Wine-producing region or type of wine
⑥ Country of origin
⑦ Vintage year
⑧ Quality control number/official seal
⑨ Wine style
⑩ Brand name
⑪ Name of wine-producing property
⑫ Name of producer/bottler
⑬ Where the wine was bottled
⑭ Alcohol by volume
⑮ Content by volume

GERMANY

WEINGUT
Dr. Bürklin-Wolf

1994
Wachenheimer Gerümpel
Riesling Kabinett
TROCKEN

Qualitätswein mit Prädikat · A. P. Nr. 5 142 043 012 95
Gutsabfüllung · D-67157 Wachenheim

Pfalz
11,5% vol
e 750 ml

FRANCE
CRU BOURGEOIS

CHÂTEAU
Loudenne

MÉDOC
APPELLATION MÉDOC CONTROLÉE

1988

W. H. Gilbey Ltd
PROPRIÉTAIRES A ST YZANS DE MÉDOC GIRONDE
MIS EN BOUTEILLES AU CHÂTEAU 12.5% vol
PRODUCE OF FRANCE
750 ml e

SPAIN

RIOJA
DENOMINACION DE ORIGEN CALIFICADA

Faustino V

EMBOTELLADO POR
BODEGAS FAUSTINO MARTINEZ
OYON · RIOJA ALAVESA · ESPAÑA

75 cl.
12,5% vol.

ITALY

COLLE PAPA®

DENOMINAZIONE DI ORIGINE CONTROLLATA

FRASCATI
Superiore

IMBOTTIGLIATO DA G.I.V. s.c.a.r.l.
NELLE PROPRIE CANTINE DI MONTEPORZIO CATONE - ITALIA

PRODUCE OF ITALY
12% vol
750 ml e

Interpreting wine label information

182

● Germany bases its higher level on the time the grapes were harvested and the amount of sugar in the grapes. QmP wines will have words like *Kabinett, Spätlese, Auslese, Beerenauslese* and *Trockenbeerenauslese* after the grape variety on the label to indicate these features.

Quality levels and terms for some EU wines

Quality level	France	Germany	Italy	Spain
Higher quality level	Classed growths (Cru) from select vineyard sites (Premier and Grand Cru)	Qualitätswein mit Prädikat (QmP)	Denominaziòne de Origine Controllata e Garantita (D.O.C.G.)	Denominaciònes de Origen Calificada (D.O.Ca)
Quality wines produced in a specified region	Appellation Contrôlée (AC) V.D.Q.S.	Qualitätswein bestimmter Anbaugebeite (QbA)	Denominaziòne de Origine Controllata (D.O.C.)	Denominaciònes de Origen (D.O.)
Table wines with geographical description	Vin de Pays	Landwein	Indicazione Geografica Tipica (I.G.T.)	Vino de la Tierra
Table wine	Vin de Table	Tafelwein	Vino da Tavola	Vino de Mesa

'Vintage' wines

Some people believe that a wine described as 'vintage' will be in some way very special and expensive. However, any wine made from grapes harvested in a single year will be a vintage wine. A wine made from grapes harvested in two or more separate years will be a non-vintage wine like some wines from Champagne.

The importance of the vintage year of a wine is because grapes, like many other crops, depend on good weather conditions to grow and develop. If the year in which the grapes grow has good weather, the harvest or vintage will be good, as will be the wine made from the grapes. If the weather conditions are bad with little sunshine and a lot of rain, the harvest will be poor and the quality of the wines will suffer.

Basically, in some years the vintage will be better than others. The wines made in the good years will be of a better quality and the wine producers will ask for and obtain higher prices for them.

Do this

1 Study the labels of six wines offered by your establishment. Note down:
   (a) the vintage year
   (b) the quality level of the wine
   (c) the name
   (d) the bottler or supplier
   (e) any label information related to the colour or sweetness/dryness.
2 Find out if your supervisor or *sommelier* has a chart showing the vintages of the major wines. Some diaries contain them. Find out the best vintage years for
   (a) red Bordeaux
   (b) white Burgundy
   (c) red Burgundy
   (d) Rhône wines.

MEMORY JOGGER

What are the major characteristics of wines that you should use when describing them to customers?

DESCRIBING THE CHARACTERISTICS OF A WINE

Descriptions given to customers either in the wine list or by the service staff are usually based on aspects such as the bouquet, the appearance or colour, the body, the sweetness, dryness and acidity and the flavour.

Bouquet

It is not always easy to describe the bouquet or smell of a wine as it will depend on several factors, especially the age of the wine and where the grapes were grown.
● A wine served highly chilled will have little bouquet.
● Some red wines need to be opened for several hours before they are drunk to allow the bouquet to develop.

There are some classic descriptions of the bouquet of wines. See the following table.

Grape varieties and their associated bouquets

Grape variety	Associated bouquet
Chardonnay	Smoky, tropical fruit in Australian and American wines
Sauvignon Blanc (Fumé)	Raw gooseberries, smoky, blackcurrant leaves
Sémillon	Honey and flowers: honey, over-ripe grapes in older wines
Riesling	Flowery, fruity when young; 'petrol' in older wines
Gewürztraminer	Spicy, peppery, herby
Cabernet Sauvignon	Blackcurrants, cedar wood, 'cigar box'
Pinot Noir	Raspberries when young: 'farmyard' when aged
Merlot	Spices, plums, 'fruitcake'
Syrah (Shiraz)	Old leather, burnt rubber, 'sweaty saddle'
Grenache	Spicy, herby, peppery

● Wines which have been aged in oak barrels will often have a hint of vanilla in their bouquet.

All wines should smell 'clean'. Any smell of mustiness, vinegar, green apples or yeast in a wine suggests that it is not in good condition and not fit for service.

Colour

Red wines can vary in colour from a deep purple, almost black colour when young through various shades of red to a mahogany or chestnut colour. Older wines tend to become browner in shade with age. This is most noticeable at the rim of the glass.

White wines can be virtually colourless or a pale yellow-green when young. The majority of dry white wines will be straw yellow in colour. Sweet and older wines tend to have a golden colour. A brown tinge in a white wine may indicate a fault with the wine.

Rosé wines are made to be drunk while young and fresh. They may range in colour from a pale purple-red to an orange-pink. An orange tinge in a rosé wine often indicates that it was made in a warm area like the South of France or Portugal.

Body

Wines are often referred to as being light-, medium- or full-bodied. A light wine will probably have less than 10% alcohol and also feel light in the mouth. A full-bodied wine will have an alcohol content of around 12.5% or above and will feel heavier and have a more intense flavour in the mouth. Medium-bodied wines will fall between these two. See the following table for examples.

Light-bodied	Medium-bodied	Full-bodied
German QbA wines from Mosel-Saar-Ruwer Beaujolais Anjou Rosé	Most white Burgundy, Bordeaux and Alsace Most red Bordeaux clarets Rioja red and white Californian, Australian and S. African Chardonnay Tavel and Provence Rosé German *Spätlese*	Brunello di Montalcino Barolo Rhône reds Red and some top white Burgundies Châteauneuf-du-Pape Californian Cabernet Sauvignon and Pinot Noir Australian Shiraz

Sweetness, dryness and acidity

One of the most noticeable characteristics of the taste of a wine is its sweetness or dryness and the amount of acidity in the wine. The acidity in a dry wine makes it crisp and refreshing in the mouth. It can also balance the sweetness of a wine and prevent the wine feeling sticky in the mouth. Some ways of describing the degree of sweetness and dryness and examples of wines are given in the following table.

Wine styles and example wines

Style	Examples of wines
Very or 'bone' dry	Red Loire wines like Bourgueil and Chinon. White wines like Muscadet, Sancerre, Pouilly Fumé and Chablis
Dry	A large group including about 90% of all red wines, white Burgundy, most Alsace wines, Soave, Tavel Rosé
Medium-dry	Vouvray, Frascati, most German QbA wines, most New World white, Anjou Rosé, Lambrusco, Californian Cabernet Sauvignon and Zinfandel
Medium-sweet	Late-harvest Alsace and Australian wines, German *Auslese,* Coteaux du Layon and Bonnezeaux, Asti Spumante and Italian Moscato wines
Sweet and very sweet	Sauternes, Barsac, German QmP wines at *Beerenauslese* and *Trockenbeerenauslese* levels, Australian liqueur Muscat

Flavour

When describing the flavour of a wine to customers, you should mention the dryness or sweetness of the wine and acidity. However, one of the main characteristics of the taste is the amount of fruit flavours in the mouth. What is important is the intensity of these flavours and how long the impression lasts in the mouth, often called the 'length' or 'finish'. A typical description might be that the wine has intense fruit flavours and a long finish.

● Red wines have more flavour than most white wines and usually the more full-bodied a wine is, the more intense its flavours will be.

Alcohol content

The Food Labelling Regulations require the wine list to include information on the alcohol content of the wines advertised. The information should also be on the bottle on either the front or back label.
● It is important that you give the customer accurate information about the alcohol content of a wine to comply with the Trade Descriptions legislation.
● If you do not know, find out by consulting the wine label.

Price

The Price Marking (Food and Drink on Premises) Order requires a price list to be displayed. It is also illegal to charge more than the advertised price for a product.
● Make sure that any prices displayed on the wine list or a notice board are accurate.
● Make sure that you know the prices of the wines on your list.

If new stock of a wine is bought, it may cost more. Check with your supervisor that the prices advertised are accurate.

Essential knowledge (1NC10)

It is important that customers are given accurate information about any wine on your list, especially about the price, strength and quality:
● to comply with the Trade Descriptions Act and other consumer protection laws
● to prevent customers becoming dissatisfied and feeling cheated or misled
● to prevent customers consuming a larger amount of alcohol than they wish, especially when drinking no or low alcohol products
● to ensure that customers receive an efficient and high quality service.
However, you should not reveal details such as the cost price of wines, profit margins or the mark-up on wines in your establishment. This type of information should be kept confidential.

Essential knowledge (2NC3)

When describing wine to customers, you should not give detailed descriptions. You should confine your description to short statements about:
● the bouquet
● the appearance or colour
● the body
● the sweetness or dryness and acidity
● the flavour.
If you have not tasted the wine, you should find out the information from other sources such as the wine list, the labels on the bottle and the comments of other customers. If in doubt, consult your supervisor.

Do this

Either by checking the labels, consulting the wine list or asking your supervisor, write down the descriptions you would give to customers of:
(a) three white wines
(b) three red wines
(c) one rosé wine

LICENSING LAW AND WINE SERVICE

The licensing laws describe who you can sell wine to and who you must refuse to serve with wine. The laws related to who can purchase wine are different in Scotland from those in the rest of the United Kingdom.

- In England, Wales and Northern Ireland, you may not sell wine to any customer whose age is less than eighteen years.
- In Scotland you may sell wine to a person older than sixteen years as long as it is in an area set aside for table meals and not in a bar.

Although persons younger than those described above may **consume** wine with a meal in a restaurant – it is legal for any person over five years of age to do so – the wine can only be **purchased** by persons of the ages given above as part of a substantial meal in an area set aside for that purpose like a restaurant. However, your employer may not wish to sell wine to people under eighteen years of age.

There are some customers you may not serve wine to apart from those described above. See the following *Essential knowledge*.

Essential knowledge (1NC10)	In the restaurant or other area set aside for table meals, you may only take orders from and serve wine to customers who comply with the licensing laws. You should not sell wines to:
	- any person who you suspect is under eighteen years of age in England, Wales and Northern Ireland
	- any person you suspect is under sixteen years of age in Scotland
	- any customer who is drunk or any person attempting to buy more wine for that customer to drink on the premises
	- any person behaving in a violent or disorderly manner or who is under an exclusion order or barred from the premises.
	You should also not sell wine to be drunk either on or off the premises unless it is within the permitted hours of your establishment's licence.
	Failure to comply with the licensing laws will result in your employer (the Licensee) being prosecuted and fined and the licence endorsed. After several offences, the licence can be withdrawn and the premises will not be allowed to serve alcohol to its customers.

ESTABLISHING A RAPPORT WITH CUSTOMERS

It is important for all food service staff to establish a good relationship with the customer. A major part of this is answering customers' questions about the dishes on the menu and advising them about the appropriate wines.

- Make sure that you know the main ingredients of menu dishes and especially those of sauces and flavourings.

Giving the appropriate signals

It is essential that the wine waiter uses the appropriate verbal and non-verbal signals with the customer. If the customer is unfamiliar with wines, they may not feel confident with you and be afraid of showing their lack of knowledge in front of their guests. The customer must be treated with respect and courtesy at all times, even if you feel under pressure.

- Allow the customer time to read the wine list and make their choice.
- Be patient if customers are indecisive or change their minds.

If you have to serve other customers, excuse yourself and tell the customer that you will return shortly. Apologise for the delay when you return to take the order.

Make sure that you also send the appropriate non-verbal signals.
- Face the customer whenever possible and smile. Maintain a reasonable level of eye contact, but don't stare or keep darting your eyes around the restaurant.
- Don't raise your eyebrows or frown if a customer makes an unexpected choice or mis-pronounces the name of a wine.
- Keep your tone of voice friendly and look attentive if customers wish to talk to you.

Once you have established a rapport with the customer, it can be maintained throughout the service when you occasionally check back with them and seek feedback from them on your wines and other products.

Advising customers about wines

It is important to remember three points which were mentioned earlier in this element when advising customers.
- Don't do or say anything that is going to embarrass the customer such as making them appear stupid or ignorant or correcting them.
- There are no hard and fast rules about which wines match certain types of food. Even if you think a customer's choice is not suitable, you should remember that the customer is always right.
- If you are unsure what to recommend, consult your supervisor or a more experienced member of staff. A wrong recommendation from you could ruin a customer's enjoyment of their meal.

When advising customers on the choice of wine, there are four factors you should consider: the customer's preferences, wine and food complements, the suitability of wines for the occasion and your establishment's requirements for sales.

Customer preferences

Some customers will be unfamiliar with the wines on your list. Their experience may be restricted to times when they go out for meals or have sampled local wines while on foreign holidays. There are several ways that you can find out about their tastes and experience which can help you in deciding which wine to recommend. You can ask them:
- What type of wine have they enjoyed previously?
- Have they drunk wine while on holiday?
- What other types of alcoholic drinks they enjoy?

For example, a customer who normally drinks draught bitter or dry vermouth might appreciate a dry, aromatic wine. A customer who prefers a dry full-bodied drink like a stout might appreciate a dry, full-bodied red wine. The section on describing the characteristics of wine above can be used to question the customer about their tastes.
- Check if they like dry or sweet drinks, light- or full-bodied drinks, delicate or fruity flavours.

If you are unsure what to recommend and cannot obtain advice, choose a medium-dry red or white wine such as Australian, Californian or Bulgarian Cabernet Sauvignon or Chardonnay. These will match a wide variety of customers' tastes and foods.

MATCHING WINE AND FOOD

The traditional view of matching wine and food is white wine with fish and poultry and red wine with meat. While in many respects this may be correct, there are many examples of red and rosé wines that go well with some fish dishes and white wines which go well with some types of meat. Basically, the choice is not a matter of the colour of a wine, but of dryness/sweetness, acidity, body and flavour.

Always be ready to give advice and assistance

Contrasts and complements

A wine should either contrast with or complement a food. For example. a white fish dish with a creamy sauce would be contrasted by a dry white wine with crisp acidity. The acidity of the wine would cut through the creamy taste and clean the palate. On the other hand, a Rhine *Spätlese* with a hint of sweetness and some acidity would match or complement the sweetness of the sauce.

Matching the intensity of flavours

When choosing a wine to recommend, you should also consider matching the flavours of both the dish and the wine.
● A delicately flavoured dish would be overwhelmed by a richly flavoured wine.
● A highly flavoured dish such as a curry or chilli would overwhelm almost any wine except the heaviest and most robust reds.

Ideally, light, fragrant wines like a Mosel Riesling will match delicately flavoured foods such as trout. Highly flavoured red wines will match rich dishes like beef stews and venison.

Regional wines and foods

Another method of deciding wine and food matches is to offer the wines of the region as matches to the food. For example, you could offer Chianti as appropriate to a Bolognese sauce, red Burgundy with coq au vin or a South of France rosé with a dish served Provençale.

The information above highlights one key point: the need to know details of the dishes on your menu. For other suggestions, see the following table.

Food and wine complements

Dish	Wine style	Examples
First course Salads (Seafood, Nicoise, Caesar) Oysters, Prawns, Shrimps Chicken/duck/ goose pâté	Fresh dry white Dry white Medium-dry white, smooth red	N. Italian Chardonnay, Bordeaux Sec Chablis, Muscadet, Sancerre Alsace Gewürztraminer or Pinot Gris; Pomerol or Beaujolais-Villages
Soups Bouillabaisse Seafood bisques Minestrone	Very dry white or rosé Medium dry white Medium-bodied dry red	Tavel or Provence rosé Australian or Californian Chardonnay or Sauvignon Chianti, Zinfandel
Main courses White fish (sole, skate, turbot) – with creamy sauces or *beurre blanc*/black butter Oily fish Fresh salmon Trout Roast poultry Game birds Beef (including stews) and venison Lamb and pork	Dry or medium-dry white Very dry white Sharp, dry white Medium- to full-bodied white Light, delicate white Dry or medium-dry white Medium- or full-bodied red Medium- to full-bodied red Medium-bodied red	Chablis, white Burgundy Muscadet, Sancerre Sauvignon de Touraine white Rioja, Muscadet White Burgundy, Californian or Australian Chardonnay Mosel or Saar Riesling Chablis, Rhine *Kabinett* or *Spätlese* Bordeaux claret, Burgundy Barolo, Rhône reds, Californian Cabernet Sauvignon or Pinot Noir Bordeaux claret, Rioja
Desserts Cheesecake Fresh fruit Fruit flans/sweet soufflés/ strawberries and cream	Semi-sweet and sweet white Sweet white Sweet white	Vouvray, Anjou, Rhine *Auslese* Coteaux du Layon, liqueur Muscat Sauternes, Barsac, sweet Champagne

Matching wine with the occasion

This subject was mentioned in a previous section where certain styles of wines were suggested in relation to special occasions and groups. In addition to these points, you should also consider:
- It is not appropriate to promote fine, expensive wines with routine or fast food dishes.
- Generally, everyday wines such as *vin de pays* are more appropriate with everyday dishes.
- Try to match the price of the wine you recommend to the price of either the average main course of an à la carte menu or the full price of a table d'hôte menu.

Customers will be dissatisfied if the cost of the wine exceeds the cost of the food, especially as the wine will seem to be the less substantial part of the meal. Generally, you should try to match the finer, more expensive wines on your list with the more complex, more expensive items on your menu.

The need for sales

Part of the service role is to promote the establishment's products and services. As more profit is usually made on wine and other drinks than on food, you should be alert for the opportunity to promote and sell wine to your customers. You should read again the section above on promoting wines, if necessary.

Essential knowledge (2NC3)	When advising customers on the type of wine to choose, you should take into account: ● the customer's preferences for wines or other alcoholic drinks ● the nature and ingredients of the menu dishes and which wines will contrast with or complement them ● the nature and price of the food ● whether or not the occasion of the meal has any special significance for the customer ● the need to promote the establishment's products and services and to increase sales and income.

Much of the information required to build a relationship with the customer can be obtained through listening attentively (if you have time), friendly questioning and polite recommendation.

Do this

1 Obtain samples of recent menus offered by your establishment and discuss with your supervisor what the appropriate wines would be for a selection of the main course dishes.
2 Using the table of food and wine matches above, find out which wines on your list you could match with the examples of dishes given.

TAKING DOWN CUSTOMERS' ORDERS

After presenting the wine list to the customer and either having given them time to consider it or advised them of an appropriate selection, you should record the order on a beverage pad. You should record:
● the bin number if that is included on your wine list
● the name of the wine
● the vintage year
● the price.

Ask the host:
● if they have any preferences about service temperature
● when they wish you to serve it
● if a red and a white wine have been ordered, whether the host wants them both offered to their guests at the same time or the red wine served after the white.

Wine lists can be constructed in several different ways. Some establishments:
● give each wine in the list a number, often called a 'bin number', because it refers to a location where the wine is normally 'binned' or stored
● put red, white, rosé and sparkling wines in separate sections
● group both red and white wines together by country of origin
● arrange wines in the list from the lowest priced to the most expensive.

It is important that the order you take is recorded accurately:
● so that the correct wines can be obtained from the cellar or dispense point
● to ensure that the correct type and vintage is presented to the customer
● to prevent having to return to the customer for further information and appearing inefficient and unprofessional
● so that the customer's bill can be made up correctly.

MEMORY JOGGER

Why is it important that you should take down customers' order accurately?

Taking the wine order

It would be inadequate to arrive at the dispense point with an order for simply 'Bordeaux'. This does not specify the colour and there may be several red and white wines from that region on the wine list. Some wine lists may also have several vintages of the same wine on offer, some of which will be more expensive. If a customer orders one of the less expensive vintages and is later charged for a bottle of a more expensive one, they will not be pleased. They could also refuse to pay the difference.

The waiter or *sommelier* should record the price of each wine ordered on the beverage pad and total them. This is normally a duplicate pad and the top copy is either left at the dispense point or taken to the cashier who will add it to the record of the food order. Follow your establishment's procedure with regard to billing customers for wine.

Do this

Find out:
(a) How the wine list is constructed and if red and white wines from the same regions are recorded on separate pages.
(b) Whether your establishment offers more than one vintage of certain brands of wine.
(c) What are the procedures for obtaining wines from the dispense point and for billing customers for wine.

CUSTOMER INCIDENTS

Occasionally, there will be events which cause customers to become upset or create problems for staff. If a customer reports a problem to you:
● acknowledge the incident and apologise to them, if necessary
● remain calm and listen carefully without interrupting and making comment
● show them that you are taking the incident seriously
● start to deal with the situation immediately and tell the customer what action you intend to take.

Resolve any incidents that you can within your own authority. However, you should always act within your organisation's procedures and report all incidents to your supervisor. Remember:

● Some incidents such as theft from or accidents to customers may require the emergency services to be called and have legal implications.
● Do not admit responsibility for an incident or you might create legal liabilities for your establishment.

If you encounter problems with customers such as those described in the early section of this element, inform your supervisor.

Problems with the availability of wines

If, after taking an order, you find that the stock of a particular wine has run out, take the wine list and inform the customer immediately, apologise and suggest an alternative wine similar to the wine chosen. Inform the customer about the price of the different wine, especially if it is more expensive. You should also inform other service staff so that new customers can be informed when the wine list is presented.

● Inform your supervisor if stock of a wine runs out so that new stock can be ordered.

Case study

It was a busy evening session in an expensive city-centre restaurant. The sommelier had reported in sick and one of the station waiters had been told to take over her job for the evening. He was taking his responsibilities very seriously. He presented the wine list to two elderly gentlemen. They ordered a bottle of 'Old Lunch Bags'. The waiter was confused and, raising his eye-brows, asked them to point out the wine on the wine list.

'Oh!' he said pompously. 'You mean the 1989 Lynch-Bages'

The customers looked at him and nodded. When he went to the dispense point to obtain the wine he was told that the last bottle had just been sold, but the 1985 was still available. He told the bar man to give him a bottle and that the customers would never notice. He presented the wine quickly, opened it and served it. He placed the bottle on the side table so that the customers could not examine the bottle.

Later he was called to the table by the Restaurant Manager. The customers had queried the price charged for the wine. They pointed out that they had ordered the 1989 and were being charged £15 more than the price advertised on the wine list. The waiter then explained what had happened. The customers refused to pay the difference.

(a) What mistakes did the waiter make when taking and serving this order?

(b) What action should he have taken when the 1989 vintage was not available? What had he forgotten? What law was he in breach of?

(c) How would you resolve the situation of the customers refusing to pay the difference?

What have you learned

1 Give three examples of behaviour that could embarrass customers.
2 Give three examples of ways in which you might identify the host of a party.
3 When and how should you present the wine list?
4 At what stage of a meal would you promote:
  (a) a dry sparkling wine
  (b) a still dry red or white wine
  (c) a sweet wine.
5 What is the difference between a non-alcoholic (alcohol free) wine and a low alcohol wine?
6 Wines from which regions and countries are traditionally bottled in:
  (a) a square shouldered bottle?
  (b) a tall green flûte?
  (c) a circular flask wrapped in woven straw?
7 Give three examples of information:
  (a) which **must** be on a wine label
  (b) which is **optional** but often included on the label

(continued)

8 What is the highest quality level for:
   (a) German wines?
   (b) Italian wines?
9 What is a vintage wine? How is the vintage of a wine important?
10 What would a brown tinge suggest to you about:
   (a) a red wine
   (b) a white wine.
11 Why is it important that you should give customers accurate information about any wines you serve?
12 What types of customers do the licensing laws forbid you to sell wine to?

ELEMENT 3:   (2NC3) Present and serve wines; (1NC10) Serve bottled wines

---

PREPARING TO SERVE WINE

Having taken the order, you should make sure that the service areas, such as the customer's table and your side table or sideboard, are correctly prepared.

- Check that the correct glasses are on the table. Depending on the table setting, you may have to obtain and place an additional glass at each cover if two wines are to be served or a tall flute if a sparkling wine is to be served first.
- Place a side plate on the table to the right of the host's cover and/or an ice bucket and stand to the right of the host's chair. If a chiller or wine cooler is to be used, this should be placed either on the table or at a side table if there is inadequate space. The ice bucket should be filled with a mixture of ice and water up to approximately two-thirds of its height. See the following section.
- Make sure that you have the necessary equipment to open the wine after it has been presented and deal with any problems that might occur. You should have a sharp knife or foil cutter, a corkscrew or bottle opener, a small spoon and a broken cork extractor if one is available. If a sparkling wine is to be served, you should also have pincers and a bottle stopper available.
- Either obtain or make sure that you have the necessary number of service cloths for the number of wines to be served.
- A clean tray or salver, covered with a fresh napkin, should be available on the side table or sideboard to bring additional clean glasses to the table and to clear used glasses during service.

Once your service areas and equipment are ready, you should obtain the wine(s) from the dispense point. Make sure that each bottle is clean and undamaged.

Essential knowledge (2NC3)

The main points to remember when handling glassware are:
- Clean glasses should be brought to the table on a covered salver. Glasses are carried upside down during mise-en-place, but upright on the salver during service.
- When placing and clearing glasses, you should always handle them by the stem. Never put your fingers on the bowl, near the rim or inside a glass.
- Set out glasses in the order of usage from right to left at the right-hand side of the cover. The size and shape of the glassware required will depend on the type and style of wine to be served.
- White wine is served in a clear glass containing around 15 to 20 cl.
- Red wine is served in a slightly larger glass than white wine containing 20 to 25 cl.
- Sparkling wines can be served either in a wide, shallow coupe or 'saucer' or a tall, slender flute.
- A fortified wine such as sherry is served in a small glass holding between 7.5 and 10 cl such as an Elgin schooner.

ADJUSTING THE WINE TEMPERATURE FOR SERVICE

In Element 1, it was mentioned that the service temperature of wines was largely a matter of customer preference and that white wines were often stored at the service point at around 10 °C which keeps them lightly chilled. Red wines are normally held at the service point at room temperature. The ideal service temperature for a range of wines was given in that Element.

In Element 2 you were recommended to ask the customer if they had any preferences regarding the service temperature of the wines when you had taken the order. If your customer requires you to adjust the service temperature, you may have to either further chill or warm up the wine.

To chill wines for service: varying the ice to water ratio

The method most frequently used to chill wines is in the ice bucket. This is not a rapid method and it can take twenty to thirty minutes to lower the temperature of a wine by two or three degrees. The speed of cooling and the final temperature of the wine can be changed by varying the amount of ice to water in the ice bucket.
- The higher the proportion of ice mixed with the water, the lower the temperature of the mixture will be. This will cool a wine quite quickly.
- If little ice is mixed with the water, the higher the temperature of the mixture will be. This mixture is more suitable for holding the wine at its original temperature and keeping it lightly chilled.

If the bottle is unopened, you can speed up the cooling by turning the bottle upside down in the ice bucket for a short while to cool the wine in the neck of the bottle.

Placing a bottle of wine in a freezer or ice maker is not recommended because of the dangers of contamination being passed from the bottle to other foods or ice. This would be a breach of the food safety and food hygiene regulations.

To warm wines for service

Heating a wine too quickly makes it cloudy and undrinkable. Red wines should be brought up to room temperature as gently as possible. This is normally done by standing the wine in the room in which it is to be served for several hours.
- In an emergency, you can raise the temperature of a red wine by transferring it to a decanter or clean spare wine bottle which has been filled with warm (not boiling) water for a short time.
- Never place red wines into boiling water, onto a hotplate or radiator or in a hot cupboard to raise its temperature quickly.

Do this

Try an experiment in your establishment with three wine buckets. Put the same quantity of water in each ice bucket. Using the scoop from the ice maker, add one scoop to one bucket, two scoops to the second and three scoops to the third. Borrow a temperature probe from the kitchen or use a thermometer to measure the temperature in each bucket. Make a note of the water temperature in each bucket after 5, 10 and 20 minutes.

PRESENTING THE WINE

Essentially there are two ways of presenting bottled wines: on the service cloth or in a wine cradle or decanting basket. Presentation in a cradle is usually limited to mature wines which contain a sediment. The wine bottle is always presented unopened in case there has been a mistake with the order or the customer has changed their mind.

Using the service cloth

When you collect the wine from the service point, try to keep mature red wines in their original position. If they have been stored horizontally or upright, try to keep them in that position and try to avoid agitating the wine by sudden or rapid movements.
● Hold the bottle by the neck in your right hand with the front label facing upward. Using a folded service cloth in your left hand, support the body of the bottle.
● Present the bottle to the host with the label uppermost from the right-hand side at a suitable distance to allow them to examine the label.
● Name the wine to your customer: 'Your 1988 Château Loudenne, Sir.'
● When the customer confirms that the order is correct, the wine can either be opened at the table or taken to the side table or sideboard to be opened. White or rosé wines can be placed in an ice bucket or cooler to be opened. Follow your establishment's procedure.
● If further chilling is required the host should be informed and the wine left in the ice bucket until it is ready or the host requires it to be poured.

Presenting wine

Using a cradle or decanting basket

The cradle or basket should be lined with a clean napkin. When the bottle is moved from the shelf or rack, it should be kept in the same position and placed onto the napkin. Try to keep any movements as smooth as possible during the transfer.
● Present the bottle with the label uppermost to the customer. If the customer confirms the order, either place the cradle on the table or remove it to a side table or sideboard.
● The bottle should be kept in the cradle and be opened at the angle it is held in.

If the host has ordered both a red and white wine, present the white wine first. This reflects the normal order of tasting and serving the wines.

OPENING STILL AND SPARKLING WINES

Still wines

The precise method that you use will depend on the type of corkscrew or bottle opener you are using. Generally, the procedure you should follow is:

MEMORY JOGGER

What procedure should you follow when opening a bottle of still wine?

Remove the capsule
- Locate the collar on the neck of the bottle which is usually between one and two centimetres below the lip.
- With a small sharp knife, the blade of a 'Waiter's Friend' or a foil cutter, cut the capsule neatly by holding the blade firmly under the collar and turning the bottle slowly. Remove the plastic or foil above the cut to expose the cork.
- Clean the cork and the rim of the bottle with a clean cloth to remove any dust, mould or lead salts and prevent debris from the rim falling into the bottle when the cork is withdrawn.

Withdraw the cork
- Place the top of the corkscrew vertically in the centre of the cork. Applying a slight downward pressure, turn the corkscrew clockwise slowly and smoothly to prevent damaging the cork.
- Do not drive the corkscrew completely through the cork. This can dislodge small pieces of cork into the wine or cause a thin veil of cork dust to settle on the surface of the wine.
- Gently lever the cork from the bottle until about one centimetre of cork remains in the bottle neck. Using your thumb and forefinger, twist the remaining section of the cork out of the bottle. Try to avoid a loud pop as the cork is extracted.
- After drawing the cork, wipe around and inside the lip of the bottle with the service cloth to remove any remaining debris.

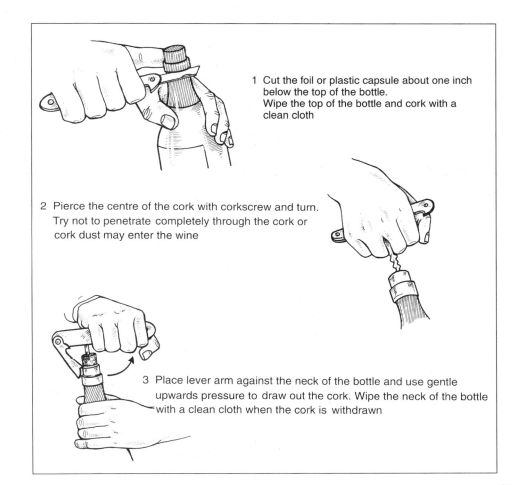

1 Cut the foil or plastic capsule about one inch below the top of the bottle.
Wipe the top of the bottle and cork with a clean cloth

2 Pierce the centre of the cork with corkscrew and turn. Try not to penetrate completely through the cork or cork dust may enter the wine

3 Place lever arm against the neck of the bottle and use gentle upwards pressure to draw out the cork. Wipe the neck of the bottle with a clean cloth when the cork is withdrawn

Opening a wine bottle with a 'waiter's friend'

Handling the cork

It is the practice in some establishments to present the host with the cork at this point so that they can sniff the cork to check for any unpleasant or vinegary smells. Other establishments may attach the cork to the neck of the bottle or place it on a side plate along with the bottle. Do not sniff the cork yourself unless invited to do so by the host. Follow your establishment's procedure regarding this aspect of the service etiquette.

● The cork of some wines is branded with the bottler's trade mark or a number. Presenting the cork to the customer is also a method of authenticating the wine by proving that an incorrect label has not been placed on the bottle.

Wine in cradles

When opening a bottle of wine held in a cradle, follow the same procedure described above. However, try to avoid shaking or moving the bottle while cutting the capsule and removing the cork.

Sparkling and semi-sparkling wines

Great care should be taken when opening sparkling and semi-sparkling wines. The sparkle in the wine is caused by carbon dioxide gas which is trapped in the bottle and dissolved in the wine. For example, the pressure inside a bottle of Champagne can be between 4 and 6 bar (atmospheres), the equivalent of between 60 and 90 psi (pounds per square inch). This is similar to the air pressure in the tyre of a heavy lorry or double-decker bus.

Sparkling and semi-sparkling wines are made in several different ways. However, there are two ways that you can assess the degree of pressure in a bottle.

1 By the weight of the bottle. To contain a wine with a lot of pressure requires a thicker glass than for a still wine. The higher the inside pressure, the heavier the bottle will feel.
2 By the label terms. Wines made by a similar method to Champagne will have a high internal pressure. Look for label terms such as 'traditional method' or their equivalent, such as the French 'Méthode Traditionelle', Spanish CAVA or Italian 'Metodo Tradizionale'. Some Australian and Californian sparkling wines may use the phrase 'fermented in this bottle'.

The pressure inside the bottle can expel the cork violently and this can injure any person who is struck by the cork.

Procedure

● Tear away the foil cover to reveal the wire muzzle covering the cork.
● Hold the bottle at an angle between 30 and 40 degrees from the upright. Point the cork away from your body and away from the table area, other members of staff or windows.
● Keeping your hand over the cork, carefully untwist the wire muzzle. Slide your thumb up under the wire and lift off the muzzle and any cap over the cork. Once the muzzle is removed, you should not take your hand off the cork.
● Holding the cork with your left hand, wrap the bottle in a service cloth.
● Keeping your left hand on the cork, gently turn the bottle not the cork.
● As the cork eases out, release it slowly until it gently pops out.

Make sure that you have a glass close by in case the wine begins to fizz out. Serve immediately by pouring into the customers' glasses. With each glass, wait until the froth subsides then fill each glass about two-thirds full. Seal an unfinished bottle with a stopper.

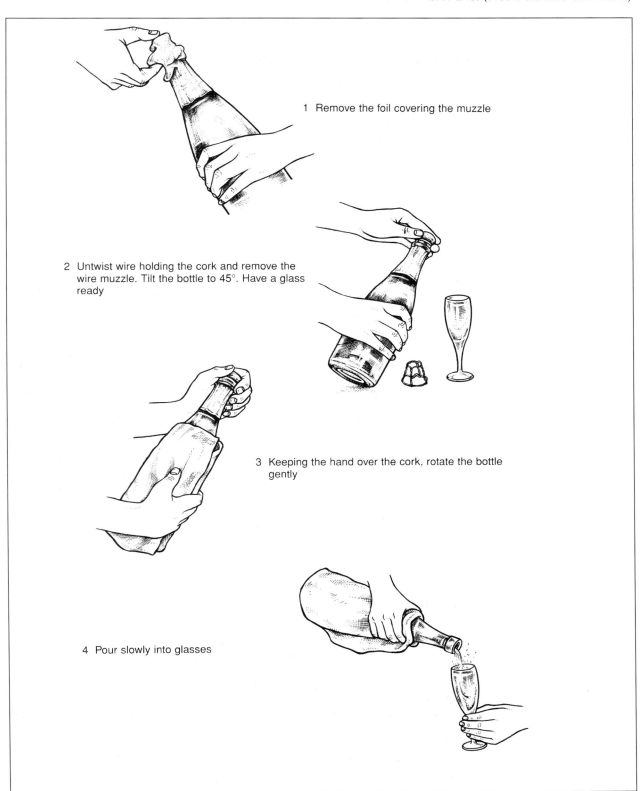

1 Remove the foil covering the muzzle

2 Untwist wire holding the cork and remove the wire muzzle. Tilt the bottle to 45°. Have a glass ready

3 Keeping the hand over the cork, rotate the bottle gently

4 Pour slowly into glasses

Opening a bottle of sparkling wine

Essential knowledge (2NC3)

In order to handle a bottle of Champagne or other sparkling wine safely:
- serve the wine well-chilled as this helps to keep the carbon dioxide gas dissolved in the bottle
- do not shake or agitate the bottle while carrying and presenting the wine
- do not point the bottle towards your face or body, any other person, the area where guests are seated or glass while opening the bottle
- keep a firm grip on both the cork and bottle at all stages of the opening procedure.

Do this

1 Find out if your establishment holds a stock of mature red wines which have to be handled and presented carefully. Make a note of their names and the vintage year.
2 Examine the stock of sparkling and semi-sparkling wines held in your establishment.
   (a) Compare the weight of the bottles. Are some heavier than others?
   (b) Examine the labels. Which wines are made by the traditional method or fermented in the bottle? Use the table of common label terms in Element 2 to establish the degree of sparkle.

DECANTING WINE

You may have to decant a red wine if the customer requests it or if the wine has been brought up from a cool cellar and needs to be warmed up. Decanting sometimes helps to bring out a wine's full bouquet. It is not usually necessary to decant a white wine except very old ones which can have a thin layer of sediment inside the bottle.

The procedure you follow will depend on the equipment that is available to you or whether you have to decant by hand and eye.

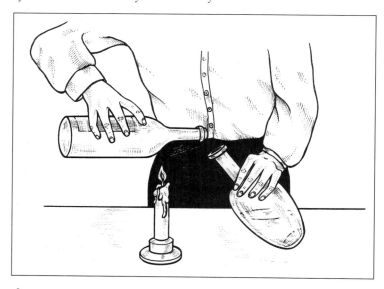

Decanting wine over a light so that the sediment is visible as it approaches the neck of the bottle

Procedure

1 Handle the bottle carefully or use a cradle or decanting basket to prevent disturbing the sediment.
2 Present the bottle to the customer to confirm the wine is correct.
3 Obtain a clean, dry decanter at room temperature. Warm the decanter if you need to raise the temperature of the wine. If you are using a straining funnel, place it inside the neck of the decanter and, if necessary, line it with clean, dry muslin.

4 Open the bottle following the procedure for still wines described above. Take care not to turn or jerk the bottle.

5 Use a candle or other light as a background to highlight the level of wine in the bottle.

6 Raise the bottle slowly and pour the wine gently, holding the bottle against the light so that you can see inside. As soon as the sediment, which appears as a dark cloud in the wine, gets near to the shoulder of the bottle, slow down and stop pouring to prevent the sediment entering the decanted wine.

If you have not decanted the wine at the table or in sight of the customer, present the empty wine bottle and cork to the host when you bring the decanter to the table. This is to confirm to the customer that the wine in the decanter is the wine which they ordered.

MEMORY JOGGER

What procedure should you follow when decanting from the bottle?

SERVING WINE

There are several aspects of the service etiquette or procedure that are important to the professional service of wine. These include obtaining the host's approval and the service order as well as the service method.

Approval

After the bottle has been opened or the wine decanted, ask the host if he would like to taste the wine before it is served to the guests. If he agrees proceed as follows.

● Stand to the right of the host and pour a small sample into the appropriate glass. This allows the host to check that the wine is in good condition, at the required service temperature and to check and comment on the bouquet and flavour.

If the host approves, you should begin to serve the guests. Note that the host may ask another member of the party to taste the wine.

Service order: guests

The traditional order of service is that female guests are served first, then male guests and finally the host.

● Moving around the table in an anti-clockwise direction, serve the first lady to the right of the host and then the other female members.

● Then serve the male guests, again moving around the table in an anti-clockwise direction.

● After all the guests have been served, return to the host (male or female) and fill their glass to the correct height.

There are two variations to the service order which can operate in some establishments.

● When serving the guests, the eldest ladies are served before the youngest and the eldest gentlemen before the youngest.

● At private functions the host's wife is sometimes served after the guests, but before the host's glass is filled.

It is important that you follow your establishment's procedures.

Service order: wines

If the host has ordered both a white and red wine, you should offer the white wine first for their approval. The bouquet and flavour of most white wines tend to be more delicate than those of red. A white wine tasted immediately after a red would appear to be very light and relatively tasteless.

Pouring bottled wine

The general procedure when pouring wine is as follows.
● Where possible, serve from the right of the person whose glass you are filling.
● Support the base of the bottle with one hand with the label uppermost; hold the service cloth in your other hand under the neck of the bottle.
● Place the lip of the bottle above the rim of the glass without touching it and tilt the neck of the bottle down slowly until the wine starts to flow.
● When the wine reaches the correct fill height, ease the neck of the bottle upwards, twist the bottle slightly to the right and slide the service cloth up towards the lip to catch any drips.
● Even in difficult situations such as corner tables or where tables are next to a wall, always take the bottle to the glass and not the glass to the bottle.

Fill height

When filling customers' glasses, you should:
● fill the smaller white wine glass between one-half and two-thirds full
● not fill the larger red wine glass more than half full.

Remember, you must leave space above the wine to hold the bouquet and red wines usually have more pronounced and complex bouquets. Depending on the glass sizes, there will be approximately the same quantity of wine in a white wine glass which is two-thirds full and a red wine glass which is half full.

Glasses per bottle

The standard bottle sizes offered by most establishments are the half-bottle containing 37.5 cl, the standard bottle which contains 75 cl and a magnum which contains 1.5 litres or two bottles. For the number of glasses that can be obtained from these sizes, see the following *Essential knowledge*.

Essential knowledge (2NC3)	If the average serving of wine in each glass is around 12.5 cl, you should obtain:
	● three glasses from a half bottle containing 37.5 cl
	● six glasses from a standard bottle containing 75 cl
	● twelve glasses from a bottle containing 1.5 litres
	With a mature red wine which contains a sediment, the last part of the wine is not poured, giving only five and a half glasses from a standard bottle.

Pouring wine from a decanter or carafe

The procedure for pouring decanted wine or wine from a carafe is the same as the general procedure for pouring bottled wines described above. There is one addition. With a bottled wine, the customer can see the label, but there is no label on a decanter or carafe. When serving from these, you should name the wine to the customer. For example: 'A glass of Château Loudenne, Madam?' or 'Would you like a glass of the House Red, Sir?'

As the size of carafes differs from most bottle sizes, the number of 12.5 cl glasses that can be obtained are different. These are approximately:
● two from a 25 cl carafe
● four from a 50 cl carafe
● six from a 75 cl carafe
● eight from a 1 litre carafe.

Essential knowledge (2NC3)

When presenting and serving wine, it is important that you use the correct service etiquette (procedure).

- Bottled wines should be presented and served with the label uppermost to authenticate the wine and be visible to the host and his or her guests.
- The service cloth should be used as a background when presenting the wine and to prevent drips staining the table linen during service.
- The host should be invited to sample each wine before it is served to the guests. A white wine should be offered before a red.
- Wine in a decanter or carafe should be named before being poured.
- The white wine glass should be filled between half and two-thirds full and the red wine glass half filled.

It is important that you follow the correct service etiquette with customers to create a good impression of the professionalism of your service and maintain the standard of service expected by your establishment.

Do this

1 Find out what equipment is available in your establishment for decanting wine. Ask your supervisor to demonstrate the method used.
2 Find out the service order for filling guest's glasses which operates in your establishment.
3 Using a lined glass or thimble measure, find out the appropriate fill height in the glasses used for red and white wines in your establishment.

Who are you permitted to serve?

Provided that the wine has been purchased by a person over eighteen years of age (sixteen in Scotland), you may serve wine to any person over the age of five years. However, this is at the licensee's discretion and your establishment's procedures may differ from the law.

However, if a customer becomes drunk or disorderly, you are not allowed to continue serving them or allow other people to buy drink for them. Before refusing to serve a customer, you should consult your supervisor. See *Essential knowledge* on page 187 of Element 2 to refresh your memory, if necessary.

Faults with wine

Because of the widespread use of modern technology in wine-making and processes such as flash pasteurisation and sterile filtration when bottling wines, it is relatively rare to find major faults with wine. However, when opening and serving bottled wines, you should be alert for some of the more obvious signs that there is a fault with the wine.

Off-odours
- Reject any wine which has a distinctly musty smell, has a smell of bad eggs, 'mousy' smells, smells of vinegar or apples or yeast. All these are signs of chemical or bacterial problems with the wine.

● The smell of a struck match is sometimes apparent when a bottle is opened and the first glass is poured. This is sulphur dioxide, which is often used as a preservative in wine. If the wine is left for a while, the smell will disappear and the wine should be drinkable.

Appearance

All wines should be clear and 'fall bright' when poured into a glass.

● Any cloudiness or haze in a wine will indicate that it is unfit for service. This may indicate a second, undesirable fermentation has taken place in the bottle and there may be an off-odour as well. Bubbles in a still wine which has not been shaken up can also indicate a problem.
● An orange-brown colour and a 'burnt' smell in a white wine can indicate that it has oxidised and is unfit for service.
● If wines are stored in cold conditions, small sugar-like crystals can form in the bottle. These are harmless and do not affect the quality of the wine. However, customers often mistake them for 'glass' in the bottle.

If you detect any fault in a wine, apologise to the customer and offer to replace it. Remove any glasses into which the wine has been poured and replace them. Report any faulty bottles to your supervisor who may be able to reclaim the value of the wine from the supplier or obtain a replacement bottle.

● Ask the customer if they wish to have a new bottle of the same wine or if they wish to order a different wine.
● Pour any wine from glasses back into the bottle and re-seal it with the cork. Mark it as faulty and remove it from the service area.

STORAGE AFTER SERVICE

After the guests and host have been served, the wine should be left either on or near the table. The place and conditions of storage depend on the type of wine and the method of service.

Chilled wines

● A chilled white, rosé or sparkling wine should be placed in the ice bucket positioned at the right of the host or in a cooler placed on the table or side table.
● The service cloth should either be draped over the neck of the bottle or inserted through the ring at the side of the ice bucket according to establishment procedure.

Red wine, decanters and carafes

● These should be placed on a side plate to the right of the host close to their wine glasses. Do not place the wine close to a table light or candle which may heat the wine.
● The service cloth can be folded onto the side plate under the bottle or carafe or a clean napkin can be used to cover the plate. The cork is often left on the side plate as well.
● The label of a bottled wine should face towards the host.

You should follow your establishment's procedures regarding the placing of service equipment and wines after service.

<table>
<tr>
<td>

*Essential
knowledge (2NC3)*

</td>
<td>

It is important that you should try to hold any wine remaining in the bottle at the appropriate service temperature.
● Chilled wines should be returned to the ice bucket or cooler immediately after service.
● Red wine should be placed on the table away from any direct sources of heat.
When the room temperature is very high, as in the summer months for example, you can attempt to control the temperature of wines during service by:
● adding additional ice to the ice bucket to replace any melted ice or preparing a new ice bucket to replace the first.
● removing the red wine, with the host's permission, from the table and storing it on a side plate on the side table wrapped in a clean service cloth which has been soaked in iced water and squeezed to remove any excess.
Also see *Essential knowledge* on page 171 of Element 1 for the appropriate service temperature for a range of wines.

</td>
</tr>
</table>

MAINTAINING RAPPORT WITH THE CUSTOMER

Having established a relationship with the host and their guests during the process of taking the order and serving the wine, you should remain aware of what is happening at the table. If two different wines have been ordered, you should have agreed with the host at the time of taking the order when the second wine was to be served.

As the first wine is finished or a new course is served, check with the host if he wishes you to serve the second wine. Pour it into clean glasses and remove any empty glasses used for the first wine. Ask each guest politely if you can remove the empty glass.
● If guests have not finished the first wine and refuse the second, offer to refill their glass with the first wine.

Refilling glasses

Regularly check the level of wine in the customers' glasses. When the glasses of most of the guests are nearly empty, return to the table and refill them.
● When you lift a bottle from the ice bucket, let any surplus water drain from it first. Wrap the body of the bottle in the service cloth to prevent water dripping onto the table.
● Ask each guest if they would like more wine. Try to ensure each guest receives a small amount.
● Do not pour out the last portion of a mature red wine. This contains the sediment and will ruin any wine it is poured into.

When a bottle of white, rosé or sparkling wine is empty, it is customary to place it upside down in the ice bucket. The red wine bottle is removed from the table with the side plate. In both instances, this is a signal to the host that the wine is finished.
● At this point, ask the host politely if another bottle is required.

If the host orders another bottle of the same wine, bring fresh glasses to the table and offer to replace the guests' glasses.
● As customers eat and drink during the meal, the inside and outside of their wine glass will become smeared with lipstick, grease and small particles of food. Replacing the glasses allows the second bottle to be served in the best condition possible and not be affected by any previous contamination.
● It is not necessary to present the second bottle of the same wine, but you should ask the host if he wishes to taste the wine from the new bottle before you serve it.

While it is important that you remain alert to what is happening at each table, avoid behaviour which can embarrass or irritate customers.

- Don't hover around tables. Customers require a degree of privacy and may not wish their conversations to be overheard.
- While waiting to serve customers or refill their glasses, don't interrupt them. Stand patiently and speak during a break in the conversation or when the customer becomes aware of you.
- Remember to smile and use a friendly tone of voice.

Checking customer satisfaction

After the customers have finished, you should ask their opinion of the wines they were served. A simple question such as, 'Did you enjoy the New Zealand Chardonnay?' will allow you to learn about the customers' tastes and preferences. You can also use this occasion to mention alternative wines and suggest that the customers should try them on their next visit to your establishment.

DEALING WITH UNEXPECTED SITUATIONS

If an unexpected incident occurs, you should deal with it promptly and efficiently. If customers are involved, any action you take should cause as little disruption as possible. An efficient response is often required to reduce any annoyance to customers and encourage them to return to your establishment.

All accidents and spillages should be reported to your supervisor, especially if there is any damage to customers' property or clothing. A written report is often required of any complaints or incidents and a record is usually kept of wastages and equipment faults.

Faults with corks

A common problem during wine service is a cork breaking while it is being extracted from the bottle. Common causes are:

- bottles being stored in an upright position for long periods allowing the cork to dry out
- failing to penetrate the cork to a sufficient depth or to keep the corkscrew in the centre of the cork
- corks which have deteriorated in storage, especially in older bottles of wine.

A related problem is particles of cork being pushed into the wine if the corkscrew goes completely through it.

The best method of extracting a broken cork is to use a pronged cork extractor. This is barbed like a fish hook and is pushed down the side of the cork to catch under the base. If this type of equipment is not available, try to penetrate the cork diagonally with the corkscrew. This will give it more grip on the remaining cork.

- Always turn the corkscrew gently into the cork. If you apply too much pressure, you may push the remaining cork into the bottle.

If the cork disintegrates or is pushed into the bottle, you can either inform the customer and ask if you can decant the wine or consult your supervisor about replacing the damaged wine with a new bottle.

If any pieces of cork have fallen into the wine and are poured into a customer's glass, lift the glass and take it to the sideboard. Use a clean spoon to extract the pieces and return the glass to the customer.

Spillages

If you are responsible for a slight spillage of wine at the table:
- Check with the customer to see if their clothing has been stained. Apologise to the customer.
- Remove any items such as plates, cutlery or napkins which have been soiled or which will be in your way when cleaning up. Return any hot food to the hot-plate.
- Clean the spillage with a clean damp cloth. If a table cloth is being used, place something beneath the stain to absorb any surplus liquid and prevent the table-top being marked. Several layers of paper napkins could be used.
- Cover the stain with something non-absorbent like a plastic menu insert and unfold a clean service cloth or napkin over it.
- Replace any items which have been removed and return any food.

If you or the customer have knocked over a glass of wine, replace the glass and refill it as required. Major spillages may require the table to be completely cleared and re-laid. See *Unit 2NC2* for details of this procedure.

Essential knowledge (1NC10)	You should report all spillages to your supervisor as soon as possible.
	• If customers' clothing or property has been damaged, your establishment may have liability to clean or replace it.
	• If you have to replace wine that you have spilled at a table, you will need your supervisor's permission to draw replacement stock.
	• If you spill stock before serving it, your supervisor may need to witness the fact and record it in a wastage book.
	• If spillages are recorded, your employer may be able to recover some of the cost against tax and V.A.T. payments.
	If spillages are not reported and witnessed, staff may be wrongly accused of stealing stock.

Case study	It was David's first evening in the restaurant. When he came to set out his wine glasses, he found that there were no white wine glasses left. He decided to use a 20 cl red wine glass for white wine and a 25 cl water glass for red wine. A party of four arrived at his table and the host, who was celebrating his wedding anniversary, ordered a bottle of Australian Chardonnay. David presented the wine and, after opening it, asked the host to taste it. The host declined and David began to fill his glass to within one centimetre of the rim. He proceeded to do the same with each of the guests as he went around the table. He placed the bottle in the ice bucket. When the host indicated that he wanted his glass refilled, the bottle was empty.
	The host looked surprised and a little annoyed, but ordered a second bottle. David proceeded to pour the wine exactly as he had done before. When the customer was later presented with the bill, he did not have enough cash and had to ask his wife to write a cheque for the meal.
	1 How many faults can you identify with David's service?
	2 How did his choice of glasses and his service method contribute to the customer's embarrassment when paying the bill?
	3 How would you have dealt with the situation?

Do this

1 Find out your establishment's procedure regarding serving wines to people under eighteen years of age, even if the wine is purchased by an adult.
2 Find out how experienced members of staff maintain their relationship with customers during service. How do they check customer satisfaction with the wines they have served?
3 Find out your establishment's procedures for:
   (a) recording details of faulty wines
   (b) dealing with wastages or wine unfit for service
   (c) dealing with a situation where a spillage damages a customer's clothing.

What have you learned

1 Why is it important that you check the glasses on your customer's table before serving wine?
2 Give three points you should remember when handling glassware.
3 What are the key points to remember when presenting a bottle of wine?
4 What is the procedure for opening a bottle of still wine?
5 What is the correct procedure for opening a bottle of sparkling wine?
6 How should you handle a bottle of Champagne or other sparkling wine in order to open it safely?
7 What are the main points you should remember when decanting a mature red wine?
8 How and why should you seek the host's approval before serving wine to his/her guests?
9 What are the main points to remember when serving bottled wines?
10 How many glasses can be obtained from a half bottle, a standard bottle and a magnum of wine?
11 Give two examples of faults with wines that would make them unfit to serve.
12 Why is it important that you should hold wine at the correct service temperature after you have poured the first glasses.
13 Why should you not pour out the last part of a bottle of mature red wine?
14 Why is it important that you report spillages to your supervisor?

Get ahead

1 Study the labels of the wines stocked by your establishment. Ask your supervisor to explain any label terms you do not understand.
2 Local colleges often run courses in Wine Appreciation or the Certificate course of the Wine and Spirit Education Trust. Find out if any courses are available in your area and try to attend one.
3 Obtain a copy of an introductory textbook about wine from your local library or one of the many guides to wine and wine tasting. Read about the wines offered in your establishment.
4 Most off-licences will hold a wider stock of wines than most restaurants. Visit your local off-licence and study the labels on the bottles. Note the country and the region of origin, their quality levels and prices.
5 If you have the opportunity while on holiday abroad or visiting the South of England, visit a vineyard and find out how they make their wines. See if you can taste samples of the wines.

Provide a carvery/buffet service

This chapter covers:
ELEMENT 1: **Prepare and maintain a carvery/buffet display**
ELEMENT 2: **Serve customers at the carvery/buffet**
ELEMENT 3: **Maintain customer dining areas**

What you need to do

- Deal with customers in a polite and helpful manner.
- Keep the carvery or buffet table clean, free from damage and correctly positioned for food service.
- Arrange appropriate table linen, utensils and decorative display items, keeping them clean and free from damage.
- Present and display food items appropriately.
- Portion, serve and arrange food in accordance with laid-down procedures and customer requirements, using the correct clean and undamaged equipment.
- Replenish food items at appropriate times.
- Keep the carvery or buffet and dining areas tidy and free from food debris.
- Clear customer tables of soiled and unrequired items and any left-over food or accompaniments, as necessary.
- Remove soiled table linen and replace it with clean linen as required.
- Store and display food items in accordance with food hygiene legislation.
- Deal with spillages and breakages in an appropriate manner.
- Correctly deal with left-over food items.
- Work in an organised and efficient manner to meet daily schedules.
- Carry out work causing minimum disturbance to customers.

What you need to know

- How to identify customer requirements and provide them with accurate information, promoting establishment products and services.
- Why it is important to replenish and correctly display food items throughout service.
- Why dining and service areas must be kept clean and tidy.
- Why portions should be controlled when serving food to customers.
- Why information given to customers must be accurate.
- How to deal with spillages and breakages.
- Why waste must be handled and disposed of correctly.
- Why table items should be checked for damage and cleanliness before use.
- Why and to whom all incidents/breakages should be reported.
- How to deal with unexpected situations.

INTRODUCTION

Carveries and buffets are both types of service where the customers leave their tables to choose from a range of dishes and/or roast joints of meat on display. Customers may either be served by food service staff or chefs (who may stand behind the buffet or carvery) or they may help themselves.

Attractive presentation is essential when preparing a buffet

Carvery and buffet types of service require less staff because customers serve themselves; this in turn helps to keep the cost of the meal down. However, as with other types of self-service, it is important that standards of presentation and hygiene remain high at all times.

When providing both buffet and carvery service you need to remain particularly aware of special customer needs: elderly and disabled customers should always be offered extra assistance.

ELEMENT 1:   Prepare and maintain a carvery/buffet display

CARVERY SERVICE

Carvery service offers the guest the opportunity of choosing a starter and sweet from a table d'hôte type menu and a main course from the carvery display. Customers are greeted and seated by the head waiter or receptionist, the menu is presented and the first course is ordered. After the first course, the customer is invited to the carvery where they choose from a variety of roast meats or vegetarian alternatives. The chef carves the customers' choice of meat and the customers then help themselves to vegetables and accompaniments before returning to their table. After the main course has been cleared, customers order a sweet from the menu.

Positioning the carvery

When positioning the carvery, give careful consideration to the following:
● *access to the kitchen*. You need to be able to carry dishes to and from the kitchen and carvery easily and smoothly

- *space behind the carvery*. There needs to be enough space behind the carvery for staff to move around freely
- *customer access*. Customers should be able to reach the carvery, move along to make their selection and then return to their tables easily and safely
- *position of electric sockets*. Portable carvery units need to be situated close to suitable electric sockets

Preparing the carvery

- Before setting up the carvery table, make sure that the plate warmer or hot cupboard is switched on in plenty of time for the plates to warm before the start of service.
- Check that all plates are clean and free from damage before setting up the carvery table.
- When setting up the carvery, check that there is an adequate supply of plates, carving utensils and equipment, and that these are in a clean and undamaged condition.
- When the main foods are brought to the carvery in readiness for service, check that the appropriate sauces and accompaniments are present.

Presenting and displaying food items and accompaniments

The carvery should be clean and large enough to hold all the food items without overcrowding. Display the food in an attractive manner, bringing it out for display at the last possible moment to ensure that the food is in peak condition and to comply with food hygiene legislation. Joints of meat are often displayed under infra-red lamps to keep them hot during service and to improve the display.

Joints are usually positioned at the beginning of a carvery display and nearer to the carver than the customer (to prevent the carver having to lean across the display). Smaller items (such as Yorkshire puddings) are often displayed in front of the joints. The number of joints on display varies according to the establishment, price, occasion, etc.

When preparing the carvery, do not display cold food items such as salads too early as this can cause them to look 'tired'. Replenish food items (including accompaniments) as necessary. This ensures the smooth running of the operation and avoids causing customer delays and dissatisfaction.

Make sure that the carvery and the area around it is kept tidy and free from food debris at all times. This is important to prevent accidents or injury to yourself, your colleagues and customers and to prevent contamination risks.

The carvery menu

This includes a first and third course usually served to the customer at the table, and a middle (second) course where the customer approaches the carvery itself to select a dish. An example carvery menu is given on page 212.

Food hygiene: carveries

All hot food displayed on a carvery must be maintained and served at a temperature of 63 °C (145 °F) or above, because bacteria are unable to survive at these high temperatures. When working on a carvery, use separate implements for each dish, and ensure dishes remain covered for as long as possible to prevent cross-contamination. Remember the dishes must only be displayed for a maximum of four hours.

MEMORY JOGGER

Why must table items be checked for damage and cleanliness before use?

MEMORY JOGGER

Why must hot food be maintained and served at 63 °C or above?

Oven hot Garlic Mushrooms
with Bread
Mousse of Smoked Salmon & Spinach
Melon Boat Gruyère
Chef's Country Pâté
with Oatcakes or Granary Rolls

* * * * *

Decorated Whole Fresh Salmon
Sugar Baked Decorated Danish Gammon
Roast Rare Ribs of Beef
Seasoned Loin of Pork
Roast Prime Turkey with Cranberries
Salad Bowls to Include:
Nicoise, Broccoli & Yoghurt,
Tomato Vinaigrette with Dill, Coleslaw,
Waldorf with Carrot, Beetroot,
Curried Rice & Pimento, Egg Mayonnaise

Dressings:
Mayonnaise, French, Thousand Island, Blue Cheese

Breads:
Granary, Sesame Twist, French
Hot Buttered New Potatoes in Season

* * * * *

Apple Strudel
Orange & Lemon Soufflé
Strawberry Shortcake
Hazelnut Cheesecake

* * * * *

English Country Cheeses
with
Crisp Green Apples, Celery, Grapes

Coffee with Cream

Mints & Sweetmeats

An example carvery menu (reproduced by kind permission of Joseph Bell)

Essential knowledge

Food items should be replenished and displayed correctly throughout service in order to:
- maintain speed and efficiency of service
- avoid cross-contamination of foods
- ensure correct temperatures for hot and cold foods
- provide an attractive display.

BUFFET SERVICE

This method of service is used successfully in a wide range of catering establishments. Customers visit the buffet table, select food items and then either sit down to eat or (at more informal occasions) remain standing.

There are three types of buffet: finger, fork and carved.

Finger buffets
Here customers help themselves to food from a buffet table or choose from food offered on dishes by staff circulating the room. The type of food offered at a finger buffet must be capable of being eaten without a knife and fork; the choice is usually

Danish Open Sandwich Selection
prepared on French Bread, Ryebread,
or Pumpernickel as preferred:
Danish Gammon
Smoked Salmon
Seafood
Salami
Beef Remoulade
Herrings
Blue Cheese
Pâté

* * * * *

Deep Fried Chicken Drumsticks
Seafood Barquettes/Seafood Quiche
Pinwheels of Smoked Salmon
Hovis & Asparagus Rolls
Cucumber & Cream Cheese Rings
Assorted Crudités with Spicy Dips

* * * * *

Fresh Cream Gâteau or Pavlova
Chocolate & Cognac Mousse
Dairy Cream

Cheeseboard
with Celery & Biscuits

Coffee with Cream

An example finger buffet menu
(reproduced by kind permission of Joseph Bell)

An example of a hot fork buffet menu
(reproduced by kind permission of Joseph Bell)

Seafood & Avocado Cocktail
OR
Melon with Cream Cheese & Peaches
OR
Hors D'Oeuvres Variés
Granary Roll

* * * * *

Select two from:
Beef Stroganoff
Chicken Marengo
Scampi Provençale
Pheasant Casserole
Veal Fricassée with Cream
Venison & Game Pie with Cumberland Sauce
Coq au Vin
Braised Kidneys Turbigo
Whole Poussin Princesse
Fresh Salmon Pie with Asparagus
A Selection of three fresh Salads
Saffron Rice with Pimento
Baked Jacket or New Potatoes
A Medley of Seasonal Vegetables
Bread rolls – Butter

* * * * *

Sweet Table to include:
Fresh Orange & Grand Marnier Soufflé
Tipsy Trifle
Raspberry Pavlova
Belgian Apple & Cinnamon Flan

Cheeseboard with Celery

Coffee with Cream
Mints & Bon Bons

quite varied and can include: sandwiches, rolls, bouchées, canapés and open sandwiches. An informal finger buffet allows people to circulate and is ideal for cocktail parties, product launches and family occasions.

Fork buffets
In this instance, although some seating is provided at unlaid tables, the customers usually stand. They collect their food, a napkin and a fork from a buffet table. Presentation of food is similar to a finger buffet (above) but also includes items which can be eaten with a fork only, such as vol-au-vents, chicken pieces, veal and ham pie, goujons of fish and salad items.

Carved buffets
This style of buffet involves a more formal seating arrangement at tables which have been laid with cutlery appropriate to the menu. The guest visits the buffet table and selects the food he or she would like to eat for each course. When the guest has finished, each course is cleared away by food service staff.

The main course usually consists of decorated joints of meat, poultry and fish, carved at the buffet and served with a selection of salads and accompaniments. This type of service may be adapted according to establishment, customer and menu requirements. It is often used in hotels as a method of serving breakfasts and afternoon teas.

Preparing the buffet

Whichever type of buffet service is being used, there are certain basic principles to follow:
- the buffet should be set up in a *prominent position* in the room
- there should be *enough space on the buffet* to display and present all the food without overcrowding
- the buffet should be *within easy access of the kitchen* and wash-up so that food items may be replenished and dirty plates removed with the minimum disturbance to guests
- there should be *enough room* for guests to circulate freely
- there should be *sufficient occasional tables and chairs* for guests who may wish to sit down
- the *total presentation of the room* should be attractive and promote the correct atmosphere

Arranging the table linen

Traditionally the buffet table is covered with suitable white tablecloths falling to within 1.25cm ($\frac{1}{2}$ in) of the floor at the front and sides of the buffet. If more than one cloth is used, the creases should be lined up and the overlaps should run in the same direction: away from the entrance to the room or the main approach to the table (this makes them less noticeable). The ends of the buffet should be boxed in either by folding or by using pins; this gives a more favourable overall presentation.

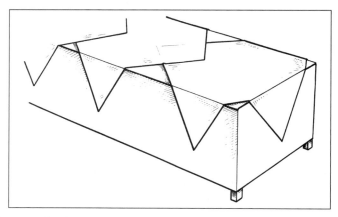

A boxed in buffet cloth

Banquet rolls may also be used, where the required length is cut from the roll and then conveniently disposed of after the buffet has been cleared away. Slip cloths can be placed over the top of the buffet table to provide additional colour contrast to the table.

Do this

- Find out what types of buffet are offered by your establishment.
- Find a sample menu of each of the types of buffet mentioned earlier.
- Ask your supervisor to show you how to box in a buffet cloth.
- Find out what types of display items are used on carveries and buffets in your establishment.

ARRANGING FOOD ON THE BUFFET

By considering the following points and reaching appropriate decisions you can achieve the maximum effect from a buffet-style presentation.

- Food is displayed in this way to make it look more appetising, so avoid over-crowding the display with overly elaborate arrangements which distract attention from the food.
- Buffet tables usually have a main focal point with food items arranged and displayed around it. Items which are often used as a focal point are flower displays, fruit baskets, decorated hams or ice/butter carvings.

A buffet focal point

- Colour, height and shape can add interest to the buffet table. Try to use a variety of these dimensions to provide contrast without making the buffet look messy.
- Food which is difficult to serve should be positioned where customers can gain easy access to it.
- Hot foods should be positioned towards the end of the buffet so that they do not go cold on the plate while customers are making further choices.
- In order to maintain the effectiveness of the display, empty dishes should either be removed or replenished as necessary.

Arranging utensils and accompaniments

- Appropriate accompaniments should be placed next to the food items, so that customers can match them to the correct food.
- A sufficient number of clean plates may be arranged either at one end of the table, at appropriate places along the table or on a smaller separate table.
- Depending on the style of buffet, tables will either be pre-laid with cutlery, napkins, condiments, etc. or these will be available at or near the buffet display, usually at the end.

Food hygiene: buffets

The maximum time food may be on display is four hours; after this time any bacteria present could multiply to significant numbers, increasing the risk of food poisoning. Ensure that food is kept at appropriate temperatures prior to service and remember to avoid airborne contamination by keeping foods covered until the last possible moment.

215

Essential knowledge	Dining and service areas must be kept tidy and free from rubbish and food debris in order to:
	• prevent the transfer of bacteria to food
	• prevent pest infestation in dining areas
	• avoid the risk of fire
	• maintain customer satisfaction
	• comply with the law

Case study

The restaurant where you work operates a carvery on Sunday lunchtimes and you have been asked to set up the appropriate display in the restaurant:
1 *Describe where you would place the carvery in your own establishment.*
2 *Draw a diagram of the display unit and indicate on it where you would place the items from the example menu on page 212.*
3 *Make a list of other items which will need to be placed on the display and suggest the most appropriate position for them.*

What have you learned

1 Why should careful consideration be given to the positioning of a carvery?
2 At what temperature should hot food be maintained and served?
3 Why should food items be replenished and displayed correctly throughout service?
4 Briefly describe the three types of buffet.
5 Why must dining and service areas be kept tidy and free from rubbish and food debris?
6 Why is it important to consider access to the kitchen and wash-up when preparing a buffet?

ELEMENT 2: Serve customers at the carvery/buffet

CUSTOMER REQUIREMENTS

MEMORY JOGGER

Why is it important that accurate information is given to customers?

When serving food at a carvery or buffet you are representing your establishment, so it is important that you know how to deal effectively with customers and promote your restaurant's products and services correctly.

Always greet customers politely as they approach the buffet or carvery and be prepared to answer any questions they may have. Some customers may have special dietary requirements, so it is essential that you know what ingredients have been used in the dishes on offer and how they have been cooked. Customers will often want to know which dishes are suitable for vegetarians and which, if any, are low in fat.

Essential knowledge	Information given to customers should be accurate in order to:
	• ensure efficient customer service is maintained
	• ensure that the establishment's products and services are correctly promoted

SERVING FOOD

Before starting to serve food, check that you are familiar with the portion control methods you need to use (see *Portioning food* below) and that you have all the necessary serving utensils to hand in a clean and undamaged condition.

When serving food, take care to arrange food items on customers' plates attractively. Try to place food items on the plate in such a way that the colours contrast in an appealing way. Remember to offer appropriate accompaniments.

Lift the lids from any hot dishes carefully, keeping your head away from the dish; steam rising from the opened dish can cause burns. Always replace the lids when you have finished serving each portion to ensure that the dishes keep hot.

Remember to use different carving knives and forks for each joint, and service spoons and forks for each other item to prevent cross-contamination. If you are unable to leave service utensils in the appropriate dish between serving customers, (e.g. because of heat) keep a service plate available for holding them.

As dishes become empty, remove them and/or replenish as appropriate.

Do this

- Find out what portion sizes are used in your establishment and the most common way of establishing these when serving.
- Watch your supervisor serving food at a buffet or carvery and notice how they arrange the food on the plate for maximum appeal.
- Find out what dishes are normally offered to vegetarians on buffet or carvery menus in your establishment.

PORTIONING FOOD

Portion food correctly; this is important for several reasons:
- to maximise profits
- over-filled plates look unattractive and create wastage
- under-filled plates may create customer dissatisfaction
- it is important to ensure that all customers receive similar quantities of each dish.

MEMORY JOGGER

Why is it important to control portions when serving a buffet or carvery?

Establishing portion size

There are several ways to identify the correct food portions:
- use of pre-portioned pies, flans and other food items
- use of measured quantity serving utensils
- use of garnishes or decorations to indicate portions (e.g. a rosette of cream may indicate a portion of gateau)
- plate size.

Essential knowledge

Portions should be controlled when serving food to customers in order to:
- control costs
- avoid wastage
- maintain customer expectations and satisfaction

Case study

A wedding reception is being held at your establishment. The menu is buffet style. Before service is due to start, you notice one or two items are missing from the buffet and you return to the kitchen to get them. When you return you find that the customers have arrived and started to serve themselves. There is a long queue at the buffet table, many of the dishes look depleted and you hear customers complaining about the lack of choice and waiting time.

1   Describe how this situation could have been avoided.

What have you learned

1   Describe how you would greet a customer approaching the carvery.
2   Why should portions be controlled when serving food to customers?
3   What methods may be used to ensure portion control?
4   Why should information given to customers be accurate?

ELEMENT 3:   Maintain customer dining areas

PROVIDING AN EFFICIENT SERVICE

Buffet and carvery service usually involves customers leaving their tables, selecting food items from the buffet or carvery and returning to their tables with each course.

However, in certain situations, such as wedding buffets or hotel carveries, it may be necessary to prevent queues forming by 'inviting' individual tables to the buffet while assuring others that you will invite them in a 'moment'.

It is important for food service staff to be aware at all times, particularly at the end of each course, so that plates and cutlery can be cleared away promptly and efficiently along with other table items as appropriate; this should be carried out with the minimum disturbance to customers.

When all the customers have finished their meal, the buffet or carvery should be cleared of dishes, cutlery and crockery. Soiled table linen and breakages should be dealt with in the appropriate manner (see also *Unit 2NC2: Provide a table service*).

Dealing with spillages
If a spillage should occur on the buffet table during service it should be dealt with as quickly as possible to maintain the overall appearance of the display.

1   Remove a liquid spillage by mopping it up using a clean absorbent cloth. Remove a solid spillage (e.g. part of a food item) by scraping or lifting it onto a clean plate.
2   Remove the cloth or plate containing the spillage to the kitchen.
3   Cover the spillage stain on the linen with a clean slip cloth or napkin.
4   Place an old menu card or napkin underneath the slip cloth to help absorb excess liquid.
5   Remove any soiled linen to a service area and deal with it in accordance with establishment procedures.

See also page 158 on dealing with larger spillages.

MEMORY JOGGER

Why must spillages be dealt with promptly?

WORKING SAFELY

The restaurant must be kept tidy and clean at all times. Check the dining and service areas for potential hazards before service begins, and be aware of any developing problems during service. Waste, whether it is a small spillage, left-over food item, discarded tissue or something larger (such as an empty cardboard box), should be regarded as potentially hazardous. It can cause accidents, contamination, encourage pest infestation and pollute the dining environment. You are legally required to dispose of it safely and correctly.

Remember that you are responsible for your own, your colleagues' and your customers' health and safety. Work safely and efficiently, allocating your time appropriately to avoid any 'last minute rushes'.

DEALING WITH UNEXPECTED SITUATIONS

During a carvery or buffet operation, unexpected situations may arise; it is important that you are able to take appropriate action as soon as possible. Make sure that you are familiar with the correct first aid treatment for cuts and burns, either of which might be suffered by customers or staff. Always inform your supervisor of any accidents and ensure that the Accident Book is completed correctly.

Case study

At the end of a buffet function in your establishment, a customer asks if they may take some of the leftovers home to have for their lunch the following day. It was a fork buffet consisting of cold meats and salads and a variety of sweets and had been on display for three and a half hours.
1 *How would you react to this request and why?*
2 *Describe how you would clear down the buffet table and how you would dispose of any waste?*

What have you learned

1 Describe how you would deal with a small spillage on a table.
2 Why must waste be disposed of correctly?
3 Why must dining and service areas be kept tidy and free from rubbish and debris at all times?
4 What should you do if a colleague accidentally cuts him/herself?

Get ahead

1 Investigate how breakfast and afternoon tea buffets may operate and what items would be included on the menu for these occasions.
2 Find out what specialised knives and other pieces of equipment might be used by the carver working behind a carvery.
3 Find examples of buffet menus that would be charged at varying ranges of prices. What kind of items and/or types of service increase costs?

Provide a silver service

This chapter covers:
ELEMENT 1:   **Silver serve food**
ELEMENT 2:   **Clear finished courses**

What you need to do

- Prepare equipment and items for service.
- Clear courses to satisfy establishment and health and safety standards.
- Portion, serve and arrange a variety of food using the appropriate equipment.
- Check that all service equipment is clean and placed ready for service.
- Identify and meet customers' requirements while causing the minimum of disturbance.
- Clear courses from the table at the appropriate time with assistance from other staff.
- Deal with surplus food and used service equipment in accordance with laid-down procedures.
- Carry out work in an orderly and efficient manner taking into account priorities and laid-down procedures.

What you need to know

- How to deal with customers correctly.
- Why care has to be taken to serve and arrange food correctly.
- What sequence to follow when clearing.
- Why food has to be carefully portioned during service.
- The procedures of service.
- What action to take when dealing with unexpected situations.

INTRODUCTION

Silver service, sometimes known as *English service* is a form of table service where the food is served from a flat or dish onto the customer's plate at the table. The food is usually transferred using a spoon and fork, although occasionally the food is served using two forks, two fish knives or some other type of specialist service equipment. Some restaurants have moved away from this style of service, but within the hotel industry as a whole the skill is still required for many occasions. It is almost always used, for example, for a banquet, and for meals in many top class hotels, restaurants and cruise liners.

Silver service has both advantages and disadvantages. The main ones are listed below and overleaf.

Advantages
- Many portions of food can be carried and served by one person.
- Portions can be controlled by the food server.
- The service is flexible, and can be used with a combination of other types and styles of service.
- Customers feel they are getting special service.
- It is a quick form of service when organised, trained staff are used.
- It presents an opportunity to demonstrate quality food, presentation and service.

Disadvantages
- It is more expensive to provide, requiring well-trained staff.
- There may be a high initial cost for specialist equipment (if needed).
- More space is needed between tables, which reduces the number of covers to be served.
- When groups of people are served, the presentation of food to the final guests served can be adversely affected.

Skills

When training to be a silver service waiter you need to develop certain skills in addition to the technical ones required, such as:
- local knowledge (customers may ask you about local facilities, attractions, etc.)
- menu knowledge (customers may need dishes translating or explaining, or may require information concerning special dietary requirements)
- a polite, and courteous manner
- a sense of urgency
- communication skills.

You will generally spend a considerable amount of time in contact with customers, so attention to personal hygiene and customer care is imperative. Remember also that you are the direct representative of the establishment and the person best placed to meet the customers' requirements and needs.

When clearing courses, always act in a professional manner, as this also reflects the standard of the establishment.

PLANNING YOUR TIME

A well-planned and efficient service will keep your customers satisfied. When thinking about how to carry out your tasks effectively, take into account both national and establishment procedures, and consider health, safety and hygiene points as well as the task in hand. The following principles will help you to maintain a time-efficient service:
- ensure you are fully prepared for service
- make journeys worthwhile; for example, you could return dirties on a journey back from the restaurant to kitchen/wash-up
- while customers are eating one course, prepare for the next; make sure any necessary cutlery, crockery, glassware is clean and ready
- keep sideboards fully stocked
- coordinate service if serving several tables; for example, serve one table and then clear the next
- before leaving the kitchen make sure you know the portioning of the dishes to be served; this will avoid waste and control costs
- anticipate your customers' needs and time your service accordingly (e.g. serve cold food before hot).

ELEMENT 1: Silver serve food

PREPARING FOR SILVER SERVICE
- Check any dishes or flats to be used for the service *before* service to make sure they are clean and undamaged. If they are to be used for the service of hot food, they must be hot themselves; likewise cold if for cold food.

MEMORY JOGGER

What final checks can be made at the hotplate before serving food to the customer?

- When using dishes, prepare underliners of the appropriate size.
- The portioning of food is very important. As the food server, you must be able to identify the number of portions on the flat. Portions can easily be identified if, for example, two slices of meat are garnished on the flat slightly further away from the next two slices. If the portions are not identifiable, you may serve two portions instead of one by mistake and have to return to the kitchen for more. If in doubt, ask.
- Ensure that your sideboard is fully prepared with all necessary equipment and has space for you to place down loaded trays.
- Check that food which has been heated on flats has not stuck to the flats, making service difficult and possibly spoiling presentation.
- The speed of service is very important. An experienced food server could be expected to serve between 10 and 15 customers from one flat for functions and banquets; this means that the food would have to be very hot when coming from the kitchen and the food server would need to serve quickly enough for even the last customer served to have hot food.

YOUR SERVICE CLOTH

A service cloth is a very important part of your service equipment as well as a part of the food server's uniform. It must be kept clean and ironed at all times and only used as a service cloth for such things as:
- carrying hot plates
- final polishing of plates and cutlery
- wiping small spills
- brushing crumbs onto a service plate
- wiping the underside of plates before placing them on the table
- protection against hot service dishes.

Carrying clean plates

ADJUSTING CUTLERY

The adjusting of cutlery is done as soon as the customer's order has been taken or before each course is served. This is to ensure that the cutlery on the table is correct for the dishes chosen. For a table d'hôte cover you would need to remove any unnecessary items from the cover and relay any extra items after taking the customer's order. For an à la carte cover, however, you would lay the cutlery required for each course just before serving that course.

There are several points to note.
- You will need a service plate or salver covered with a napkin. Cutlery is placed on the service plate or salver when it is being moved, because this is safer, easier for distinguishing the different pieces of cutlery and more hygienic than carrying it in the hand or pocket. Always tuck the top of knives under any forks for safety reasons.
- You need to work around the table, removing and placing cutlery from the left of one customer, then turning and removing and placing cutlery on the right of the next customer.
- You must not go between two customers who are having a conversation.

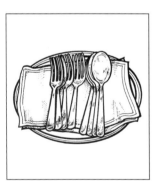

Carrying cutlery

PLACING PLATES ON THE TABLE

Full silver service will require you to place hot and/or cold plates onto the table before serving food items. The method for carrying this out correctly is given below.
- Cover the palm of your hand with one end of your service cloth.
- Place the plates in that covered palm and wrap the rest of the cloth round the plates.
- On reaching the table, wipe the top plate, then pick it up using your thumb and

fingers on the rim. Place the plate carefully in front of the customer, bending your knees slightly and leaning gently forward.
● Continue around the table repeating the sequence for each plate. Serve female guests first, working anti-clockwise around the table, then serve the male guests and lastly, the host.
● Place the plates onto the table following any establishment procedures. For instance, if the plates are decorated with a company crest or logo, the plate would normally be placed so that the crest is at the top of the cover.

TECHNICAL SILVER SERVICE SKILLS

MEMORY JOGGER

How can the service of delicate and rounded items be made easier?

Silver service is a skill which can be learned quickly, but needs practice to acquire competence. Occasionally you will need to use some specialist service equipment, but your principal items of service are the service spoon and fork.

Using a serving spoon and fork
● With the curve of the fork in the bowl of the service spoon, hold both handles in the palm of the hand.
● Push your first finger between the handles so pinching the fork between your finger and thumb.
● By making a slight adjustment to the holding position, you will be able to keep the spoon supported while being able to lever the fork open and closed.

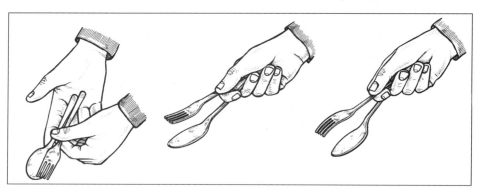

Holding a spoon and fork for silver service. Far right: the fork is inverted to serve round objects

Useful tips
If the fork is inverted (i.e. with the prongs facing down) it is easier to serve round objects such as potato; while peas, for example, need only the spoon. For delicate flat items, such as fish fillets or omelettes, two splayed-out service forks or fish knifes are sometimes easier to use. Some dishes involve special service equipment such as tongs, sauce ladles, etc.

Do this ✔
● In order to become a competent silver food server you will need to practise and master the skills of using the service spoon and fork. Select different sized items of various types to simulate food items and practise picking them up and placing them down, adjusting the spoon and fork as necessary.
● Use an old customer order to practise adjusting cutlery at an empty table.

PERFORMING SILVER SERVICE

1 Hold the service flat or dish on the palm of your left hand cushioned by your service cloth. (If you are left-handed, hold the dish in your right hand.)
2 Present the dish to the customer/s before actually serving, generally while standing to their left (see *Service side* on p. 225). By doing this you allow customers to

admire the dish fully arranged and decorated, and to confirm it is the one ordered. If lids or cloches are used take care when lifting them off as condensation can drip onto a customer or the tablecloth.

3 Bring the flat or dish to the level of the customer's plate and hold it just over the rim.
4 Carefully lift the food with the spoon, using the fork to hold the item and then place it on the customer's plate. Transfer any garnishes in the same way.
5 If a sauce or gravy is on the flat, this can be served by tilting the flat and using just the spoon to serve the sauce or gravy.
6 On completion, thank the customer and move on to the next.

Service side

There is no hard and fast rule on which side of the customer you should serve from, although each establishment has its particular procedures and rules. There are however, two methods that may be adopted in part or full:
● *English service*: all food is served from the left and cleared from the right. All beverages are served and cleared from the right
● *Continental service*: plates and glasses are placed from the right; coffee and food from the left; drinks are served from the right; and all items are cleared from the right.

There are occasions when a food server should be allowed to judge this for themselves; for example, if a customer is sitting next to a wall, it would be wrong to ask another customer to move so that the server had room to reach. However, it is important to be consistent to avoid confusing the customer.

SERVICE PRIORITIES

The following points need to be considered when determining priorities of service:
● serve female guests first and the host last
● serve hot food on hot plates, cold food on cold plates
● warn customers of hot plates
● serve cold food before hot food
● do not touch food on the plates
● serve accompaniments (e.g. sauces) as soon as all other food items have been served
● serve from the left unless establishment procedures or seating positions require you to act otherwise
● if a customer asks for a larger portion than allowed, serve the normal portion to that customer and place a supplementary order. Do not serve another guest's portion, leaving them to wait
● use clean cutlery for each food item.

Talk to your customers and take note of their likes and dislikes. If you do your job well they are more likely to return to the restaurant on another occasion. As a food server your work includes public relations, sales and marketing through efficient service.

SERVING PARTICULAR DISHES

Serving soup

Before serving soup you will need to lay the correct cover: soup spoon for soups, dessert spoon for consommés.

For one portion of soup an individual soup tureen is often used.
1 Approach the customer from the left, holding the soup tureen on a service salver

or underliner and the soup bowl and its liner on your forearm.

2   Place the soup bowl (with liner) in front of the customer, then position the service salver so that it just covers the rim of the soup plate.

3   Keeping the service salver level, pick up the individual tureen, move to the edge of the service salver and pour slowly into the soup bowl away from the customer. The tureen is placed on an underplate/flat to act as a drip plate so preventing any spillage going on the table or customer.

4   Return the tureen to the sideboard and offer the customer the appropriate accompaniments.

For multiple portions of soup a large soup tureen would be used. The soup would then be served, using a service ladle, at the sideboard or from a service table (guéridon) at the table, and the soup bowls then carefully placed in front of the customer.

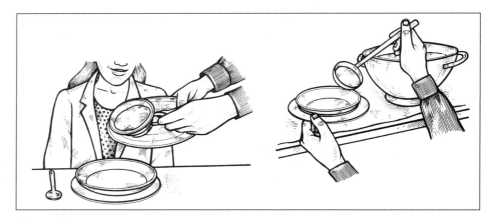

Left: serving soup from an individual tureen. Right: serving multiple portions of soup from a large soup tureen

Serving fish and large or delicate items

Before serving fish, check that the correct cutlery has been laid; i.e. a fish knife and fork. When serving, you will sometimes find that fish fillets or large thin slices of meat are difficult to serve with a spoon and fork and it may be necessary to adopt one of the following options:

1   use two forks or two splayed fish knives

2   cut across the middle with your service spoon, serve and reassemble on the customer's plate remembering to arrange it attractively.

Serving meat or poultry

Before you start, check that the correct cutlery has been laid; i.e. a joint knife and fork with a hot joint plate for hot food, and a cold plate for cold food.

1   If some cold dishes have been ordered take them to the sideboard or serve them first.

2   Approach each customer from the left and present the dish. The customer can then see the presentation work of the chef as well as seeing the completed dish.

3   Lower the service dish or flat so as to slightly cover the rim of the joint plate.

4   Using your service spoon and fork, place the meat portion onto the customer's plate at the 'half past six' position along with any garnish. If there is a sauce or gravy on the flat, tip the flat slightly forward and use your spoon to serve the sauce.

5   If more than one portion of meat is being served from the same flat, rotate it so that the portion to be served is nearest the plate each time. If the meat portion is correctly positioned there should be plenty of room for any potatoes and vegetables.

Serving meat

Serving potatoes and vegetables

The general rule is to serve potatoes before vegetables, although each establishment will have its own procedures.

1 Place the serving dish on a salver or service plate.
2 Have a separate service spoon and fork for each different type of dish to be served.
3 Present the dish, then lower the service dish so as to slightly cover the rim of the customer's plate.
4 Using your service spoon and fork, serve each potato dish starting from the far side of the customer's plate and working your way back. Remember to rotate the dish as you serve each item with its own service equipment.
5 Once the potatoes have been served, use the same procedure to serve the vegetables.

Once you are practised and competent, service time can be speeded up by placing the potatoes and vegetables onto a large service salver or underflat. In this case, you would serve from the front of the salver or flat and then rotate it, to bring the next type of vegetable to the front of the flat before serving it.

Serving potatoes and vegetables

Essential knowledge	Care has to be taken to serve and arrange food correctly in order to maintain: ● cost controls ● the attractive appearance of dishes ● customer satisfaction.

Accompaniment sauces

The sauce should be served from a sauce boat placed on an underplate with a ladle.
1 Position the sauce boat so that it is over the rim of the customer's plate and pointing towards it.
2 Take a ladle full of sauce, then run the under-edge of the ladle on the side of the sauce boat to remove any drips which may otherwise fall on the cloth or customer.
3 Pour the sauce gently over the portion of meat. (Note that for certain dishes the sauce should be poured on one side of the plate.)

Ladling gravy onto food

Do this

- Watch experienced food servers serving soup in your restaurant, noticing equipment and techniques used.
- Ask your supervisor what implements are used in your establishment for serving fish and large or delicate items.
- Practise serving, using different items which are similar in size, shape and weight to the food items you might serve.
- Practise ladling liquid from a sauce boat to a dish.

Serving cheese

Before serving cheese, check that the correct cover is laid and that the correct accompaniments are placed on the table: i.e. a side plate and side knife, a dish of butter, celery and cruets. Other accompaniments may be offered according to establishment procedures. Check that you have a clean knife for the service of each cheese.
1 Present the cheese board from the customer's left-hand side.
2 When the customer has made their choice, rest half the board on the table edge while holding the other half in your hand; this will give a firm base for cutting as well as freeing a hand to cut with.
3 Cut a portion of the chosen cheese and place it onto the customer's plate using the double prongs.
4 Offer a selection of cheese biscuits or place a selection on the table either in a basket or on an underplate.

When cutting cheeses, care should be taken to achieve the correct portioning so as to satisfy the customer while controlling costs. For each type of cheese there is a special method of cutting; see the illustration on page 151.

Serving cheese

Essential knowledge

Food must be carefully positioned during service in order to:
● control costs
● avoid wastage
● maintain customer expectations and satisfaction.

PLATING FOOD FROM A SIDE TABLE OR TROLLEY

This type of service is a little easier as both hands are free, allowing you to hold a piece of service equipment in each hand. This is helpful when serving or arranging delicate items such as hors d'oeuvres, pies, puddings, flans and gâteaux.

● Collect all the equipment required for service before starting to serve.
● Wheel the service table or trolley to the customers' table, positioning it so that they can see the tasks have been carried out. Besides serving and arranging food, these tasks could include carving and jointing of meats, filleting of fish, the making of salad dressings or the portioning of desserts.
● Present the dish/es to the customers.
● Working quickly, serve each customer by transferring the portion from the dish to the customer's plate together with any accompanying garnish.
● Pick up the plate by the rim and place it carefully in front of the customer.

Plated service (from side trolley to table)

SERVICE AND TIMING

MEMORY JOGGER

What procedures should you follow to maintain a smooth, efficient service?

In order to maintain customer satisfaction and ensure a speedy and efficient service, the timing of service is critical. The following points will help to maintain a smooth, time-efficient service:

● place any cold accompaniments required onto the table before serving
● as soon as possible after taking the order, serve the first course
● inform the customer if there are going to be any delays
● as soon as everyone has finished eating, clear that course
● take the dessert order promptly
● suggest coffee and liqueurs after the dessert course has been cleared.

UNEXPECTED SITUATIONS

The type of unexpected situations that might occur during silver service are covered in *Unit 2NC2: Provide a table service*, pages 157–158.

Case study

A customer has ordered, for his main course, a grilled darne of salmon and a mixed salad to be served with a French dressing.

The salmon will be presented on a service flat and then skinned and boned by you from a service table in front of the customer. You will also have to prepare the French dressing for the salad.

1 *What ingredients/equipment will you need to have on the side table for the preparation of the French dressing?*
2 *What equipment will you need to skin and bone the darne of salmon?*
3 *What procedures and order of work would be followed to carry out the full service of this customer's choice?*

What have you learned?

1 Why is the adjusting of cutlery carried out?
2 What points need to be considered when deciding on priorities of service?
3 Why must food be carefully portioned during service?
4 Why should you take care to serve and arrange food correctly?
5 Why are dishes presented before they are served?
6 How can the service spoon and fork be held to make it easier to serve round items?
7 How can the service of fish fillets be made easier?
8 What point on the plate is meat placed?
9 How can a cheese board be supported for the service of cheese?

ELEMENT 2: Clear finished courses

WHEN TO CLEAR

Each course should be cleared once all of the customers have finished eating. If the host of a party is known, clear their plate last. Clearing should be systematically carried out round the table.

At a function where a large number of people are eating together, the supervisor will give a signal for clearing to start.

CLEARING MAIN COURSES

*Carrying dishes and
underplates*

1 Approach each customer from the appropriate side; this is usually the right.
2 Lean forward slightly and take hold of the plate by the rim; remove the plate from in front of the customer, leaning back and away as you do so.
3 Turn slightly away and back from the customer (so that you are out of his or her vision). Put the plate into your other hand with your thumb on top, two fingers underneath, and the other fingers held back and pointing upwards (see the illustrations on page 154).
4 Scrape any left-over food items to the front of the plate and arrange the knife and fork at right angles to each other with the knife blade tucked under the bridge of the fork. This prevents the cutlery from sliding around or falling to the floor.
5 Remove the second plate as before, but this time place it on the platform made by your held-back third and fourth fingers, thumb base and inside wrist checking its balance as you do so.
6 Place the second knife under the fork on the first (lower) plate.
7 Scrape any food items forward onto the first plate.
8 Place the second fork with the first on the lower plate.
9 If more plates have to be cleared, continue as above, collecting only as many plates as you can safely carry. While scraping and stacking always turn away from the customers.
10 Once you have collected all the plates and stacked them neatly onto your fore-arm, move the first plate with all the debris, knives and forks onto the other (top) pile.
11 Hold the whole pile with both hands and remove it to your sideboard or wash-up area.

Clearing plates or dishes with liners

This procedure is much the same as above, except that there is another plate or dish to stack in each case.

Once the second plate is in position on the forearm (Step 5 above), the cutlery from the first dish is moved up and into the second dish, then the second dish (holding the cutlery) is placed onto the lower dish leaving a liner plate on the forearm.

Clearing dishes with liners

The sequence is repeated until all dishes are cleared. The lower stack can then be placed on to the forearm, collected into both hands and removed to the sideboard or wash-up area.

Clearing by salver

On some occasions it may be appropriate to use a salver to help with clearing. The salver is held in one hand and the cleared plates stacked onto it.

Key points

- Clearing should be done as quietly as possible; noise can unsettle customers.
- If there is a lot of debris, clear a few plates at a time; large piles of waste can become unsightly.
- Carry out clearing as quickly as possible, making as few visits to the table as you can. Working with assistants as a team will help give speed and efficiency of service.
- If you do drop something when clearing, do not bend over to pick it up while you have plates stacked; remove them to the sideboard or wash-up then return to pick up the item.
- Each time you clear a course, look at the table to check that the cutlery and crockery is in order for the next course. If it is not, correct it before serving the next course.

Do this ✔

- Practise clearing two or three plates without food, until you feel confident that you can do it without dropping cutlery or plates or spilling waste.
- Notice how often cutlery is cleared or changed during a meal in your restaurant.

CRUMBING DOWN

Crumbing down is a task that is normally carried out after the main course has been cleared although it should be done whenever the table needs it, whichever course has been cleared. The purpose is to remove crumbs and debris from the table. The items of equipment needed are a service plate and a service cloth. After the course has been cleared:

- approach the customer from the left-hand side
- position a service plate just under the table lip
- working from the centre of the cover position, use a folded service cloth or small brush to brush any crumbs onto the service plate
- If an à la carte menu has been served, there will not be any cutlery left on the table. However, if a table d'hôte cover has been used the dessert spoon and fork will be at the top of the cover: move the fork down to the left-hand side of the cover
- move round to the right-hand side of the customer and repeat the same crumbing down procedure. On completion move the dessert spoon down to the right-hand side of the place setting for a table d'hôte cover.

When the service cloth is not in use, hold it with your fingers under the service plate. During the whole crumbing down procedure do not reach across a customer: if this is unavoidable, excuse yourself first.

CLEARING OTHER TABLE ITEMS

Ashtrays
If during the meal an ashtray is dirty yet not being used it must be changed or removed. To do this you will need a service plate or salver with a napkin on top and a clean ashtray.

To change or remove an ashtray:
● approach from the nearest point to the ashtray
● stand side on to the table holding the salver in the hand furthest away from the table
● hold the clean ashtray upside down in the other hand and place it on top of the dirty ashtray
● pick up both together (this will prevent cigarette or cigar ash from being blown onto the table) then place them onto the salver
● return the clean ashtray to the table, turning it up the right way.
● before moving across the room, cover the dirty ashtray with the napkin.

Glasses
As courses are cleared, and depending on the wine served, it may be necessary to clear glasses. If you need to do this, approach the table from the right-hand side of each customer and pick up the glasses by their stems or bases. Place them on a salver before removing them to the sideboard, wash-up or bar area.

Condiments, accompaniments and table decorations
Condiments and accompaniments for each dish should be removed when that course is cleared. Cruets are normally left until the main course is cleared. Table decorations, in most cases, are left throughout the meal although some establishments remove them before coffee is served.

Maintaining sideboards

It is important to keep the sideboard clear throughout service and at no time to allow debris, dirty crockery and cutlery to be on the sideboard at the same time as dishes to be served. This would increase the risk of contamination and food poisoning. The sideboard should also be kept fully stocked throughout service so as to provide a speedy and efficient service.

Case study

You are working as a food server in a very busy silver service restaurant serving a table of two couples. During the clearing of the first course, your colleague knocks over a full glass of red wine. It was a genuine accident that causes no injury, but does make quite a mess of the table and some has spilt onto a lady's dress. One of the gentlemen at the table reacts in an aggressive manner. You can immediately see that your colleague is panicked and upset by the incident and reaction of the gentleman.
1 What is to be your immediate action and why?
2 From this point what other procedures should be followed so that the customers can continue their meal?

What have you learned

1 What action should you take if you drop an item during the clearing of a course?
2 When is crumbing down carried out?
3 Why should you cover a dirty ashtray with a clean one when removing the dirty ashtray from the table?
4 When should you begin to clear a table?

Get ahead

Although silver service is regarded as the higher standard of service, flambé work is the most impressive to watch and requires a skilful and informed performer. By working through the list below you can begin to build up your knowledge of this skill.

1 Find out what the term *flambé* means.
2 Look through a catering equipment supplier's brochure. Find the pieces of equipment required for a basic flambé operation and cost them out.
3 Find out what principal characteristics must be present in food items to enable them to be cooked at the table.
4 What precautions need to be considered before flambé work can be carried out?
5 Apart from flambé, what other work is carried out in front of the customer at a guéridon?
6 What is *Canard à la presse* and how is it done?

Index

Page references in italics indicate illustrations.